"The mainstream media have a fundamental role in our democratic process, one that it is essential to the health of the Republic, not to put too fine a point on it. So it is in everyone's interest that they not only survive, but also be widely respected.

"This book is *not* about proving the existence of liberal bias in the media…Ultimately it is about making things better. The naked emperors can continue to deny and dissemble on the bias question, proudly marching on with their privates dangling in the breeze, but while they've been marching, the ship has already sailed. And the fat lady stopped singing a long time ago.

"They need to be saved—*from themselves.*"

Acclaim for
ARROGANCE

Arrogance

Rescuing America from the Media Elite

BERNARD GOLDBERG

WARNER BOOKS

NEW YORK   BOSTON

Warner Books

Time Warner Book Group
1271 Avenue of the Americas, New York, NY 10020
Visit our Web site at www.twbookmark.com.

Printed in the United States of America
Originally published in hardcover by Warner Books
First Trade Printing: November 2004
10 9 8 7 6 5 4 3 2 1

The Library of Congress has cataloged the hardcover edition as follows:
Goldberg, Bernard.
    Arrogance : rescuing America from the media elite / Bernard Goldberg.
      p. cm.
    Includes index.
    ISBN 0-446-53191-X
      1. Journalism—Objectivity. 2. Television broadcasting of news—United States.
    I. Title.

    PN4784.O24G63 2003
    302.23'0973—dc21

2003052597

ISBN: 0-446-69364-2 (pbk.)

Book design by H. Roberts Design
Cover design by Flag

For my pal Asa Baber, an honorable man and a very funny guy
who made so many of us feel like the luckiest people
on the face of the earth . . . rest in peace, my friend

Contents

Arrogance

"We are simply, I'm afraid, disliked by far too many—perceived by them as not only smug but arrogant and as critics of everybody but ourselves."

—LATE CBS NEWS ANALYST ERIC SEVAREID

Introduction

S o I'm sitting in a very nice conference room in the very nice Time & Life Building, high above bustling West Fiftieth Street in Manhattan, for my first meeting on this book. There are about ten big shots from Warner Books sitting around a very nice long table waiting to hear what I have in mind, which basically is to use my earlier book *Bias* as a jumping-off point to examine the powerful behind-the-scenes forces that have turned too many American newsrooms into bastions of political correctness; to examine those forces and see why they generate bias in the news and how they sustain it; and to tell the media elites, who are too arrogant to see for themselves, the ways they'd better change if they want to stay relevant. Because if they don't, they'll cease to be serious players in the national conversation and become the journalistic equivalent of the leisure suit—harmless enough but hopelessly out of date.

But as I'm sitting there I'm not thinking about any of that. To be perfectly honest, what I am thinking is, before *Bias* caught on with so many Americans, before it became such a hit, no one in the liberal, highbrow book business would have thrown water on me if I were on fire. None of them would have dirtied their hands on a book that would have dismayed their smart, sensitive liberal friends. Before *Bias* I would have been the skunk at their garden party. *But now they can't wait to hear what I think?*

But about fourteen seconds in, I am brought back to earth when one of the participants informs me that a friend of his thinks the whole idea of liberal bias is bogus.

I smile the kind of insincere smile I detest in others and look at the guy, wondering if I'm also looking at his "friend." I'm also wondering if everyone else in the room also thinks that bias in the news is just the stuff of right-wing paranoia. I am in Manhattan, after all, the belly of the beast.

And besides, Manhattan is one of those trendy places where the hot media chic thing is not only to dismiss the notion of liberal bias in the news, but actually to say, with a straight face, that the real problem is . . . *conservative bias!*

This is so jaw-droppingly bizarre you almost don't know how to respond. It reminds me of a movie I saw way back in the sixties called *A Guide for the Married Man.* In one scene, Joey Bishop plays a guy caught by his wife red-handed in bed with a beautiful woman. As the wife goes nuts, demanding to know what the hell is going on, Joey and the woman get out of bed and calmly put on their clothes. He then casually straightens up the bed and quietly responds to his wife, who by now has smoke coming out of her ears, "What bed? What girl?" After the woman leaves, Joey settles in his lounge chair and reads the paper, pausing long to enough to ask his wife if she shouldn't be in the kitchen preparing dinner!

Joey's mantra in such situations is simple: Deny! Deny! Deny! And in this scene his denials are so matter-of-fact and so nonchalant that by the time the other woman leaves the bedroom, leaving just Joey and his wife, her head is spinning and she's so bamboozled that she's seriously beginning to doubt what she just saw with her own two eyes. She's actually beginning to believe him when he says there was no other woman in the room!

Just think of Joey Bishop as the media elite and think of his wife as *you*—the American news-consuming public.

You have caught them red-handed over and over again with their biases exposed, and all they do is Deny! Deny! Deny! Only now the media have become even more brazen. Simply denying isn't good enough anymore. Now they're not content looking you in the eye and calmly saying, "What bias?" Now they're just as calmly turning truth on its head, saying the real problem is *conservative bias.*

What's next? They look up from their paper and ask why you're not in the kitchen preparing dinner?

Having been on the inside for as long as I have, twenty-eight years as a CBS News correspondent, I should have known it would be just a matter of time before they would stop playing defense and go on the offensive. Given their arrogance, I should have known that sooner or later they would say, "*We* don't have a bias problem— and if you think we do, then that proves that *you're* the one with the bias problem." Never mind that millions of Americans scream about liberal bias in the media; all the journalists can say is "You're the one with the bias!" The emperors of alleged objectivity have been naked for quite some time now, and sadly, they're the only ones who haven't noticed. Or as Andrew Sullivan, the very perceptive observer of all things American, so elegantly puts it, "Only those elite armies of condescension keep marching on, their privates swinging in the breeze."

But to deny liberal bias, the elites not only have had to brush off their own viewers, they also have had to paint their critics as wild-eyed ideologues—and then completely misrepresent what they say. For example, on March 4, 2003, this is how Nicholas Kristoff began his column in the *New York Times*: "Claims that the news media form a vast liberal conspiracy strike me as utterly unconvincing." Well, they strike *me* as utterly unconvincing, too. Exactly who, Nick, is making those "claims"? Got any names? Because I travel all over the country and speak about bias in the media, and I haven't met one serious conservative—not one—who believes that a "vast liberal conspiracy" controls the news. And for what it's worth, I write on page four of the introduction to *Bias* that "It is important to know, too, that there isn't a well-orchestrated, vast left-wing conspiracy in America's newsrooms." What I and many others do believe, and what I think is fairly obvious, is that the majority of journalists in big newsrooms slant leftward in their personal politics, especially on issues like abortion, affirmative action, gay rights, and gun control; and so in their professional role they tend to assume those positions are reasonable and morally correct. Bias in the news stems from *that*—not from some straw man conspiracy concocted by liberals in the supposedly objective, mainstream media.

Yet the idea that socially liberal reporters might actually take a liberal tack in their reporting is a proposition too many journalists on the Left refuse even to consider. Better to cast conservatives as a bunch of loonies who see conspiracies under every bed, around every corner, behind every tree, and, most important of all, in every newsroom.

In fact, right on the heels of the Kristoff column, the conspiracy thing pops up again in—surprise, surprise—the *New York Times*. This time in a book review: "The notion that a vast left-wing conspiracy controls America's airwaves and newsprint [is] . . . routinely promoted as gospel on the right."

Wrong again! But they are right about one thing: There is plenty of paranoid talk about a "vast left-wing conspiracy" in the newsroom. The problem is, the paranoids dreaming it up aren't conservatives—*they're liberals!*

And the uncomfortable truth—uncomfortable for ideologues on the Left, anyway—is that there now exists "a huge body of literature—including at least 100 books and research monographs—documenting a widespread left-wing bias in the news," according to Ted Smith III of Virginia Commonwealth University, who has done extensive research into the subject. And much of the evidence comes *not* from conservatives with axes to grind but straight from the journalists themselves, who in survey after survey have identified themselves as liberal on all the big, important social issues of our time.

Despite the overwhelming evidence, despite all the examples of bias that were documented in my book and others, despite the surveys that show that large numbers of Americans consider the elite media too liberal, *despite all of that*, the elites remain in denial. Why? Well, for starters, as I say, a lot them truly don't understand what the fuss is all about, since they honestly believe that their views on all sorts of divisive issues are not really controversial—or even liberal. After all, their liberal friends in Manhattan and Georgetown share those same views, which practically by definition make them moderate and mainstream. So, the thinking goes, it is all those Middle Americans who take the opposing view on, say, guns or gay marriage who are out of the mainstream, the ones who are "fringe." Journalists don't usually use the word—not in public anyway—but those supposedly not-too-sophisticated "fringe" Americans are smart enough to pick up on the condescension.

But there's another reason journalists refuse to come clean on liberal bias—one that Dr. Freud would have a field day with. To be honest with the American people *and themselves*, you see, would be to shake their world to its very foundations. And that, as you might imagine, is not something they're anxious to do, introspection not being their strong suit. By and large, these are people who see themselves as incredibly decent, even noble. They're the good guys trying to make the world a better place. That's why many of them went into journalism in the first place—to make the world a better place. Bias is something the bad guys are guilty of. So rather than look honestly at themselves and their profession, they hang on for dear life to the ludicrous position, *to the completely absurd notion*, that they, among all human beings, are unique—that only they have the ability to set aside their personal feelings and their beliefs and report the news free of any biases, "because we're professionals," they say.

But so are cops, and they can't keep *their* biases in check is what journalists tell us all the time. If a cop is biased, sooner or later that bias is going to come out on the job, is what reporters say. And they're probably right. It's human nature, after all. It's the same with judges and corporate executives with biases. No way they have the ability to set *their* personal feelings and beliefs completely aside—not for long anyway. And, as we all know, no white southern male over the age of five can keep his biases under control, certainly not as far as the elites are concerned. But journalists alone, the guys in the white hats, somehow can do what no other group can. Somehow, all of their life experiences can neatly be set aside as they go about bringing us the news, absent any preconceived notions and prejudices—because "we're professionals."

It's unbelievable. Literally.

Deny! Deny! Deny! By now it's not only their mantra, it's practically official newsroom policy. In one way or another Dan Rather, Peter Jennings, and Tom Brokaw have all dismissed the very idea of liberal bias in the news. Rather has called it a "myth" and a "canard" and has actually said that "Most reporters don't know whether they're Republican or Democrat." Jennings thinks that "It's just essential to make the point that we are largely in the center, without particular axes to grind, without ideologies which are represented in our daily coverage." Ditto Brokaw, Couric, Lauer, Stahl, Wallace, and Bradley. The list, as they say, goes on and on.

But as strategies go, this new wrinkle—*"There is no liberal bias in the news, but there is a conservative bias"*—is far better. This is what you say if you're a media liberal who is not only tired of playing defense but wants to put his critics on the defensive for a change. This is what you say if you're trapped in a corner, and you don't know what else to do and you think you're fighting for your life.

❖   ❖   ❖

It was Tom Daschle, the Democratic leader in the Senate, who fired the first shot (unless you want to go back a few years to Hillary Clinton and her warning about the vast right-wing conspiracy) when he went after every liberal's favorite punching bag, Rush Limbaugh, in November 2002. That was right after the Democrats got hammered in the midterm elections and lost control of the Senate. Daschle accused Limbaugh and other conservatives on talk radio of inciting violence against liberals like himself. How would that work? you ask. Well, apparently Senator Daschle thinks the people who listen to talk radio are a bunch of crazy, drooling, scary rednecks who— *if they're in a good mood*—merely send out death threats to the liberals Rush was complaining about. If, on the other hand, Rush riles them up—*and they're in a foul mood*—well, then, who the hell knows what those morons might do?

This was so pathetically lame that it would have just been a one- or two-day story, except up popped Al Gore to stir the cauldron. Gore expanded the target list from Limbaugh to an entire Conservative Axis of Evil—an unholy trinity made up of talk radio, Fox News, and the *Washington Times,* whom Gore said were nothing more than mouthpieces for the Republican Party. "Most of the media [have] been slow to recognize the pervasive impact of this fifth column in their ranks," he declared, "that is, day after day, injecting the daily Republican talking points into the definition of what's objective as stated by the news media as a whole."

Once Al Gore spoke the gospel of conservative bias, it took only seconds for left-of-center journalists to start hopping on board the bandwagon.

"Al Gore said the obvious," wrote the left-wing *New York Times* columnist Paul Krugman.

"The legend of the liberal media is finally dead," proclaimed Joe Conason, the liberal columnist of the *New York Observer.*

"Sooner or later, I think we're all going to have to acknowledge that the myth of liberal bias in the press is just that, it's a myth," according to Jack White, one of *TIME* magazine's liberal columnists.

The true "new bias," according to E. J. Dionne Jr., one of the many liberal columnists at the *Washington Post,* "adds up to [a] media heavily biased toward conservative politics and conservative politicians."

Then on January 1, 2003, a weary world woke up to a page-one story in the *New York Times,* a story that made it all official. According to the *Times,* liberals are so sick of being beaten up by pro-conservative media, like talk radio and Fox News, that they are looking to create liberal outlets of their own for "balance"—everything from "progressive" radio talk shows, as the *Times* described it, to "a cable network with a liberal bent."

This seems like a good place to state the obvious: Yes, Republicans do indeed have friends in some conservative places like talk radio, Fox News, and the *Washington Times,* whom I'm sure they use to get their talking points out. But what Al Gore and his pals in the media forget to mention is that Democrats also have friends, in some very powerful *liberal* places, and the Democrats use them to get *their* talking points out. Places like major newspapers in every big city in the country, big-circulation mainstream news magazines, television networks with their millions and millions of viewers—all very large platforms that journalists use, intentionally or not, to frame the national debate on all sorts of big important issues, in the process creating "conventional" and "mainstream" points of view. *That* is what media power is really about.

The fact is, Rush Limbaugh, Fox News, and the *Washington Times* might not even exist if weren't for the routine (and the generally *unconscious*) liberal tilt of the mainstream media. Liberal journalists may indeed try to keep their biases in check (as they keep telling us), but—mainly because they don't even recognize that their liberal views are liberal—they often don't succeed. As I once told Bill O'Reilly, he should send a case of champagne to Rather, Brokaw, and Jennings with a nice little note that reads, "Thanks a lot, guys, for sending over all those viewers."

Why do you think liberals like Mario Cuomo, who had a Saturday morning show on radio, and more recently Phil Donahue, with his nightly show on television, flat out failed as talk show hosts, along with a bunch of other liberals including Jerry Brown and Jim Hightower and a few more you probably never heard of? Why do you think there's no current liberal talk show host in the entire United States of America who comes within light-years of Rush Limbaugh's or Sean Hannity's ratings? The Left, self-servingly, says it's because conservatives (unlike civilized liberals, of course) are loud and angry and make complex political and social issues moronically simple for their moronically simple listeners, many of whom, of course, live in simple-minded Red State country. Here's another theory: Maybe liberal talk shows keep failing because the American people don't think they need yet one more media megaphone coming from left field. Maybe they flop because the American people are saying, "We already have plenty of those, thank you." Or as Jay Leno put it one night: "A group of venture capitalists are in the process of developing their own liberal radio network to counter conservative shows like Rush Limbaugh. They feel the liberal viewpoint is not being heard—except on TV, in the movies, in music, by comedians, in magazines and newspapers. *Other than that, it's not getting out!*" The joke got a great big laugh, which ought to tell us something, since the audience wasn't made up of the Young Right-Wing Conservatives of America—just your regular Middle-American types. You think maybe just about *everybody* by now thinks it's funny when the Left complains that, "the liberal viewpoint is not being heard"?

But the success of conservative talk shows isn't just about America's disaffection with the liberal media; it's about America's disaffection with liberalism itself: with liberals' abiding respect for diversity (except, of course, diversity of opinion); with their reflexive tendency to blame America first for whatever is wrong in the world; with their deep suspicion of America's military; with their titanic hypocrisy (as in their enthusiastic support of affirmative action (as long as it doesn't adversely affect their own kids); with their self-righteous support for "art" seemingly designed to do nothing more than offend sensible people, often sensible people of faith. Remember *Piss Christ* and that other *masterpiece* that portrayed the Virgin Mary surrounded by elephant crap?

This is why liberal talk on television and radio has failed. And far more important, it's also why liberalism in our culture—once such a great American treasure—has lost so much of its luster over the years. Half the time I find modern-day liberalism sad; the other half, I just find it silly.

So, in the world of media, if Republicans have the *Washington Times,* a relatively small second newspaper in a two-newspaper town, the Democrats have the most influential newspaper on the planet, the *New York Times,* whose editorials—and recently even some of its news stories—sound an awful lot like Democratic talking points.

And we're supposed to fret about *conservative* influences on the news?

No matter. While the Left gears up to start its own national liberal radio talk show network (and maybe a liberal cable TV network, too, possibly starring Al Gore), using seed money from fat-cat Democratic Party contributors, this is the new mantra, the number one talking point for all those solid thinkers who for so long have denounced Rush Limbaugh's ditto-heads as mindless automatons: *"There is no liberal bias in the news, but there is a conservative bias."*

Yes, it seems that right-wingers these days not only control Big Oil and Big Tobacco and Big Tires and Big Business in general and the military-industrial complex and the White House and both Houses of Congress and on some days the Supreme Court of the United States . . . *but now those conservative SOBs also control Big Media!*

The very sound of it is comforting: *"There is no liberal bias in the news, but there is a conservative bias."* Say it enough times and, who knows, maybe it will actually start to be true.

Perhaps the charge liberals have been making most often to back their claim of conservative bias is that the media have given George W. Bush a free ride on some very important issues involving foreign policy and national security. For a while you could hardly open up a liberal magazine or go to a liberal Web site without finding some bitter screed about how the press was sucking up to the president on everything from the war in Iraq to supposed civil liberties abuses at home. But the truth is, all the news media were doing was what the media always do in times of war: They were rallying 'round the flag. September 11 had a devastating impact on the national psyche. America had been attacked—not at our embassies in Africa and not even at Pearl Harbor. We had been attacked in New York City and Washington and Pennsylvania. The way the media covered the president wasn't proof of a *conservative* bias so much as it was evidence of a post–September 11 *pro-American* bias. This may not please some on the Left, but that's the way it's always been. And, just for the record, this *misplaced sense of patriotism,* as some on the Left saw it, didn't stop those *lapdogs* in the press from challenging President Bush on a million other issues, from environmental policy to the always popular "massive tax cuts for the rich."

"Well, what about all those media outlets with right-wing points of view?" the guy in the conference room wants to know, repeating what his friend (who doesn't think there's a liberal bias in the news) told him. "There's Bill O'Reilly; there's talk radio; there are a bunch of conservative syndicated columnists . . ."

I'm not sure if he or anyone else in the room notices that my eyes are rolling around my head in lazy circles. I have heard this one about 40 million times.

I find it both tiresome and disingenuous when liberals say, "Stop your whining about liberal bias; you've got plenty of conservatives in the media." Of course there's a conservative media. There's Rush Limbaugh and Sean Hannity and George Will and Robert Novak and Cal Thomas and Fred Barnes and Bill Buckley. But let's not forget that just about every editorial writer and columnist at the big powerful mainstream news outlets like the *New York Times, Los Angeles Times, Washington Post,* and *Boston Globe* are *liberals!* So conservatives have clout in the world of opinion and liberals have clout in the world of opinion. Wonderful! But, fundamentally, that's not the point. The point is that opinion is one thing and news is another. So telling me that there are all those conservative commentators out there and that I should stop my whining doesn't make me feel even the slightest bit better about the liberal bias of supposedly objective *news* reporters. News reporters are supposed to play it straight. It's that simple!

But even beyond that, in the media world, power and influence come from numbers. So consider these: The evening newscasts on ABC, CBS, NBC, and PBS total about 35 million viewers a night compared to *Special Report* with Brit Hume—Fox's evening newscast—which (right before the war in Iraq) was averaging about 1.3 million viewers. (Over an entire twenty-four-hour news cycle, Fox averaged about 1.058 million viewers; again, that's just before the war began.) Yes, it's true that Brit Hume brings certain conservative sensibilities to his newscast, but then Dan Rather brings certain liberal sensibilities to his. So, let's review: 35 million for the supposedly mainstream, nonliberal, nonbiased media, and just over a million for conservative Fox News. I repeat my earlier question: And we're supposed to fret about *conservative* influence on the news?

Of course, part of what *really* bothers so many liberals—though you can bet very few have actually thought about it this way—is that there even exists a more conservative alternative to the mainstream news outlets. Liberals, you see, had the playing field to themselves for so many years, controlling the rules of the game, that to them it had come to seem the natural order of things. It's ironic, isn't it, that liberals, who are always telling us that they're for change, that they're against the status quo, that *that* is what largely defines liberalism and (of course) makes liberals better, don't really mean it when the change doesn't quite suit them, when it means they will have a little competition—irreverent, edgy competition at that—to contend with. That's when they embrace the status quo with everything they've got and pine for the good old days, the days before those annoying *outsiders* got into the act, when the Big Three networks had to compete only with themselves. So while many Americans are encouraged that there's now some genuine diversity out there, many liberals regard this news as distressing—even *disorienting*, especially since ratings at the old news networks have been dropping for years while the upstart Fox News has been coming on strong, picking up new viewers just about every month since it went on the air in October 1996.

"Then what about the mainstream media's treatment of Clinton? You can't possibly think they went easy on him, can you?" is what liberals always ask.

It's a fair question. And the answer is, no, they didn't go easy on Clinton. The truth is, reporters will go after any politician—liberal or conservative—if the story is big enough and the politician is powerful enough. Still, all things being equal, there's no question the media elites salivate more when they're going after Republicans and conservatives—even the elites would admit to that, I think, after a few drinks.

But the entire premise of the question is wrong, because party politics is not primarily what liberal bias is about. What media bias is mainly about are the fundamental assumptions and beliefs and values that are the stuff of everyday life. The reason so many Americans who are pro-life or anti–affirmative action or who support gun rights detest the mainstream media is that day after day they fail to see in the media any respect for their views. What they see is a mainstream media seeming to legitimize one side (the one media elites agree with) as valid and moral, while seeking to cast the other side as narrow, small-minded, and bigoted. Even the editor of the liberal *Los Angeles Times* noticed that. On May 22, 2003, John Carroll wrote a scathing memo to his staff about political bias in the paper, singling out what he considered a liberally biased page-one story on abortion. "I'm concerned about the perception," he wrote, "and the occasional reality that the *Times* is a liberal, 'politically correct' newspaper. Generally speaking, this is an inaccurate view, but occasionally we prove our critics right. . . . The reason I'm sending this note to all section editors is that I want everyone to understand how serious I am about purging all political bias from our coverage. We may happen to live in a political atmosphere that is suffused with liberal values (and is unreflective of the nation as a whole), but we are not going to push a liberal agenda in the news pages of the *Times*."

Three cheers for John Carroll of the *Los Angeles Times*! The only part I'd take issue with is where he says, "generally speaking, [it] is an inaccurate view" to think the *Los Angeles Times* is a "liberal, 'politically correct' newspaper." No, generally speaking, it's quite an accurate view to believe the *Times* "is a liberal, 'politically correct' newspaper." And then there's the only "*occasionally* we prove our critics right." I don't think so. But I don't want to quibble. And besides, I understand he's got to live with these people.

Bias in the media isn't just about what they cover; it's also about what they don't cover. Sherlock Holmes once solved a particularly thorny crime using as his key piece of evidence the dog that *didn't* bark. It's the same with the news media. What they don't make noise about also tells us a lot about their preconceived notions and their biases.

We get lots of stories, for example, on racial discrimination. And we should. It's a valid and important subject. It also fits certain liberal assumptions about America—that bigotry is not just alive and well here and there, but that it's everywhere. Yet we don't get the kind of equally valid, legitimate, and important stories about race that make liberals feel uneasy. We hear almost nothing, for instance, about the powerful link between family dysfunction—especially children growing up without fathers—and violent crime. This isn't some partisan issue—far from it—this is the kind of thing that should concern all

Americans. As a matter of fact, it wasn't a conservative at all but William Galston, an assistant to Bill Clinton, who said that in order to avoid poverty, just do three things: finish high school, marry before having a child, and don't have that child until you're at least twenty years old. Only 8 percent of people who do all three of those things wind up poor, but a staggering 79 percent of those who fail to do them wind up in poverty.

The fact is, poverty shouldn't be a racial issue, either, since it and its social consequences cut across racial lines. But since a high percentage of those below the poverty line are black, liberal reporters do treat poverty as a racial issue, with the result being that it is rarely dealt with honestly.

It seems to me that the undeniable connection between poverty and the three key behaviors Galston cites would make a great story for the networks, the kind of story that might actually save lives. But we need more than just *a* story on the subject; the link between poverty and behavior should be part of the subtext of almost *every* story reporters do about poverty, about how the poor are always supposedly getting screwed by the system—or by overt racism. Do that kind of honest reporting enough times and we would start to really understand the nature and causes of poverty in America. That, for crying out loud, would be a much-needed public service for our country! But these are *inconvenient* stories that politically correct journalists pretty much stay clear of. It's sad but true that stories about personal responsibility and behavior—especially when poor people are involved—don't fit neatly into liberal journalists' preconceived notions about poverty and race and discrimination. Which is to say, the very absence of such news in the mainstream press is itself evidence of bias. It's the dog that doesn't bark.

So, that's what bias in the news is really about: what they report, how they report it, and what they choose *not* to report. The problem is groupthink. Outside the newsroom, the elites hang out with too many people who think just the way they do about the big issues of the day. Inside the newsroom, they surround themselves with still more like-minded people. They need a few pains in the ass around, a few newsroom renegades to keep them on their toes. But nervous news executives don't like people like that, so they wind up with orthodoxy. It's worse than a conspiracy.

Which is precisely why it's so hard to fix.

And I'm thinking as I sit in that conference room high above West Fiftieth Street in Manhattan that the only people who at this late date still don't know there's a bias problem are the naked emperors of alleged objectivity and those poor saps determined to defend them at any cost. And if you listen closely, you can hear all of them, calmly chanting their mantra in perfect unison: "What bed? What girl?" Sorry. *"There is no liberal bias in the news, but there is a conservative bias. There is no liberal bias in the news, but there is . . ."*

Still, as I'm sitting there in the conference room, I realize all of this is helpful. The elite media are once again making things easy for me. They have made my point—that they will do anything to avoid facing up to this problem. *Anything!*

Even the good guys give you reason to despair. In early 2003, David Shaw of the *Los Angeles Times,* who is one of the top media writers in the country, came up with an earth-shaking theory. There is no significant liberal bias in the news, he told us, but there *is* another kind of bias, one that is far more dangerous. "We're biased in favor of bad news, rather than good news. We're biased in favor of conflict rather than harmony. Increasingly we're biased in favor of sensationalism, scandal, celebrities and violence as opposed to serious, insightful coverage of important issues of the day."

There's a scoop, huh? Anyone who has tuned into *48 Hours, 20/20,* or *Dateline* for two or three seconds knows all of that. But now we're being told that just because there's a bias toward crap in the news—which there most certainly is—we need to worry far more about that than "about any ideological infiltration" in the news, as David Shaw puts it. Sorry, David, I can walk and chew gum at the same time. And I can worry about two kinds of bias at the same time, too, because, despite what you seem to think, *both* exist.

But I don't want to make this point, or any of the others, simply to people who already know it. Which is why one of the things I'm hoping this book will do is reach beyond the traditional conservative "ghetto" to reasonable and well-intentioned people across the political spectrum—to people with an open mind, no matter what their politics. To be sure, in today's highly polarized world, that will not be easy. Too often we talk right past each other in our culture—and no one, liberal or conservative, has clean hands on this one. Still, it seems to me that liberals—the very people who take such pride in seeing themselves as civil and open-minded—have, in a sad kind of way, become precisely what they accuse conservatives of: being close-minded and nasty. Many liberals these days—and ironically, especially the elites who think of themselves as worldly and sophisticated—are even narrower and more provincial than they imagine the rest of America to be. How can this be? It's easy when you live in a bubble, surrounded by others who think the same way about almost everything.

Yes, it's true that many conservatives also spend too much time in their own bubble, surrounded by like-minded souls who are always agreeing with one another. But here's the difference: Liberal culture in America is pervasive. You get it in movies and you hear it in music and you read it in magazines and you watch it on TV, in sitcoms and dramas as well as on the news. In America, unless you live in a cave, it's nearly impossible *not* to be exposed to liberal attitudes and assumptions on all sorts of issues ranging from guns to gay rights. Liberals, on the other hand, if they avoid just a couple of spots on the radio and TV dial—and especially if they live in liberal ghettoes like Beverly Hills or the Upper West Side of Manhattan—can pretty much stay clear of conservative attitudes and assumptions *and even conservative people,* secure in the knowledge that they're not really missing anything worth knowing.

Examples of this are not hard to come by, but some, like the following, are just amazingly telling. On February 6, 2003, while America was deeply divided on whether we should go to war with Iraq, veteran *Washington Post* columnist Mary McGrory wrote these remarkable words: "Among people I know, nobody was for the war." Imagine that. What a single-minded little world she must live in where, among all the people she knows, nobody—absolutely *nobody*—thought that invading Iraq was a good idea.

They live in a world, these bubble people, that is reassuringly uncomplicated and blissfully unchallenged by new ideas. As far as many liberals are concerned, all that's necessary to know is that different ideas can be dangerous ideas, embraced by the narrow-minded and intolerant, a threat to everything that good and decent people (like themselves) believe in.

In fact, the only reason so many smart liberals are convinced there is no liberal bias in the news in the first place is that this is what they keep hearing from the mainstream media they rely on for so much of their information. Since almost no one in these liberal circles ever risks exposure to another point of view, they truly don't understand why so many Middle Americans are so upset with Big Media. Yet what I have often found is that when liberals, for whatever reason, actually do come face-to-face with some of these scary ideas, they surprise themselves by how much they agree with them.

So, for all my frustration that so many intelligent people on the Left still don't get it, I also see this chat with the bigwigs in the big conference room as an opportunity. Among the hundreds of letters that showed up in my mailbox after *Bias* came out, there was the one from Stephen DeBock of Bayville, New Jersey, who said, "Your book reminds me of Ralph Nader's *Unsafe at Any Speed,* not so much in content as in the industry's reaction. When *Unsafe* blasted GM's coffin-on-wheels Corvair, the company responded not by fixing the product but by hiring a private investigator to ferret out whatever information it could use to discredit Nader. The tactic failed. In like manner, CBS and its stablemates have responded to *Bias* not by fixing the problem but by trying to discredit you. I wish them the same success General Motors had."

It's funny, because as I started to outline this book, I had also been thinking about Nader's classic work. What Ralph Nader understood was that the first order of business was to expose the industry's ingrained culture of denial, because until that happens there will be no meaningful change.

That, my friends, is a very tall order, and I make no claim that this book will have the influence that Nader's did. Still, as I told the executives in that conference room, I also intend to expose an industry's culture of denial. I intend to deal with the internal pressures that silence in-house dissent. Why is it so difficult for good and honest journalists who know there is a problem to stand up and be counted? I intend to deal with the increasingly powerful pressure groups inside the newsroom that enforce political correctness, or "authoritarian liberalism, sometimes referred to, though inadequately, as 'political correctness,'" as former federal judge Robert Bork has put it; with how liberal ideology permeates not only the networks and top newspapers but the journalism schools churning out the next generation of elite reporters; with the whole damn system that refuses to look honestly at itself.

But I also told them that I would lay out a blueprint for change. In the end, this is as important as anything in the book—because while everyone knows that you can't have a free country without a free press, what isn't said nearly enough is that you can't have it without a *fair* press, either. Not in the long run anyway. The networks, as we've mentioned, have been bleeding viewers at an alarming rate. Powerful as they still are, they are far less powerful than they used to be. And next year and the year after that they'll be even less powerful. That's not entirely because of bias, but a lot of it sure is. Once upon a time Walter Cronkite was "the most trusted man in America." Who today would describe *any* of the network anchors that way?

The reason some of us got involved with this issue in the first place is not that we're mindless right-wing media bashers, but that we care deeply about this issue of fairness—the very thing liberals always insist they, also, want. The mainstream media have a fundamental role in our democratic process, one that it is essential to the health of the Republic, not to put too fine a point on it. So it is in everyone's interest that they not only survive, but that they also be widely respected.

The fact is, I'm rooting for them to turn things around and regain the trust of the American people. Too many Americans these days say they get their "news" from talk radio. This isn't good for anybody. Rush Limbaugh is smart and knowledgeable, but he's not in the straight news business and he'd be the first one to tell you that. Besides, there aren't too many of his caliber on the air. But the elites will never be able to get things right with the American people if all they do when the subject of bias comes up is deny, deny, deny. As the *Wall Street Journal* put it: "In an era of talk radio, the Internet and ever more media outlets, denial is not a winning strategy."

And as I told the people in the conference room, that is why this book is *not* about proving the existence of liberal bias in the media, much less about the phony issue of conservative bias. Ultimately it is about making things better. The naked emperors can continue to deny and dissemble on the bias question, proudly marching on with their privates dangling in the breeze, but while they've been marching, the ship has already sailed. The train has left the station. The ballgame is over. And the fat lady stopped singing a long time ago.

They need to be saved—*from themselves.*

A (Very) Few Minutes
with Andy Rooney

There are some journalists out there, of course, who refuse to pretend that liberal bias is a myth, a canard concocted by right-wing ideologues. And they would never try to convince anybody—let alone themselves—that the real problem these days is somehow tied to the fashionable but silly notion of *conservative* bias in the news. They're way too honest for any of that.

The problem is, they're not quite honest enough—or more to the point, they're not quite principled enough—to stir things up, to make a real issue out of it, to force the guilty parties to confront their biases and then do something about them.

Which, I'm afraid, brings me to my old colleague Andy Rooney.

In the summer of 2002, about eight months after *Bias* was published, I had a couple of odd and curiously unsatisfying conversations with Andy. Have you ever noticed how sometimes you call someone and they seem just a little too eager to get off the phone? How they make a point of telling you how busy they are? Well, it was kind of like that. Only a lot more complicated. Have you ever noticed how disheartening it is when people you like and respect just plain let you down?

The reason I was calling Andy had to do with something he had recently said on the Larry King show. Andy usually ruminates on such weighty matters as how he likes peanut butter and how he likes jelly but how he can't stand peanut butter *and* jelly, but what he told Larry on June 5, 2002, was actually important.

"There is just no question," Andy said when asked about liberal bias in the news, that "I, among others, have a liberal bias. I mean I'm consistently liberal in my opinions."

Frankly, I don't care about Andy's politics. He's a commentator, not a reporter. He can be as liberal as he wants as far as I'm concerned. But what did he mean when he said, "I, *among others,* have a liberal bias"? Who were these *"others"*?

We were about to find out, and it was a bombshell.

"I think Dan is transparently liberal. Now he may not like to hear me say that. I always agree with him, too. But I think he should be more careful."

Had I heard right? Did Andy Rooney—the same one who's on 60 Minutes *every week—just go where no newsman had gone before? Did he really say that Dan Rather was "transparently liberal"?*

Now, I understand that Dan Rather's liberalism will certainly come as no big surprise to a lot of people. Dan has strong views on all kinds of things, and sometimes he lets those views just plain slip out.

But I also understand that Dan doesn't see it that way—at all! He's been consistently adamant in his denials and has long maintained that liberal bias is a myth, pretty much right-wing bunk. "You got a better chance hearin' Mother Goose singin' opera on a pogo stick at Carnegie Hall than you got a chance of hearin' liberal bias come out of my mouth on the news show," is how Dan might put it when he's doing his Texas thing.

But here was the beloved Andy Rooney, one of the elder statesmen of network news, admitting on national television—no, make that *worldwide* television—that Dan Rather is not just liberal but *transparently* liberal. This was extraordinary! It was huge. Even I never said anything that inflammatory.

This was more than a crack in the dam; the whole damn thing was about to burst. Andy Rooney had just acknowledged that conservatives had been right all these years, after all.

The next day papers all over the country ran big headlines, screaming that "Rooney Admits Liberal Bias at the Networks, Says Dan Rather Guilty Too." It was on *Meet the Press* and all the other Sunday morning news shows. Dan Rather was forced to issue a response.

Not really.

Exactly one newspaper picked up Andy's observations about liberal bias in television news. And that was the *Washington Times,* a conservative paper, which ran it as the "Quote of the Week." The *New York Times* didn't say a word about Andy Rooney's admission. Neither did the *Los Angeles Times.* Neither did Peter Johnson, the *USA Today* columnist who writes about all sorts of things that go on in the world of television. Neither did smart reporters like Howard Kurtz of the *Washington Post,* who writes about serious issues that affect the media and the American people. Nor did any of the many reporters who had written so passionately about really important journalistic topics like Dan Rather's haircut, Katie Couric's contract, or, for that matter, the stuff that came out of Andy Rooney's babbling brook of a mouth just a few months later about how, in his view, "those damn women" TV sideline football reporters were pretty much useless. Now, *that* was big news as far as the media was concerned; *that* made headlines all over the country!

Apparently, it was one thing to go after an old white guy who doesn't like getting his sideline football reports from damn women, and quite another to report on the same guy (in his role as a prominent media heavy hitter) admitting that he and other key members of the media elite are unabashedly liberal. Obvious as that already is to many people, it might do the one thing the media elites don't ever want to do for fear the whole house of cards might come tumbling down: *give serious credence to the charge of liberal bias.*

So before you could say, "Did you ever notice how hypocritical and shallow journalists can be?" Andy Rooney's bombshell went out, not with a bang, but with a whimper.

But before Andy himself went out, he had one more little piece of wisdom for Larry King (who had asked him specifically about my book, *Bias*). Who knows? Maybe he said it just to make sure his bosses at CBS News knew whose side he really was on. Bernie Goldberg, he said, "just has a great knack for being a jerk."

Hardly an original thought. I've been called a lot worse. So that, as they say, would have been that—because at this point, I certainly had no intention of giving Andy a call. But Andy Rooney doesn't know when to put a lid on it. So, a few weeks after he did the Larry King show, Andy devoted his syndicated column to a subject of universal interest—lying. He began by writing that "Lies are part of life." He wrote about the value of lying to your wife when she asks you how she looks in her new dress. "'It's okay' is not enough," he told us.

Then he got around to lying and his appearance on the Larry King show.

"As a guest on the Larry King show a few weeks ago, I said some things, in answer to his questions, that I would have been better off lying about or avoiding. It was not that the people who objected to what I said necessarily thought I was wrong. They thought I shouldn't have said it. In my own defense, I told a boss of mine that I thought if all the truth were known by everyone, it would be a better world. He scoffed. I think 'scoff' is what he did. I know he rejected the idea."

Let's see if I understood this: Andy Rooney thinks that when it comes to liberal bias in the news, *dishonesty* is the best policy? And this most respected and admired veteran of CBS News, whose credibility is his most valuable asset, quietly sat there while his boss—presumably that would be either Don Hewitt, the executive producer of *60 Minutes*, or Andrew Heyward, the president of CBS News—told him that even though what he'd told Larry King was not necessarily wrong, when it comes to liberal bias in the news, the best policy is to take the Fifth?

And here's the capper: After mulling it over for a while, Andy concludes right there in the column that his boss was right. "I've thought about it," Andy writes, "and in retrospect decided he was right in dismissing what I had to say. Our lives could not survive all the truth about everything."

Andy Rooney is a formidable figure, and has been since long before he joined *60 Minutes*. In his day he was a truly great reporter. He was the first American to cover a bombing raid over Germany, and he also reported on the invasion of Normandy; he was there with the troops for the liberation of Paris and later wrote a deeply moving book about that experience. Before anyone but his friends and family knew his face or his voice, back when CBS was still the industry standard of integrity and excellence, he wrote some of the network's great documentaries, as well as pieces for such legendary series as *The Twentieth Century*.

Yet here he was, not only being accused by management of disloyalty for talking honestly about a subject of great importance to millions of viewers, but working his way around to the conclusion that he *agrees* with his boss.

Andy Rooney has had many fine hours in journalism, but this was not one of them.

After my head stopped spinning, I picked up the phone to call Andy. I needed to hear one-on-one whether he could possibly have meant this the way it sounded.

Right off the bat, Andy told me he was doing his newspaper column, so we had to keep it short. Okay, I got right to the point. First of all, I asked him which boss told him that liberal bias and Dan Rather are out of bounds.

"I really don't want to answer that," he said.

Well, I said, can you tell me this: "What exactly did this boss say to you?"

"That it was disloyal for me to say what I said. I don't know whether they believe there is a bias or not; they just thought it was disloyal for me to say what I did."

That at least confirmed the identity of the boss. I'd heard that lecture myself when I first wrote about bias in the news. There's only one guy who talks about loyalty and disloyalty that way. Hint: It's not Don Hewitt.

I replied, "Look, Andy, it's one thing to lie about your wife's dress. But do you really think it's okay to lie about bias in the news?"

"I wouldn't have lied about the subject," he said. "I just would have avoided the subject."

Whatever.

Moving on, keenly aware of how mad Dan Rather gets when he's accused of liberal bias, I then asked Andy if Dan had confronted him about the "transparently liberal" comment.

"I wouldn't want to lie to you about that."

I laughed. Andy didn't.

Just a moment later, Andy repeated that he was under the gun, and the conversation was over. It had lasted only a few minutes.

But it stayed with me—because of all that had gone *unsaid.*

Fair-minded guy that he is, it's impossible to believe Andy doesn't know as well as I do just how crucial this issue of bias is. It's hard to believe that over the years he hasn't received as many letters on the subject as I have. Crusty and plainspoken as he is, Andy has that kind of credibility with viewers.

But there's another reason I'd expect Andy Rooney to bring some passion to this issue. He knows how important it is that the media encourage free and open conversation on controversial issues, rather than suppress it. And he knows—far better than most—that there's been way too much suppression in recent years of ideas that fail to pass the liberal litmus test.

He knows that, because he himself has been one of PC's most public victims. During a CBS special at the end of 1989—a wrap-up of that year's events—Andy observed that "homosexual unions" had been among the main "self-induced" causes of deaths among Americans, along with smoking and alcohol abuse. In the midst of an AIDS epidemic spiraling out of control, it was an unfortunate choice of words, seeming to indicate a callousness that anyone who knows Andy Rooney cannot believe he really felt. But it also happened to be the sort of thing a great many men of his generation—the Greatest Generation—might have said on the subject. More to the point, notwithstanding the way he expressed it, what he said was not all that far from the truth. By then even AIDS advocates were raising the alarm about "unsafe sex" within the gay community; and though most of the media was dutifully echoing the line that AIDS "was everyone's disease," to this day it has remained, at least in this country, confined almost exclusively to the high-risk groups (gay men, drug abusers and their female sex partners).

No matter. Andy Rooney was attacked as viciously insensitive and was quickly suspended by CBS News, joining the long, sorry list of so many others, from university professors to corporate officers, who have paid the price for offending PC sensibilities. At the time, I wrote Andy a letter, telling him I thought CBS News had treated him very badly, that commentators shouldn't be punished for saying unpopular things. I told him I was on his side.

I'm sure I wasn't the only journalist who felt that way. Still, a lot of the news establishment, far from resisting the suppression of speech and thought, quietly has been one of its chief proponents and enforcers.

Since this was one of the things I was writing about in this book, I decided to give Andy another shot at it. Unfortunately, our second conversation was, if anything, even more awkward than the first.

When I asked him about the trouble he got into when he was suspended for saying the wrong thing, he quickly moved to safer ground, saying there are all kinds of things people don't want talked about. "Religion is the best example of that. People don't want to talk about religion if it's negative."

I said, wasn't liberal bias one of those topics, as far as the press is concerned?

Andy basically repeated what he'd said earlier: that his boss's complaint was not that he'd talked about the media's slanting the news, but that he'd been disloyal to Dan, as if *that* were the issue of paramount concern. "I think you're overblowing it," he said.

"Well, didn't they tell you not to talk about bias?"

"They did not tell me not to talk about it," he replied, as we continued round and round; "they told me I was disloyal to talk about a colleague."

"Don't you think a discussion on these subjects with the biggest possible audience would be a good thing?" I asked, meaning not just the bias question but also all the other issues deemed off limits by the PC police.

In his response, it was impossible not to hear a world-weariness. Clearly, he just wanted to be done with me, and with these questions. "Look, Bernie," he told me, "why don't you just move on? You've had an effect. Don't make this your life. Just move on." He paused. "I'm going now; I'm late with a book manuscript."

I feel for Andy. I really do. There are things about the guy I like and admire immensely. And I know what he's gone through personally with the suspension and all.

Still, it's pretty ironic, isn't it? Journalists are always accusing government or Big Business or some other powerful institution of creating the notorious "chilling effect," which supposedly makes even the boldest in their newsrooms go mute. Yet, that's exactly what CBS News had imposed on one of its most celebrated own: a "chilling effect."

I realized there was no point continuing the conversation with Andy—when we talked, you could almost hear the tick, tick, tick, of the *60 Minutes* stopwatch as he counted the seconds until he could make his escape.

This last conversation left me with such an empty feeling that I sat down and wrote my former CBS News colleague the following letter. Ultimately, I decided not to send it. Why? Because we can go around on this forever and we will *never* have the kind of dialogue I wish were possible.

Dear Andy:

I've been thinking about your advice that I move on. I know it was well intended. But think about it, Andy: Do you suppose in the history of network journalism someone reporting on Big Oil has *ever* been urged by a colleague to drop it and move on? Or someone doing stories about threats to the environment?

I'll tell you what: Let's see some meaningful changes in network news. Let's see those points of view that run counter to PC liberal norms start getting equal time. Let's see enough changes in the way newspeople conduct themselves so that no decent citizen ever again has to feel mocked and belittled when he turns on the network news. *Then* I'll move on.

We can go back and forth about the particulars of your conversation with Larry King, and we can quibble over the precise meaning of your boss's words: Would he prefer for you to dissemble, avoid the subject, or just lie by omission? In the end, it doesn't matter. It's all bad. What does matter is, he wants to dodge the public conversation—just as we in the media have avoided talking freely about so many important issues in recent years.

My question to you is this: When did journalists become such cowards? When did they stop understanding we need *more* talk in America about issues like race and gay rights and, yes, liberal media bias—not *less?*

It's really pretty simple, Andy: It's not good for news guys to lie. Not even by omission. Not about the news anyway. If you want to lie about how many times a day Jennifer Lopez sneaks into your office and says she can't live without you, no problem.

But when you start to lie about the serious stuff—or *simply* "avoid" the subject—you cause real problems for honest journalists. I mean, our standing in the Gallup Poll of Most Trusted Professions, which already has us ranked somewhere around politicians, will push us below used-car dealers.

The bottom line, Andy, is not just whether a news media that behaves this way can survive. It's whether it even deserves to.

Your Pal,
Bernie Goldberg

File It Under "H"

You know the old saying "They can dish it out but they can't take it"?

In October 1999 the ABC newsmagazine *20/20* was about to air a story on a man named Michael Ellis, the founder and CEO of a company that markets a controversial weight-loss pill. It was the kind of investigation that doesn't always end well for the person on the other end of the camera, the one being interviewed. So, fearing his comments might be taken out of context and that the interview might be edited to make him look bad, before the *20/20* piece aired Ellis took the *unedited transcript and video of the entire interview*—which he'd recorded on his own—and put it out on the World Wide Web.

This made people at ABC News very angry. In fact, one vice president told the *New York Times,* without any hint of irony, that "We don't want other people attempting to get into and shift the journalism process."

Next to be heard from was former ABC News Vice President

Richard Wald, now teaching young journalists at the Columbia Graduate School of Journalism. Wald called the CEO's strategy "a not-so-subtle form of intimidation."

Get it? When the media disseminates information about "other people," it's news. When "other people" disseminate information about themselves, it's intimidation.

It didn't take long for the tsunami to reach CBS News, where its president, Andrew Heyward, put out the following in-house memo. I share it with you now, in its entirety.

From: Andrew Heyward
To: [The entire staff of CBS News]
Date: 11/23/99 10:23am
Subject: Addition to News Standards

CBS News has always had an informal practice of allowing people being interviewed to make their own tape if they wanted to. This is meant only to serve as their record of the interview. Now, because new technology makes it easy for sources to use this material in ways that violate our copyright, we'd like to clarify what is and is not permitted.

The following paragraphs should be added to the CBS News Standards book under Section II-3, "Interviews." They would come after the current third paragraph, the one ending with . . . "will be covered." A new printed loose-leaf page will be distributed at a future time. For the present, please print this e-mail and add it to the book of standards.

Policy on Interviewees Taping the Interview for Themselves

It is CBS News policy to allow interviewees to record their interviews. The contents, however, cannot be published in any medium without the consent of CBS News since the interview is the sole copyrighted property of CBS News. Moreover, the interviewee's tape can only be rolling when the CBS News tape is rolling. There can be no recording of off-camera or off-mike conversations.

To clarify this, the producer or correspondent should record on the CBS tape, and in the subject's presence, this statement: "We are allowing _____ to record the following interview for his/her personal use with the understanding that the contents are the legal property of CBS News and may not be published or broadcast in any medium by anyone other than CBS News and those expressly authorized by CBS News."

End of new section. 11/23/99

File that memo under "H" . . . for *Hypocrisy*.

Mauling the Messenger

Bias was *Peyton Place*, without the sex.

One was a book about narrow-minded hypocrites who inhabit a corrupt little world and will do almost anything to keep the outside world from learning their dirty little secrets. The other was a racy novel set in New England.

When *Peyton Place* was published back in the genteel 1950s, a time when sex, as a subject anyway, was still very much taboo, it touched off a furor. But Grace Metalious, who wrote *Peyton Place*, saw the book as the literary equivalent of kicking over a rock. "All kinds of strange things crawl out," as she noted in 1956. "Everybody who lives in town knows what's going on—there are no secrets—but they don't want outsiders to know."

In the town where she lived, Gilmanton, New Hampshire, they never forgave Ms. Metalious for writing about the sex and power and hypocrisy in *Peyton Place*, which of course they suspected was modeled on their own small town. Even when she died they didn't want her buried in Gilmanton. As one local newspaper writer put it, "Grace Metalious was dead but not forgiven."

Except for my refusal to cooperate on the "dead" part, *Bias* was déjà vu all over again. Liberal bias being the taboo of choice as far as the media elites are concerned, when the book came out in December 2001 it provoked a firestorm within media circles. That one of their own would expose their dirty little secrets, saying out loud what "they don't want outsiders to know," was widely seen as the ultimate act of treachery—a charge I heard a lot after *Bias* was published.

Don Imus, who has made a career out of going back and forth between kissing the media elites' collective ass one day and blasting Dan Rather as a "psychopath mental patient . . . pom-pom–waving putz" the next, called me a "backstabbing weasel" on his radio show and compared me to Sammy the Bull Gravano, who, before ratting out his pals in the mob, killed nineteen people.

Eric Engberg, a reporter in the CBS News Washington bureau, told Howard Kurtz of the *Washington Post* that *Bias* was an "act of treason," adding for good measure that I "was a selfish, self-involved guy who was not a team player."

Funny, I always thought reporters *loved* people who weren't team players. Didn't they embrace people at big companies who were not team players and who told their stories on *60 Minutes*? Didn't *TIME* magazine put three whistle-blowers on its cover as 2002 Persons of the Year? Since when did reporters vilify someone for *not* being a team player?

"CBS, after all, depends on people who aren't 'team players' for its information," as an editorial in the *Investor's Business Daily* pointed out. "Suddenly it prefers conformity to truth-telling. Engberg calls Goldberg's book an 'act of treason,' even as his job relies on similar acts of treason from his sources.

"Figures who've broken with the political right, such as John Dean, often receive plaudits from the establishment press for their willingness to tell an important truth at the expense of their personal associations.

"Why doesn't Goldberg fall into this category? Because he is pointing out the mainstream press' left-leaning bias, something that the media doesn't want to hear about."

As wearisome as some of the vitriol spewed my way was, it was obvious that the media elites' reaction to the accusation of bias ultimately says a lot more about them than it does about me or anyone else making the charge. It both reflects their colossal arrogance and, perhaps even more telling, reveals their fear of the kind of free and open dialogue that would challenge their entrenched views on all sorts of subjects.

The subject infuriates and frightens them in precisely the same way revelations about power, sex, and corruption once infuriated and frightened the inhabitants of small-town New Hampshire. Never mind that for millions of their own viewers, bias in network news is a given, and that it is steadily eroding their trust in the media; the media elites would rather dismiss those people as boobs and bigots than face up to the obvious fact that they've got a big problem on their hands.

And as I look back, I realize that is part of what bothered me for so many years—the realization that my liberal friends had forgotten how to be liberal. I was (or at least had been) one of them, after all. To this day, as I often say, I consider myself *an old-fashioned liberal*— meaning I'm a liberal the way liberals *used to be,* when they were more mainstream like John F. Kennedy and Hubert Humphrey and less left-wing like Al Franken and Michael Moore; when they were more upbeat and enthusiastic and less nasty and pessimistic. So over the years, as liberalism drifted further and further to the left, I guess I also drifted, a little anyway, in a different direction. Not long ago I was reading a piece by a Hollywood writer named Burt Prelutsky that captured the migration very nicely. The article, "Conservatives are from Mars (Liberals are from San Francisco)," ended this way: "Most of the conservatives I know, including myself, started out somewhere else on the political spectrum, and evolved through time and knowledge and experience. I personally do not know a single case of an individual evolving in the other direction. I will leave it to Darwinists to make of that what they will."

Bingo!

So, for me anyway, it's not just the bias itself but also the illiberal arrogance and the elitism and the contempt too many big journalists have for ordinary Americans. A top producer at *48 Hours,* for instance, used to call the show's audience "white trash in a double-wide making $15,000 a year." This particular producer lives in a well-to-do liberal suburb of New York City, where such an observation, if it were made about any group other than *"white* trash," would be considered hate speech, punishable by life without the possibility of ever having drinks at Phil Donahue's place.

The essayist and critic A. J. Leibling once famously said that "Freedom of the press is guaranteed only to those who own one." Though the Internet has since democratized the media in ways Leibling could never have imagined, there's still enormous truth in the observation. Except these days it's not so much the CEOs of the major media—in the case of the networks, the people who run GE and Viacom and Disney—who are calling the shots; it's the big-name on-camera journalists and their producers and the news executives who (at least nominally) work for them. Despite what liberals like to claim, the supposedly conservative influence these corporate bosses exert over guys like Dan Rather or Tom Brokaw is virtually nonexistent. The businesspeople who run those conglomerates aren't remotely involved in the daily coverage of the news, and they don't want to be.

In fact, as much as ever, it remains a tiny group of journalists who control the cameras and the microphones and the studios and the printing presses. And they abuse this tremendous power far too often. They're the ones who decide who gets on their news programs and in their newspapers and who doesn't. In the routine choices they make, they decide which voices and which opinions merit serious consideration. They decide who is mainstream and who is fringe.

And here's a big surprise: Among the ones they marginalize as a matter of course are those with the bad manners to point out their abuse of power. Indeed, Ted J. Smith III, the Virginia Commonwealth University professor and fellow at the nonpartisan Center for Media and Public Affairs, offered a detailed analysis of how the elite media neutralize their critics.

According to Smith, writing in *The American Enterprise* magazine (July/August 2002), when confronted with evidence of bias, journalists and their liberal supporters' first line of defense is almost always to dismiss such charges "as the fevered ravings of right-wing zealots." On the rare occasions when a book or an article about media bias breaks out to a wider audience, "all that's required," Smith observes, "is a bit of damage control. First, the author is rigorously excluded from the largest popular media"—meaning the network news programs and on-air magazines—so that anyone who might not have made up his mind on the subject, or even thought much about it, is never exposed to the critics—or their "dangerous ideas."

In my case, one fact says it all: Though I was on about five hundred radio programs talking about *Bias* and did about fifty cable television interviews, and despite the fact that they wrote about *Bias* in newspapers all across America and did stories about it in China and New Zealand and Australia and Brazil and Canada and the U.K. and Israel and Russia and Sweden and who knows how many other countries, there were three places I was *never* welcome: ABC News, CBS News, and (with one tiny exception) NBC News. *Dateline* wouldn't put me on to talk about liberal bias in the media, neither would *60 Minutes* or *20/20.* None of the evening newscasts would mention the book or the subject. A producer from what he described as "the Italian version of *Nightline*" wanted me on, but the one with Ted Koppel here in the States—the *Nightline* that keeps telling us how important it is—had no interest. I couldn't even get on the network overnight newscasts at three in the morning. *CBS Morning Show* wouldn't have me on, and neither would *Good Morning America* on ABC. But five months after the book came out, and only after the Associated Press ran a story about how the networks were ignoring *Bias,* the *Today* show did let me on to talk to Matt Lauer for a few minutes—but only with another guest, lefty author Michael Moore, the same Michael Moore who, less than a year later, after winning the Academy Award for Best Documentary, would launch into a tirade against America's "fictitious election," its "fictitious president," and his "fictitious reasons" for going to war with Iraq.

Aside from those few minutes on *Today,* no other Big Three network news program wanted any part of me or my book. And these are the people who say, with semi-straight faces, they have no agenda and no biases?

But while the networks were ignoring me, something happened that the media elites didn't expect. The book took off. Before it came out, I knew two things for sure: that regular Americans cared very much about the subject and that the wizards I used to work for at CBS News and their courageous counterparts at the other networks thought the only people who cared about bias in the media were right-wing dummies who had no teeth and were dating their first cousins. But even I was surprised by just how much passion a book about bias in the media actually generated. Within a couple of weeks, *Bias* hit that sacred barometer of liberal respectability—the *New York Times* best-seller list. And it kept on rising until it hit number one, where it stayed for much of the winter and into the spring.

In other words, *Bias* became almost impossible to ignore.

So what happened then? Did the major media figures who disagreed with me challenge my ideas? Did they try to begin an honest, civil discussion about liberal bias in the news?

Professor Smith could have told me exactly what was coming.

Once damage control fails, he says, "in the rest of the elite media the author is subjected to personal abuse. . . .

"Because the media have the power to set the terms of the debate, every critic can be marginalized, every study rendered 'controversial.' So journalists and their apologists can always claim that media bias has not been proved."

The fact is, despite the play *Bias* was getting on talk radio and cable television, most people at the networks continued to say nothing about the book—at least publicly. Some of my old colleagues at CBS News and the other networks were calling me privately, saying they thought I was right. But I understood why they had to whisper. They had families and jobs to protect.

But there are also those unrepentant defenders that the good professor describes, and some of them went into the kind of tizzy that Grace Metalious knew all too well. They tried to turn me into a villain for even bringing the subject up.

Take Tom Shales. Please! Shales writes for the *Washington Post,* won a Pulitzer, and, for whatever reason, is a very angry white male. Shales read *Bias* and didn't like it one bit. That's fine with me. A lot of liberal journalists didn't like it. But instead of writing an intelligent, civil review explaining *why* he didn't like it, Shales tore into me in something called *Electronic Media* (now *TelevisionWeek*), beginning his tirade this way: "Disgruntled has-beens everywhere have a new hero and role model: Bernard Goldberg, the one-time CBS News correspondent and full-time addlepated windbag."

After that, Tom pulled out one of the great clichés of all time and called me "a no-talent hack." He said I was "a flop as a network correspondent" and that I'm "a lousy writer besides." He said, "Let's face it, [Goldberg] was not a bright shining star in the firmament of CBS News." He said I "usually looked disheveled and bleary-eyed on the air." He suggested I'm stupid, that my arguments are "drivel," and he tossed around words like "lame" to describe my meager abilities.

I was really annoyed! Not because of the "has-been" shot or because he called me a "no-talent hack" or said I was "bleary-eyed." I was mad because I didn't know the meaning of the word "addlepated" and had to actually get out of my chair and go look it up. In case you care, it means having a brain that is dizzy, muddled, or confused. Tom Shales, who, it's been said, looks remarkably like the Pillsbury Doughboy with a very bad haircut, obviously doesn't realize how entertaining he is when he goes on a flamboyant romp and kicks it into hyperventilation mode.

"I can't remember the last time I saw a mainstream critic use language so vitriolic," is how Jay Nordlinger summed it up in the *National Review Online.*

"To be honest, I cannot recall having read a review that was snottier, sillier, more feeble and hysterical than this one," noted Jonah Goldberg, who is no relation, in an on-line piece called "Shrieking Shales."

By the way, a week later *Electronic Media* reported that it received more than nine hundred letters to the editor on the Shales piece and that virtually all of them took Shales to task. They called him "nasty" and "hateful," and one said he "should be ashamed of himself."

Good luck on that last one. Arrogance, in the world of elite journalism, is a far more powerful emotion, and a stronger influence on behavior, than shame can ever hope to be.

Michael Kinsley is another mainstream liberal journalist, another intelligent guy who wrote about *Bias.* Kinsley, who was the resident liberal during the early days of CNN's *Crossfire* and went on to edit the on-line magazine *Slate,* wasn't nearly as colorful as Shales, but he was almost as abusive. In a column published in January 2002 in both the *Washington Post* and *Slate,* Kinsley wrote that I was "remarkably dense," that *Bias* is a "dumb book," and he creates a fictional conversation in which a character calls me an "idiot."

If some third-grader had written a book report and called whatever he had just read "a dumb book" written by an "idiot," he'd get an F. Yet, this is what passes for intelligent analysis from this guy who went to . . . *Harvard*! About the only thing Mike Kinsley left out of his brilliant review was ". . . and Bernie Goldberg's mother wears combat boots."

To be fair, in a moment of great generosity, Mike did give me this much: "Like a stopped clock," he wrote, "Goldberg isn't always wrong."

That, at least, might have been the *start* of a dialogue. In what ways was I *not* wrong? What, in Mike's opinion, was the extent of liberal bias, and what impact has it had on trust in the media? But of course, if his column is any guide, that's a conversation Mike Kinsley is not remotely interested in having.

Bias also touched a nerve in Al Neuharth, who started *USA Today* and writes a column for the paper. After the mandatory personal insults—I "was a second-string [some say second-rate] newsman at CBS for 20 years"—Al concludes that *Bias* is "biased from cover to cover." Not that he bothers to rebut a single point I made in the book. Not one. Which leads me to believe that he probably never even read it. Still, he does manage to slip in that he is "a longtime acquaintance" of Dan Rather, Tom Brokaw, and Peter Jennings—which, I should point out (especially for anyone who doesn't understand how it works behind the scenes in Big Journalism), is the most important and most revealing tidbit in his entire review.

Editors at *USA Today* sent word to me that the Neuharth column was about to be published, and in fairness wanted to give me an opportunity to respond—"in two to three sentences." Through an intermediary I told the editors what they could do with their offer, which was translated into something like "Mr. Goldberg graciously declines your invitation to respond." My publisher, Al Regnery, however, did write a letter to the editor that read, "*USA Today* gave Mr. Goldberg the opportunity to respond in 2–3 sentences, but Al Neuharth gets 300 words? And there's no liberal bias? This is why so many people see the media as arrogant, elitist and biased, and why Mr. Goldberg's book is #1 on the bestseller list."

Every day there was another shot, but I was rolling with the punches, actually enjoying the fact that my book had not only forced some of these people to acknowledge the issue of liberal bias but had caused them so much consternation. In fact, I considered myself lucky. If Tom Shales had been one of those insecure little people who lived in Peyton Place, one of those who were harboring some dirty little secret, he might actually have shot Grace Metalious. As it was, all he did was call me names—and create even more interest in *Bias* by making people wonder what in the world I could possibly have said in the book to make a Pulitzer Prize–winning writer for the *Washington Post* so maniacal.

Then, on Saturday, March 2, 2002, I started getting E-mails and phone messages from friends around the country telling me I shouldn't let what Frank Rich wrote in the *New York Times* get to me, that what he had done was so despicable and so vile and that it reflected far more on him and the *New York Times* than it did on me.

Now, for the first time, I felt that sinking feeling in the pit of my stomach. What in the world could he have written—in *the newspaper of record*, no less—that generated so much sympathy from so many friends? I had the *Times* in my living room but had been out of the house most of the day and hadn't read it yet. So I turned to the op-ed page and saw Frank Rich's piece, a column that dragged me and my book into the tragic and savage death of another reporter, Danny Pearl of the *Wall Street Journal*, who had been executed in Pakistan.

Frank Rich wrote that just one day before "the world got news of Daniel Pearl's death, you could hear another reporter describing the perils of his profession in a talk carried on C-Span. The journalist was Bernard Goldberg, formerly of CBS News and author of the best-selling 'Bias,' and his story was tragic."

I understand that Frank Rich writes for the *New York Times* and that there might be a tendency to take him seriously. But be assured that the line about the "perils of his profession" and "his story was tragic" was simply Frank being sarcastic, in the snotty way a smart-ass child might be.

During my talk to high school kids at the Newseum in Arlington, Virginia, which C-Span carried live, I explained that after I first wrote about liberal bias in the news, way back in 1996 in an op-ed in the *Wall Street Journal*, I had become radioactive at CBS News: colleagues treated me like a pariah, and then, as Frank Rich once again derisively put it, "the ultimate indignity: Dan Rather stopped talking to him."

Rich's point was that it was in very bad taste to bellyache about what happened to me for taking on the media elites, while Danny

Pearl was being held hostage and eventually brutally murdered. "Mr. Goldberg might still be telling his tale of woe," as he mockingly wrote, "had not terrorism intervened and rendered his talk of self-martyrdom on behalf of Mr. Pearl's newspaper [the *Wall Street Journal*] ludicrous."

This did not make me laugh. This was about as ugly and un-scrupulous as it gets. I had had no idea Danny Pearl was dead, as Frank Rich well knew. Nor was I by any stretch of the imagination comparing my plight with that of Danny Pearl. As Ann Coulter smartly observes in her book *Slander: Liberal Lies About the American Right*, "You will never appreciate the full savagery of the left until you get in their way."

There is a sense of helplessness that comes over you when a prominent journalist, abusing his power in an important newspaper, slanders you this way. All I could do was write the *Times* a letter to the editor:

> When I wrote *Bias*, a book about liberal bias in the big-time media, I knew things would get ugly, given how thin-skinned so many journalists are. But I never guessed it would go this far.
>
> Frank Rich is in a huff because I recently told a TV interviewer that colleagues at CBS News shunned me years ago after I wrote an op-ed for the *Wall Street Journal* about bias in the media. For me to talk about that on TV, just one day before we learned of Daniel Pearl's death, amounted to "public griping" of the most petty and disgraceful kind. But for Mr. Rich to link, no matter how clumsily, legitimate criticism of journalism to the death of a newsman is what is truly disgraceful.
>
> I never brought up the subject of my ostracism; the interviewer did. I only answered his question. If he had asked me to compare my plight at the hands of my colleagues with Daniel Pearl's plight at the hands of his captors I would have told him it was a dumb question and that there is no comparison whatsoever.

Finally, full disclosure might have led Mr. Rich to report that I wrote about him in *Bias*, briefly, but not favorably. It might also have led him to reveal that he is best of friends with Andrew Heyward, the president of CBS News, who, as I report in *Bias*, once told me he agreed that there is a liberal bias at the networks, but also made clear he would never say so publicly. Call me crazy, but I think Mr. Rich's friendship with Mr. Heyward might have affected what he wrote about me.

This last point is a very important one, because understanding such friendships in the world of Big Journalism is crucial to understanding how the media elites operate. It's a kind of club, mostly a men's club, where club rules mandate that members behave in a gentlemanly fashion, that they never criticize one another, and that they stick together when challenged. When one is attacked, the others are expected to circle the wagons and counterattack. Andrew and Frank went to Harvard at the same time. (Kinsley was also a Harvard pal of Rich's.) They socialize. They have been close for years. If Andrew was angry, which he was because I had written *Bias*, then his buddy Frank was there to do the dirty work while Andrew could keep his own hands clean by saying he would have no comment about *Bias*.

The *Times* said it would publish part of my letter, but not the part about Frank Rich being mentioned in my book and not the part about Frank's friendship with Andrew Heyward of CBS News. So much for fair play. The *Times* not only let Frank Rich do a drive-by on me, but now its editors weren't even going to let me explain that in my view Frank was covering for his Harvard pal, the president of CBS News. So I refused to play the game and told the *Times* not to publish my letter.

A few days later, in his column for the *New York Press*, a spirited independent weekly, Russ Smith wrote that "It taxes one's imagination, but I don't think I've ever read anything in the *New York Times* as filthy as Frank Rich's March 2 column in which he exploits the execution of Daniel Pearl to smear Bernard Goldberg, author of the bestseller *Bias*."

Having a keen grasp of the obvious, I should state very clearly that there are plenty of ideologically driven nuts on the Right, too. And I ran into some of them while I was on the radio talking about *Bias*. For instance, in April 2001 I was a guest on a call-in radio show in Idaho Falls, a lovely little place with clean air and clean water and more than a few people who would fit in very nicely, say, in the twilight zone.

One of them called in to ask if I knew much about the movie *Gladiator*. Since the subject of the show was bias in the media, I wondered, *What the hell does* Gladiator *have to do with anything?* He must have been reading my mind, because he got right to the point. In *Gladiator*, he said, special-effects people had created a make-believe, computer-generated Colosseum and populated it with make-believe, computer-generated Romans to give the illusion of reality.

And?

And, he wanted to know, do they do that in television news, too? Do they use computers to generate make-believe images to slant the news to their liking? A friend of his, he said, thought that networks in fact did just that, and he was wondering, do they? I was wondering something different entirely. I was wondering if he and his friend had escaped from a mental institution.

Another caller said that when he was a young boy in Oakland, California, he witnessed a local riot on the television news. A year later, he said, he moved to Los Angeles with his family, and another riot broke out, this time in Watts. But instead of showing the Watts riot on television, he said, they were showing (Fasten your seat belts!) . . . the Oakland riot from a year earlier *and saying it was the Watts riot.*

Why would any TV station do that? I asked. I don't know, he told me, they just did. Can you be mistaken, I asked, since you were just a young boy at the time? Nope, he said. What conspiracy could the newspeople possibly be up to, I asked him, to show an *old* riot when a *brand-new* riot was happening *right now?* I have no idea, he said; all I know is that it happened.

You're wrong, I told him, annoyed, mostly at myself for talking to these lunatics in the first place. You're just plain wrong, I said. Very calmly he responded, No, I'm not wrong. You're wrong. I was there on my couch watching it on TV. You weren't.

He had a point, I thought. An idiotic point, but a point nonetheless.

Since I was on so many radio stations all over the country talking about *Bias,* there were a few other nuts I encountered, but very few, as I look back. A few people thought Rosie O'Donnell was a bigger menace than Osama bin Laden. But as I say, they were nuts. Fringe people. Like the guy from Ft. Collins, Colorado, who wrote a review for Amazon.com that said, "In *Bias* Bernard Goldberg exposes how liberals have taken over the media through the Masons, the Trilateral Commission and the incredible wealth of the Kennedy family." He also said *Bias* was "a very good read!"

Since I devoted exactly zero words in *Bias* to the Masons, the Trilateral Commission, or the wealth of the Kennedys—*zero!*—I think it's probably safe to say that my pal in Colorado would love to hook up with some of my buddies from the radio station in Idaho so they could all get together and discuss their lives on Pluto before they were transported to Earth.

But there is a difference between the nuts on the Right and the screwballs on the Left—a crucial difference. Just about everyone recognizes that the nuts on the Right are dopey and on the fringe (except for the journalists who think they're typical, mainstream conservatives). But the screwballs on the Left are not dumb at all, and even more important, they most definitely are not on the fringe. *They're members in good standing of the liberal media establishment.*

And that's why Tom Shales can go into an unbridled rage and get so hysterical that he actually makes Carrot Top seem sophisticated and brainy by comparison—and nobody in the "respectable" mainstream media cares. Or why Frank Rich can spew venom and there is not a peep from his usually sensitive liberal media pals.

But what most liberals in the media don't seem to understand is how badly they themselves are being hurt by their bias and their arrogance. What they don't seem to understand is how alienated from the big-time media so many decent Middle Americans feel. I'm convinced this alienation is precisely why *Bias* touched such a chord. It spoke to millions of Americans who think that a lot of big, important journalists don't really understand them and don't really care about them.

The success of my book and others like it might have been an opportunity for the media elites to take stock and to go beyond their knee-jerk denials and begin to seriously confront the allegations of bias. Instead they did what they always do: They tried to kill the messenger.

Of course, it didn't work. Because even if I got it all wrong, even if this whole idea of liberal bias in the news somehow really is just a crazy myth, they've still got a terrible problem on their hands—because tens of millions of Americans out there believe it! The media elites can dismiss *me,* but what do they do with *them?*

As Professor Smith nicely sums it up, "The verdict is in; the People have spoken; the media are guilty as charged. The time has come to shift the debate from whether the news is biased to what can be done to correct it."

One Cheer
for Honesty!

Just before Bill Clinton spoke at the University of Texas on February 12, 2003, a group of conservatives in Austin, including a campus group called the Young Conservatives of Texas (YCT), organized a demonstration against the former president. Hoping to get some news coverage, the Young Conservatives e-mailed a press release to news organizations throughout the state. Soon after, they got the following E-mail response signed by a reporter at the *Fort Worth Star-Telegram* named Steve McLinden.

Re: NEWS ADVISORY: YCT to Protest Bill Clinton Lecture at UT on Wednesday
Date: Mon, 10 Feb 2003
From: "Steve McLinden"
To: Young Conservatives of Texas

Ah, the heartless, greedy, anti-intellectual little fascists are mobilizing again. (Let me guess. All you frat boys saved up your allowances and monies from your McDonald's jobs for those Beemers you'll be driving to the protest, and those new jackboots you'll be sportin' enroute). Hey, don't forget all the nasty little deals that Reagan's henchmen cut with Middle East figures that got us directly into this mess today. I'm sure you'll be protesting the Reagan household any day now. By the way, is it not enough to have the White House and Congress? Would you like to stamp out all signs that we are a two-party, Democratic country? What's that? You would? How noble of you. I salute you and your polarized, little status-quo world.

I've been around newsrooms a long time and have seen lots of crazy things, but I must admit, it's hard to believe that any news reporter in his right mind would actually send an E-mail calling a bunch of college demonstrators jackboot-sportin' fascists.

So I checked with the vice president in charge of news coverage at the *Star-Telegram,* Jim Witt, to see if he knew anything about the E-mail.

Right off the bat he confirmed the E-mail was indeed real, that it indeed was sent by his reporter Steve McLinden. I was stunned.

What did he think of the E-mail? I asked him. He said he'd apologized to the Young Conservatives of Texas, telling them, "This certainly is not reflective of what we do at the *Star-Telegram,* that it is in conflict with our ethics code, that we want to have our news reporters to be unbiased."

Was McLinden still working at the paper? "As of today he is not," Witt told me.

Wow!

Let's give credit where it's due: Management at the *Fort Worth Star-Telegram* saw a blatant case of bias, and the offender was gone.

But we don't have to give them *too* much credit, because this was such an easy call. After all, Steve McLinden committed the journalistic version of a hate crime—in writing no less—then put his name to it.

But here's the real problem: Reporters express views just like McLinden's—to each other—*all the time!* Lots of reporters think conservatives are either scary or morons or both. They loathe Bush and Cheney. They have utter contempt for antiabortion demonstrators. They think people with little formal education are white trash.

One day a few years ago, I was at the CBS News bureau in Miami watching a videotape of an interview I had just done with Ralph Reed, who at the time was head of the Christian Coalition. The door to the editing room was open, and the bureau manager—the top editorial presence in the newsroom (and a Christian himself)—walked by and saw Reed on the TV monitor making some point or another in his usual quiet, gentlemanly way. "That guy makes me want to throw up," the bureau manager said as he walked right on by, offering up absolutely no explanation. And none was needed as far as he was concerned. He pretty much assumed everyone else felt the same way.

And while we're giving credit where it's due, let's also give a little to Steve McLinden. The guy may be an over-the-top, self-destructive ideologue, but at least he's an *honest,* over-the-top, self-destructive ideologue.

Root Causes

On Sunday, May 11, 2003, the *New York Times* ran a long story about deceit and betrayal—a story about a faker and a fraud, "a troubled young man veering toward professional self-destruction," as the *Times* explained it.

The story began on page one and continued for two entire pages inside the paper (plus two more entire pages detailing the errors and an editor's note), the kind of space the *Times* normally reserves for tragedies like Hiroshima or the *selection* of the president by a *corrupt* Supreme Court. Reading this piece about Jayson Blair—14,171 words in all—you would be forgiven if you got the impression that the *New York Times* thought this story was just as big—maybe bigger.

That's because the faker and fraud, the reporter who was writing fiction and passing it off as fact and who was also plagiarizing the work of other journalists, worked at the *New York Times*.

You had to know really big trouble was on the horizon when David Letterman got into the act. "You have SARS, Mad Cow Disease, the Orange Alert. The news is so bad the *New York Times* doesn't have to make it up." Two weeks later, on June 5, 2003, less than a month after the *Times* mea culpa, the paper's two highest-ranking editors, executive editor Howell Raines and managing editor Gerald Boyd, resigned. Raines and Boyd had nurtured Blair and, as the *Times* own investigation established, had given him second and third chances even when his malfeasance was evident to other editors.

In the days and weeks that followed there was a lot of talk about how the whole mess could have ever happened. What took the paper's top editors so long to finally lower the boom? What forces drove Blair to self-destruct? And—since Jayson Blair is black—what part did the *Times* obsession with diversity play in the fiasco?

These are all fair and important questions. But the elites should have taken advantage of the Blair postmortem to ask some even more telling questions, the ones involving the nature of the *New York Times* as an institution.

When Howell Raines clutched a microphone in the *Times* newsroom to tell his staff that he was leaving, some "sobbed audibly," according to the page-one story in the *Times* the next morning. But that was a minority view. By all accounts, Raines was an autocrat who made Napoleon look like Richard Simmons, and many reporters and editors at the paper clearly were delighted to see him go.

In the end Raines and Boyd had to go because American corporations—even ones like the *New York Times* that don't think much of American corporate culture—cherish stability over just about anything. And there was no stability at the *Times* after it became clear that the paper's reputation had been badly damaged.

But it would be a huge mistake to believe that the departure of Howell Raines fixes what's broken at the world's most important newspaper. A course at Dale Carnegie might have fixed whatever problem Howell Raines had; and if that didn't work, maybe a few sessions with a good therapist might at least have turned him into a better *people person*.

But the most critical problem at the *Times* goes way beyond the philosophy or management style of any one person—and what's so telling is that throughout the turmoil, no one at the paper so much as mentioned it. The simple fact is, more than anything else, the *New York Times* loss of credibility in recent years has to do with the fact that it has become so ideological. Howell Raines didn't create the problem. He only made it worse.

In its mea culpa, the *Times* called the Blair scandal "a low point in the 152-year history of the newspaper."

The *New York Times* shouldn't have been so hard on itself—or so easy. There have been *plenty* of lower points. In fact, to a lot of us outside the *Times* building, this Jayson Blair thing wasn't even the low point of the past few years, a period marked by ideologically driven coverage of all kinds of stories, including more than a few on the front page. Correcting blatantly false "facts" like those peddled by Blair is relatively easy. But what about the other distortions, usually subtle, sometimes downright glaring, that appear in the newspaper of record all the time—the ones that are born of its powerful biases? It's one thing for a liberal paper like the *Times* to load up its op-ed page with liberal columnists—and a campaign to allow women into the Augusta golf club might be perfectly reasonable on the editorial page—but it is troubling, to say the least, when closed-minded left-wing ideologues are accorded privileged positions on the most important opinion page in the country; or when a feminist crusade like that aimed at Augusta becomes an obsession that permeates the whole paper. These things can happen only at a place with an *institutional ideology*. "It's in their DNA at the *Times*," as a pal of mine puts it. "And you can't escape your DNA."

The truth is, the most powerful figure at the *Times*, the same guy who sets the doggedly PC tone at the paper—and who put Howell Raines in the editor's chair in the first place—is publisher Arthur "Pinch" Sulzberger Jr. Ideologically, Sulzberger and Raines were soul mates. In fact, Sulzberger didn't even want to cut Raines loose. And when he reluctantly gave in to the inevitable, he called it "a day that breaks my heart." So, for all those in the big media who suggested that the housecleaning, which was supposed to straighten out the *Times*, went *all the way to the top* . . . no it didn't. The top would be the office of the publisher, and Pinch Sulzberger, despite his contribution to the mess, is still there.

Indeed, for those hoping the Blair scandal would seriously alter the paper's ideological bent, there was a sobering dose of reality just three days after the fourteen thousand word–plus mea culpa. On May 14, Maureen Dowd, one of the *Times* star columnists, wrote this about President Bush: "Busy chasing off Saddam, the president and vice president had told us that Al Qaeda was spent. 'Al Qaeda is on the run,' President Bush said last week. 'That group of terrorists who attacked our country is slowly but surely being decimated. . . . They're not a problem anymore.'"

But those little dots—the ones that indicate that Ms. Dowd edited the president's words—are, on closer examination, her way of twisting the facts, almost beyond recognition. Here's what President Bush actually said, without the ellipsis. "Al Qaeda is on the run. That group of terrorists who attacked our country is slowly but surely being decimated. Right now, about half of all the top Al Qaeda operatives are either jailed or dead. In either case, they're not a problem anymore."

The president never said, nor did he remotely mean to suggest, that Al Qaeda is "not a problem anymore." What he was clearly saying, in his wry fashion, is that those members of Al Qaeda *who are either dead or behind bars* are "not a problem anymore." There is no way that Maureen Dowd did not know this; and by no stretch of the imagination (or journalistic ethics) does the fact that she's a columnist and not a reporter give her license to distort what the President of the United States is saying about a subject as vitally important as terrorism. It was, as the critic Andrew Sullivan bluntly put it, a "willful fabrication."

I don't know about you, but frankly, I think the mentality behind Maureen Dowd's little stunt is of far greater concern than the blatant dishonesty of Jayson Blair. A guy who flat out concocts "facts" is an extreme rarity in the news business, an aberration. Rightly, he has been exposed and publicly humiliated. But there's still the bigger problem—the one that involves the ideologically driven stuff that appears in places like the *New York Times* on a regular basis—the kind of journalism that they not only don't apologize for . . . but don't even acknowledge as a problem.

That is what needs to be addressed—especially *now* at the *New York Times*—if mainstream journalism is to regain the credibility it once enjoyed.

As the summer drew to a close in September 2001, just a few days after Howell Raines took over as executive editor, the *Times* ran what would prove to be one of the most embarrassing stories in the recent history of American journalism—and Jayson Blair had absolutely nothing to do with it.

Appearing on page one of the Arts section, it began:

> "I don't regret setting bombs," Bill Ayers said, "I feel we didn't do enough." Mr. Ayers, who spent the 1970s as a fugitive in the Weather Underground, was sitting in the kitchen of his big turn-of-the-19th-century stone house in the Hyde Park district of Chicago. The long curly locks in his Wanted poster are shorn, though he wears earrings. He still has tattooed on his neck the rainbow-and-lightning Weathermen logo that appeared on letters taking responsibility for bombings. And he still has the ebullient, ingratiating manner, the apparently intense interest in other people, that made him a charismatic figure in the radical student movement.

The story ran 956 words—956 words of gushing, adolescent pap about the sixties radical who admits to participating in, among other acts of terrorism, the bombings of New York City Police Headquarters in 1970, the Capitol building in 1971, and the Pentagon in 1972; who in 1970 "was said to have summed up the Weatherman philosophy as: 'Kill all the rich people. Break up their cars and apartments. Bring the revolution home, kill your parents, that's where it's really at. . . .'

". . . So, would Mr. Ayers do it all again? he is asked. 'I don't want to discount the possibility,' he said."

Far from being put off by her subject, the *Times* reporter, Dinitia Smith, is positively enchanted with Bill Ayers and his "ebullient, ingratiating manner" and his "intense interest in other people." In fact, as the piece draws to a merciful end, the former terrorist who not only doesn't regret setting bombs but feels as if "we didn't do enough" recites a poem about justice and hope and history, which prompts Ms. Smith to conclude: "Thinking back on his life, Mr. Ayers said, 'I was a child of privilege and I woke up to a world on fire. And hope and history rhymed.'"

And what rhymes with "I'm supposed to be a tough, skeptical *New York Times* reporter, who's acting like a high school girl with a crush on the captain of the football team"?

My guess is, the *New York Times* would have been a little less fawning and a little more clear-headed if, instead of helping out with the bombing of targets like the Pentagon, our charismatic bomber had done his dirty work on, say, an empty abortion clinic in the Upper West Side of Manhattan. Even as I write this I can hear the clueless editors at the most important newspaper on the planet saying, "Of course that's different; what exactly are you getting at?"

But here's the real bulletin: the *New York Times* might have actually gotten away with this adoring drivel were it not for one little inconvenient fact. *The story came out on September 11, 2001.*

You know what they say: Timing is everything. I mean, how unlucky can the Old Gray Lady get? The *New York Times* picks the very day of the worst terrorist atrocity in American history to run an admiring puff piece about . . . *a former terrorist who pines for the good old days.* But perhaps we have to cut the editors at the *Times* a little slack. How in the world could they have known just one day earlier, on September 10, when they put the paper to bed, that they would look like such despicable horses' asses the very next morning? And if the *Times* valentine to the man who can't discount the possibility that he would do it all again had appeared any other day before September 11, there's a good chance no one would have even noticed, given that the piece about Bill Ayers would have blended right in with all the other ideological stuff that had been appearing regularly in the *New York Times.*

There have been reams and reams written lately about what has become of the *New York Times*—columns, lengthy articles, entire books. Bill McGowan's *Coloring The News* alone offers numerous examples illustrating the decline of this once-great newspaper, showing how it has moved from once being "a liberal-but-fair paper of record," as one critic described it, to a politically correct parody of its former self.

But what's most important to reflect on when you talk about the *New York Times* is the matter of root causes.

This should please liberals. Liberals love to talk about root causes. The liberal reporters at places like the *New York Times* discuss root causes all the time. A quick trip through their archives reveals references both to the obvious—the root causes of poverty and homelessness and domestic violence and crime and terrorism—and to a bunch of things most people don't even think of as having root causes, like smoking and bullying and obesity. To a liberal, having a root cause means never having to say you're sorry.

So let's get to the root cause of liberal media bias in America.

You guessed it! The *New York Times,* a paper 99.5 percent of the American people do not read, yet which is still the most influential newspaper in America because the most influential people in America do in fact read it.

So, yes, the *New York Times* does indeed occupy a unique place in American journalism. And it's not just because its columns are syndicated to hundreds of local papers around the country. It's mostly because it sets the agenda for so many other news outlets, especially the networks where most Americans get their world and national news. The fact is, the Big Three news networks wouldn't know what to put on the air without it. As I've said in the past, if the *New York Times* went on strike tomorrow morning, they'd have to cancel the CBS, NBC, and ABC evening newscasts tomorrow night.

Why don't the network news divisions do more original reporting?

I am convinced you can trace the reason all the way back to our caveman days. Back then, every moron knew how to grunt, so grunting got no respect. But one day, when someone scratched something on the wall, *whoa,* everyone was impressed! A grunt disappeared into thin air, but here was something permanent. A scratch on the wall was *official!* As far as the grunters were concerned, only the smartest and most talented cavemen scratched stuff on walls!

So as we evolved, it became hard-wired into our systems that writing is more important than talking, that writers are smarter than talkers. And after a few million years of evolution the television executive producer came into being—a species genetically inclined not to trust or respect his own reporter nearly as much as he trusts and respects a print reporter, some total stranger whom he has never met in his life.

A veteran TV cameraman (a freelancer who depends on the networks for his livelihood and therefore asked that I not use his name) told me that he was in the Persian Gulf in the late 1980s covering the Iran-Iraq war when "I saw a tanker being attacked. Mobile phones were new back then, and I called the network foreign desk in New York to let the editors back there know that we had some pretty dramatic tape of the actual attack. And the person in charge in New York said to me, 'There's nothing on the wires about it.' We keep saying, 'It's happening in front of our eyes,' and New York keeps saying, 'It's not on the wires.' Because it wasn't on AP or Reuters, the editor wasn't interested."

So the cameraman did what a lot of other frustrated journalists in the field have done. "I called the [local] guy from the wire service, who then put the story out. Then I get a call from the same editor in

New York, who is suddenly interested and says, 'Send us the tape of the tanker that was attacked.'"

You see, this editor in New York wouldn't trust what his own cameraman was seeing with his own eyes. He needed to see the story in print first; then, and only then, would he know it was real, legitimate news.

Sometimes it's even more pathetic than that. Back in 1971—February 9, 1971, to be exact, at 6:01 A.M. Pacific Time—a massive earthquake hit Los Angeles. The CBS News bureau manager, a veteran journalist named John Harris, who was the only one in the office at that hour, took cover under his desk, pulled the phone down there with him, and called the radio desk in New York, literally just seconds after the quake hit. "A huge earthquake just hit us here in L.A.; roll tape, I'll give you a live report," Harris told him—this while the room was still shaking. The editor in New York told John to hang on for a moment, and when he came back to the phone he said, "I don't see anything about any earthquake on the wires."

Harris had beaten the wires. *He had beaten everybody. CBS had a shot at being first with a major story.* It didn't matter. It wasn't in print, so it was as if it hadn't happened. Once again, a few minutes later, the story did hit the wires, it became real news, and Harris finally got on the air.

Just one year later, I joined CBS News, having worked in local television and at the Associated Press in New York City. When I heard the tale about Harris, it really threw me. Why in the world would broadcasters—at CBS News, no less—feel inferior to guys who worked at the wire services? I mean, *I had worked at one of the wire services.* Did my CBS bosses have more confidence in me when I was at the AP than now that I was at CBS? It didn't make any sense. It took me years to figure it out. It wasn't that they had so much respect for *them;* it's that they had so little respect for *themselves.* It's not that TV news types have so much trust in the news judgment of print reporters; it's that they have so little trust in their *own* news judgment.

But powerful as print is in general, and as powerful as the wire services are in particular, nothing—absolutely nothing—carries nearly as much weight in network television newsrooms as the *New York Times*. There are too many examples to count where television reporters *appropriated* (read *stole*) story ideas from local newspapers in their region and pitched them to their bosses, the executive producers of the network evening newscasts in New York, who turned the stories down, until . . . *until they ran in the* New York Times, *the wall scratcher of record.*

Mike Wallace told a producer who is a close friend of mine that he wasn't comfortable with a certain story my producer pal was looking into. "What would make you comfortable?" he asked Wallace. "To read it in the *New York Times*," Wallace said. Nine months later—nine months after CBS News began checking the story out—the *Times* got around to doing it. Wallace, true to his word, suddenly was interested, and they went out and did the story for *60 Minutes*. That's what the *New York Times* means to television journalists, even those of Mike Wallace's stature.

"Once the *Times* runs a story on page one," that veteran cameraman told me, "we're told to run out and do it!"

If the *Times* decrees a story important, by definition it *is* important. And when the *Times* ignores a story—or a book or a social trend or an idea—then it is invisible. As the syndicated columnist Deroy Murdock puts it, "The cult of the *New York Times* . . . holds journalists, politicians, and other opinion makers in a Svengali-like trance. If the *Times* says the sun will rise in the west, then by golly it will!"

On a typical morning, this is how assignment editors and producers at the network news divisions begin their day. Step one: They open up the *New York Times*. Step two: They scan the paper for stories to put on their nightly newscasts. Step three: They get one of their high-priced reporters (who is in his or her own office also reading the *New York Times*) on the phone—a reporter who may not have come up with even one original story idea in his entire network career (I mean that *literally*)—and tell him or her to go out and do the

New York Times story. Step four: He or she does, and that evening a video version of the *Times* story is on the air.

And the sad fact is that the networks that shamelessly crib from the *Times* aren't even embarrassed about doing it. After all, a lot of other media are doing the same thing; such is the reach and influence of the mighty *New York Times*. And if you steal from the *Times*—and this is no small point—no one can ever give you grief about getting something wrong. It was, after all, in the *New York Times*.

Now, let's be fair—until very late in the twentieth century very few people had any problem with the *Times* role as arbiter of what mattered, because it was understood that the paper's reputation for excellence was merited. Of course it was liberal, but mostly it was sober and responsible, if sometimes a bit stodgy and boring. It didn't get that nickname "the Old Gray Lady" for nothing.

Back then the *Times* tried to cover the news straight, in a just-the-facts sort of way. Though even then it made some whopping mistakes—its chief correspondent to Moscow in the 1930s, Walter Duranty, turned out to be the media's number one apologist for Stalin, if not a Soviet agent—as a matter of policy it at least sought to be fair. This was the *Times* of journalistic giants like renowned war correspondent Homer Bigart and national correspondent and columnist James Reston, who won four Pulitzers between them; this was the *Times* the rest of the media had good reason to look to as an inspiration and an example.

That was then; this is now.

The *Times* still *looks* and *feels* like a great newspaper. It has news bureaus all over the world. The paper itself is hefty and contains all kinds of sections. And more to the point, its reporters are smart and sophisticated—probably as strong a group of journalists as you can find anywhere. And of course, the vast majority of the articles have nothing to do with ideology. Yet what's so surprising is how many do, and how ideology regularly gets shoehorned into places you'd never expect to find it—not just in pieces in the editorial or book or culture sections but, for instance, on the sports pages, too, where diversity and feminist issues are always being rammed down readers' throats. Reading the *New York Times* these days can be like taking a PC bath.

It is not easy to date with precision when the *New York Times* began its unfortunate descent into outright liberal bias, but Hilton Kramer has an idea. The paper's former culture editor, a distinguished critic and social thinker, Kramer recalls, "One day in the early seventies I was at my house in Maine, where we didn't get the paper till lunchtime. There was a big story on the front page of a Thursday paper, just below the fold, about the problem single women in New York were having finding suitable Saturday night dates. My wife was preparing lunch, and I started reading her this story from the front page and she turned around and said, 'Are you making that up? *That's really on the front page of the* New York Times?' " He laughs wistfully at the memory. "That really was the start, that period when the *Times* went from being a two-section *news*-paper emphasizing hard news, to this multisection *lifestyle* paper. Well, as soon as you move into lifestyle journalism, it's basically *all* opinion. Today there are lifestyle stories on page one almost every day. And lifestyle is an inherently liberal concept—it's a term that you only hear conservatives use sarcastically, because it implies perpetual change and the denigration of traditional standards. When standards change, they very rarely change for the better."

It is no coincidence that the beginning of the collapse of the old *Times* standards coincided almost exactly with the rise of the liberation movements of the late sixties and early seventies, particularly feminism. As the women's movement picked up steam, its appeal was precisely to the sorts of people who comprise the *Times* core constituency—privileged liberals who like to see themselves as cutting-edge and socially aware. The *Times* had always been an editorially liberal paper—responsibly and intelligently liberal. But now, as more and more of its reporters and editors emerged from the hip sixties generation, it took on an aggressive liberal-activist edge.

For committed feminists, gay activists, multiculturalists, and all the others who took their side in the culture wars that grew in intensity into the eighties and nineties, "neutrality" was nothing to be admired. The very point of the movements they supported was to attack and undermine traditional forms of thought and behavior. By, say, 1980, it's a pretty good bet that every female reporter at the *New York Times* was a fervent careerist who believed Gloria Steinem was a secular saint and that women who stayed home with their kids were brain-dead cretins and born-again losers. At any rate, this was the impression you'd get from reading the paper.

The most important figure on the editorial (as opposed to the business) side of the *New York Times* is the executive editor, the *Times* version of editor in chief. For a time the man occupying that role, a legendary, autocratic old-time newsman named Abe Rosenthal, did his best to hold the line. But Rosenthal retired on January 1, 1988. Then, four years later, young Arthur "Pinch" Sulzberger Jr. replaced his father, Arthur "Punch" Sulzberger, as the publisher and overall boss of what basically remains a family-owned newspaper.

Pinch turned out to be highly ideological in ways none of his predecessors had ever dared to be. If you're excessively open-minded, I suppose, you might be able to overlook, as a youthful indiscretion, the fact that during the 1960s he was arrested twice in antiwar demonstrations. But you'd probably have a real hard time forgiving his unapologetic support for the other side in the Vietnam War. As two ex-*Times* journalists, Alex S. Jones and Susan Tifft, reported in their recent history of the paper, *The Trust,* after one of his arrests his exasperated father asked Pinch the following question: "If a young American soldier comes upon a young North Vietnamese soldier, which one do you want to see get shot?" Pinch replied, "I would want to see the American get shot. It's the other guy's country."

That was a long time ago, you may say. And of course you'd be right. The problem is, Pinch *still* believes in all those old sixties notions about "liberation" and "changing the world, man." "He once remarked," as Jones and Tifft write, "that if older white males were alienated by his hipper version of the *Times* then 'we're doing something right.'"

These days reporters and editors at the *Times* pick up the language of the Left either without noticing or, if they do, without even caring. For example, when the *Times* says "progressive" it means "liberal." A lot of liberals these days, for all sorts of reasons, don't want to be called liberal; they prefer the sound of "progressive" instead. It's so progressive, after all. And the *Times* couldn't be more obliging.

Granted, it's not a terrible transgression, but it is revealing about the paper's mindset. Here's why: What if conservatives suddenly decide that they also want to be called "progressive" because they also like the sound and the implications of the word? Or better yet, what if one day they decide that from now on conservative ideas should be called *"visionary"* ideas? What if Republicans said to the *Times* brass, "We would like your reporters to call our conservative ideas 'visionary'—the very same way you call liberal Democratic ideas 'progressive'; we think that would be evenhanded and fair"? You think the *Times* would be so accommodating?

Neither do I.

All this begins to explain how the *Times* could have run that embarrassing, gushing profile of Bill Ayers, the former Weather Underground terrorist who wasn't at all sorry for the bombings back in the sixties and seventies and couldn't rule out that he'd get back into the terrorism business at some point. That one must have alienated a whole bunch of older white males. And black ones, too, for that matter.

In fact, the Pinch years have been a steady march down PC Boulevard, with a newsroom fiercely dedicated to every brand of diversity except the intellectual kind. In an interview with Ken Auletta of the *New Yorker,* Max Frankel revealed that soon after Pinch Sulzberger named him the paper's new executive editor in 1986, "One of the first things I did was stop the hiring of nonblacks and set up an unofficial little quota system."

By now some of the stuff the paper was running, even on its front page, was so slanted it was funny—almost. For example, during the 2000 presidential campaign, on September 12 to be exact, the *Times* ran a page-one piece headlined "Democrats See, and Smell, Rats in G.O.P. Ad." The story, which turned out to have been fed to the

Times reporter by the Gore campaign, claimed that the Republicans were trying to slip voters negative information about the Democrats subliminally, under the radar—a charge that was categorically denied by the ad's producer. Specifically, what the Republicans supposedly were trying to do was emphasize the word "rats"—which was part of the bigger word "bureaucrats" in the line "The Gore prescription plan: bureaucrats decide." During the entire thirty-second TV commercial, the word "rats" flashed on the screen—"in huge white capital letters, larger than any other word on the commercial," as the *Times* explained it—for exactly one-thirtieth of a second.

Were the Republicans really calling the Democrats "rats"? Were they using unscrupulous subliminal techniques to brainwash the electorate? Was this *The Manchurian Candidate* all over again, this time for real? In politics, as we all know by now, anything is possible, even calling the other guy a rat—for a thirtieth of a second. But there was another question, one that wasn't raised by the *Times* and should have been: Was the paper being used by the National Democratic Party to discredit their opponents?

Maybe it was a slow news day; I don't remember. But if you'd been at your supermarket checkout counter, and spotted the "rat" story on the front page of the *Weekly World News*, which had previously run a story about an alien endorsing George Bush for president, admit it—you wouldn't have been all that surprised.

So what happened when it appeared in the *New York Times*?

That evening, it led the news at ABC and CNN and got prominent play on CBS, NBC, and MSNBC. When the *New York Times* speaks, everyone in network television listens!

But morally and intellectually corrupt as the *Times* had become, it had farther to fall.

A lot of people—and not just conservatives—think it hit rock bottom in 2001, when Howell Raines took over as executive editor.

Raines was a veteran *Times*man, as proudly leftist in his beliefs— and as openly contemptuous of conservatives—as Pinch himself.

Pinch and Howell, the dynamic duo—a marriage, as one writer put it to me, made in journalism hell.

Raines was famously quoted as saying that "the Reagan years oppressed me." In contrast, there was his view of Bill Clinton: "Huge political talent," declared Raines when Charlie Rose asked how he thought history would regard Clinton. "Huge political vision . . . I think President Clinton's role in modernizing the Democratic party around a set of economic ideas and also holding on to the principles of social justice, and presiding over the greatest prosperity in human history—those would seem to me to have to be central to his legacy."

Assuming his new position shortly before 9/11, Raines immediately began imposing his iron will on the paper. Friends were in, enemies out. Some of the paper's best writers all but disappeared from its pages. Known for encouraging sycophancy (a fancy way of saying "ass-kissing") and brooking no dissent, Raines soon surrounded himself with what one commentator, Mickey Kaus, calls "a castrati chorus." According to a profile of the new executive editor in the *New Yorker*, staffers in the paper's "Washington bureau started referring to the masthead as the Taliban, and to Raines as Mullah Omar."

As former culture editor Hilton Kramer says, "There was, no pun intended, a real *reign* of terror in the newsroom. Nobody felt secure in his job anymore. In my day, it was almost unheard of for someone with a job at the *Times* to leave it. When I left in '82, several of my colleagues came to my office to give me the names of their psychiatrists because they thought I was having a nervous breakdown. These days when someone leaves, more power to him."

The most public head to be lopped off during Raines's first year was that of Andrew Sullivan, the gifted writer under contract to the *New York Times Magazine* who announced he had been "barred indefinitely from writing" for the paper. A gay conservative with a provocative mind and a serious independent streak, Sullivan had been among the most respected writers in the magazine, the paper's most visible section. But now he was excommunicated.

His crime? In his well-regarded Web site, andrewsullivan.com, he had dared to question the liberal tilt Howell Raines's *Times* was bringing to its coverage of certain stories, notably those involving President Bush and his battles with congressional Democrats. In response to his banishment, Sullivan responded with a grace and dignity altogether lacking in Raines's heavy-handed approach: "Not writing for the *New York Times*," he wrote, "is a better fate than not writing what I believe."

But Sullivan was only one of a mounting number of observers who were now talking about how routinely (and even shamelessly) the *Times* was injecting its editorial views into its news coverage. For instance, a poll taken by the *Times* in the summer of 2002 found that 70 percent of those questioned approved of President Bush's job performance, and 80 percent agreed that he "shared their moral values." The *Washington Post,* itself certainly no political ally of the president's, accurately headlined its story: "Poll Shows Bush's Ratings Weathering Business Scandals." In contrast, the *Times* headline read, "Poll Finds Concerns that Bush Is Overly Influenced by Business." As Sullivan observed, "It's as if the *Times,* tired of waiting for the nation to turn against the president, had decided simply to write the news it wanted to see."

But that was nothing. The issue that really got Raines and the *Times* going was the looming war with Iraq, as the paper went out of its way to attack and undermine the administration at every turn. Yet on Friday, August 16, 2002, the *Times* did something that stunned even its severest critics: In a front-page story headlined "Top Republicans Break With Bush on Iraq Strategy," it literally turned a prominent supporter of the administration's policy, Henry Kissinger, into an opponent. As the *Washington Times* observed, "The other, lesser names mentioned in the article—Brent Scowcroft, Sen. Chuck Hagel and Rep. Dick Armey—actually had broken ranks. But most of the public hasn't heard of them, and none have the worldwide prestige and respect of Mr. Kissinger. So, the *New York Times* kidnapped Mr. Kissinger's name and reputation on behalf of its opposition to the President's strategy."

This astonishing attempt to invent news was obvious to anyone who cared to see. Kissinger had written an op-ed piece on the subject just a few days before in the *Washington Post,* making his support for the Bush policy clear. No matter. Lemminglike, all three of the networks followed the *Times* over the cliff, with both CBS and NBC prominently featuring Kissinger's "break with the administration" in their lead story of that evening's newscasts.

Yet incredibly, the embarrassments kept on coming—and not small ones but whoppers. The next *Times* crusade, this time on the domestic front, involved the fight to get (multimillionaire) women admitted to the all- (multimillionaire) male Augusta National Golf Club. Given the depth of the feminist influence at the paper, this was no surprise. Still, for all the attention Raines and his staff gave this story, you'd have thought it was the ultimate crusade for human rights and dignity—Montgomery and Selma all over again. The paper ran editorials and news stories, including more than a few page-one features; when the time of the tournament came around in April, the *Times* had run close to a hundred pieces in all. Even to liberals, it began to look like a crazed PC obsession. In fact, in the ultimate indignity, *Newsweek* ran a piece saying just that. Headlined "The Changing 'Times,'" with the damning subhead "A hard-charging editor's crusading style is coloring the Gray Lady's reputation." The *Newsweek* piece was a startling critique of what Howell Raines had done to the paper. It quoted one *Times* staffer— unnamed, of course; he probably has a family to feed—saying that the coverage of the Augusta controversy was so obviously slanted, "It makes it hard for us to have credibility on other issues." Raines, added another unnamed *Times* reporter, was "in danger of losing the building."

The *Newsweek* piece continued: "It's not just the newsroom that's concerned. From conservative activists to everyday readers, many people around the country are noticing a change in the way the Old Gray Lady covers any number of issues, from the looming war with Iraq to the sex-abuse scandals in the Roman Catholic Church to the New Jersey Senate race. Raines, the hard-charging executive editor, has an almost religious belief in 'flooding the zone'—using all the paper's formidable resources to pound away on a story. But increasingly, the *Times* is being criticized for ginning up controversies as much as reporting them out. 'This is certainly a shift from the *New York Times* as the "paper of record,"' says Alex Jones, a former *Times* media reporter and coauthor of *The Trust,* a book about the paper. 'It's a more activist agenda in terms of policy, especially compared to an administration that's much more conservative.' Or as *Slate* press critic Jack Shafer puts it, 'The *Times* has assumed the journalistic role as the party of opposition.'"

In April 2003, Cynthia Cott, the media reporter for the left-of-center *Village Voice,* joined the chorus. Since succeeding Joseph Lelyveld, she wrote, Raines has "engaged in a rolling purge, systematically pushing out editorial employees with ties to the past. . . . According to insiders, Raines is the kind of 1950s-style autocrat who manages through humiliation and fear." Cott goes on to quote one *Times* insider who says that old-timers at the paper "say they have never seen anyone be so arrogant, so petty, so mean. Vindictiveness is in." Another source says, "'It's no longer about managing down. It's about paying obeisance to the king.' Among cognoscenti, 43rd Street is now known as the 'republic of fear.'"

Cott went on to report that "In the 19 months since Raines took over, so many high-ranking *Times* people have stepped down that cultural custodians are scrambling to keep track of the body count."

Andrew Sullivan had a more succinct indictment of the paper: About a year after Raines took over, he wrote, "The rot began to sink in."

Sullivan came to that conclusion even before the *New York Daily News* reported that two of the paper's own sportswriters who had written columns disagreeing with the paper's editorial stance on the

Masters, including respected Pulitzer Prize winner Dave Anderson, had had their work spiked by Howell Raines's *New York Times,* which seemed to be censoring its own columnists for having the temerity to disagree with Raines. Even editors of college papers don't try to pull stuff like that! The *Times* took so much heat, they actually had to (at least partially) relent, and run edited versions of the two columns.

(All of this caught the mischievous eye of Dennis Miller, the comedian, who suggested that if Saddam Hussein were to open a golf club "For Men Only" in Baghdad, maybe *that* would get the sensitive editors at the *New York Times* to change their editorial mind and come out in favor of war with Iraq.)

The paper's agenda-driven mindset extended even to its formerly serious and thoughtful op-ed page. Once, the *New York Times* boasted the most esteemed social and political commentators in the business. Now, instead of Harrison Salisbury and Flora Lewis, it gives us a one-note samba left-wing ideologue like Paul Krugman and an obsessively hip Maureen Dowd, who begins a typical (and yes, it *is* typical) column like this:

> A gaggle of my girlfriends are surreptitiously smitten with Eminem. They buy his posters on eBay. They play him on their Walkmen at the gym. They sing along lustily to "Cleanin' Out My Closet" and "Lose Yourself" in the car. They rhapsodize that his amazing vignettes of dysfunctional families make him the Raymond Carver of hip-hop.
>
> They crowd into movie theatres along with teenage boys in watch caps, and then insist that Eminem's rapping his way out of a Detroit car factory in *8 Mile* is way hotter than Jennifer Beals's dancing her way out of the Pittsburgh steel mill in *Flashdance.* They put off helping their kids with homework so they can watch the rapper's trailer-park mom being interviewed on *Primetime Live.*
>
> "My 11-year-old daughter is repulsed that I like him," a friend says, as her daughter chimes in that mom is "psychotic

and weird." Mothers, the little girl explains, are not supposed to like people who talk about "drugs and sex and hard lives."

Only in today's *New York Times* will an eleven-year-old appear infinitely wiser and more mature than the columnist quoting her.

Then again, like so many at the paper these days, Dowd was only slavishly following her boss's lead. "D.M.C.'s Jam Master Jay was killed a few months ago," Raines told an interviewer in January 2003. "I had been following the debate in rap music about Snoop Dogg trying to revive his career by insulting Suge Knight. I thought this was so interesting because it was being covered in the entertainment press like it was about one guy's mother being insulted by the other guy. And, in fact, it's a business story that's touching Sony and many other companies in an industry that's had a 20 percent decline in revenues. So behind this public street conflict is this huge business story."

This prompted a prominent journalist (*not* at the *Times*) to send some of his friends in the profession an incredulous E-mail in which he asked, "What the hell is he talking about? The logic and thinking behind this quote is beyond me. *I'd been following the 'debate' in rap music . . . ?*?? What's the editor of the *New York Times* doing dropping (or even knowing) the name 'Jam Master Jay,' except in a desperate attempt to sound 'with it'?"

But here's the thing: You think the people who run the *Times* are embarrassed by any of it?

"The *Times* readership is diminishing," as Hilton Kramer points out, "but the influence it exerts is as enormous as ever. Because as long as the rest of the mainstream media keep depending on the *Times* to define what's news, its power will remain."

In early 2003, several months before the Blair scandal broke, I was eager to talk to Howell Raines about that power and to get his views on what his critics were saying about the paper under his command. But—as the *New York Times* itself might put it—several attempts to contact Mr. Raines for comment went unanswered.

Maybe it was just a coincidence, but on the very day I made my final try to reach him, Raines did indeed have something to say about his critics—but not to me, not directly anyway. Accepting the National Press Foundation's George Beveridge Editor of the Year Award (on February 20, 2003), Raines took aim at those who see a liberal bias in the news.

"We must be aware," he said, "of the energetic effort that is now under way to convince our readers that we are ideologues. It is an exercise in disinformation, of alarming proportions, this attempt to convince the audience of the world's most ideologically free newspapers that they're being subjected to agenda-driven news reflecting a liberal bias. I don't believe our viewers and readers will be, in the long run, misled by those who advocate biased journalism."

"By those who advocate biased journalism"? Is that their answer to everything: to smear their critics as agenda-driven right-wing ideologues when what some of us are trying to do is make things better? If you criticize a news organization for liberal bias in a particular story, then *you're* the one who's biased? *You're* the one who "advocate[s] biased journalism"? What I would have asked Raines, had he been willing to talk, is this: Why are the critics—*liberals and conservatives alike*—biased for coming to the conclusion that the *New York Times* appears to be largely driven by ideology? Was *Newsweek* magazine part of the "energetic effort that is now under way to convince our readers that we are ideologues" because it said your "crusading style is coloring the Gray Lady's reputation"? Was Jack Shafer of *Slate* part of the problem when he said, "The *Times* has assumed the journalistic role as the party of opposition"? Were your own staffers who have criticized your liberal activism part of the vast "disinformation" campaign?

What Howell Raines never understood during his twenty months at the helm is that it's not a bunch of right-wing nuts who are trying to subvert the minds of the readers and viewers he claimed to be so concerned about. A lot of those readers and viewers . . . *are the critics.* They—and "they" in this case is a big chunk of the American people—have been complaining about bias in the news for a long time now, long before I and others ever started writing about it. Just because Howell Raines ignored them, just because he wrote them off as disgruntled reactionary dolts, doesn't make it so. For a smart guy, it's odd that he was not able to see that he's the one who was out of touch. Way out of touch. Like so many media elites, he was part of the club. The one whose members give awards to one another all the time and tell one another how wonderful they are—and how vile their critics are.

But it's now clearer than ever that Raines should have been trying to talk to a few of those critics. He should have sat down with the least ideological among them—and *listened.* Maybe then he might have begun to understand why so many Americans are so unhappy with what we routinely call the "mainstream media."

Of course the *Times* has always been an institution with more than its fair share of arrogant blowhards—people whose whole sense of who they are is based on getting to say they work at the *New York Times.* Deroy Murdock, the columnist who once wrote that the *New York Times* "exudes an insufferable snottiness," recalls that he phoned a friend one day at the *Times* and said, "Hi, is Mark there?"

"No, he's not," a woman replied.

"May I leave a message?"

"No," she said. "You'll have to call back and speak with an editorial assistant. I'm an editor, and at the *New York Times,* editors don't take messages." Click.

But the *Times* has never been as arrogant as it is today. Or as mean-spirited. Or as disconnected.

This was never clearer than in the story that appeared on the paper's front page on December 9, 2002—more than a year after the Bill Ayers gaffe on September 11. It was a profile of a young man at Yale named Chesa Boudin, who had just been awarded a prestigious Rhodes Scholarship. And it was a disgrace.

It turns out that young Mr. Boudin is the son of David Gilbert and Kathy Boudin, two members of the sixties radical group Weather Underground, who have been in prison for more than twenty years for their part in a 1981 robbery of a Brinks truck that left two policemen and a guard dead. And because his parents were in prison, Chesa Boudin was raised by two other members of the radical group, Bernadine Dohrn and Bill Ayers.

Yes, *that* Bill Ayers.

Now it was young Chesa Boudin's turn to be canonized by the *New York Times,* whose reporter, Jodi Wilgoren, tells us about how he overcame "striking challenges" while growing up, how he dealt with his epilepsy and his dyslexia and his "temper tantrums." Chesa Boudin, of course, should not be condemned for the acts of his parents. No, he should be condemned entirely on his own merits.

An antiwar activist at Yale, he believes his parents were heroes. "We have a different name for the war we're fighting now," he tells the admiring *Times* reporter. "Now we call it the war on terrorism; then they called it the war on Communism. My parents were all dedicated to fighting U.S. imperialism around the world. I'm dedicated to the same thing."

"Now, I'm not angry," he tells the *Times.* "I'm sad that my parents have to suffer what they have to suffer on a daily basis, that millions of other people have to suffer as well."

What other people? The homeless in Chile, the poor in Bolivia, the illiterate in Guatemala—that's what other people, he tells the *New York Times.* But even more revealing is what he does *not* tell the *Times.* While we hear much about Chesa Boudin's suffering and hardships, and about the suffering and hardships of the poor around the world, neither the *Times* nor our Ivy League–educated Rhodes scholar tells us anything about the suffering and hardships of other children much closer to home—the nine children left behind by the policemen and the guard who were murdered, in cold blood, with the help of Chesa Boudin's parents.

On this the *Times* and young Mr. Boudin are silent. They say not a single word.

But just when you think it can't get any worse, the hopelessly politically correct *New York Times* is there to prove you wrong.

The *Times*, it turns out, was also silent on one other "small" point. *Not once in the entire story, beginning on page one, are the victims— the dead policemen and the guard—ever mentioned by name!*

For the record, they were Sergeant Edward O'Grady, Officer Waverly Brown, and Brinks guard Peter Paige. There was a small scholarship fund set up in their memory, for local kids who want to pursue careers in law enforcement. Maybe the Rhodes trustees, who have given Chesa Boudin lots of money for his studies, would want to make a small contribution to the fund.

Reading this story, barely more than a year after 9/11, you could only ask yourself, "What are the people at the *New York Times* thinking? Are they truly this clueless? Are they so infatuated with the infantile radicalism of the sixties that they've lost all sense of decency?"

But then you're caught short by an even more discouraging thought: that almost no one in the mainstream press is asking him or herself *any* of these questions. All they're asking is, "Is there anything in the *Times* today we can take?"

Even now, those at the *Times* will tell you how much the paper prides itself on its accuracy. After all, didn't it admirably air all its dirty laundry in the Jayson Blair case? Didn't the investigation of his fraudulent work set off a chain of events that led to the resignations of the paper's two top editors? Doesn't the *Times* run corrections all the time to show how much it cares about getting every detail right?

But here's the real question: Wouldn't the *Times* (and other mainstream news outlets that follow its lead) be far better off if they were equally concerned with that other kind of newsroom diversity—the intellectual kind? Wouldn't that help cut down on a far more insidious form of distortion than the kind practiced by Blair—the chronic undercurrent of PC evident throughout the paper? And wouldn't it begin to restore the *Times* credibility with the many readers who have learned to expect to find their attitudes and beliefs mischaracterized and belittled by the newspaper of record?

Unfortunately, those who run the *New York Times* will likely never raise those questions and will continue to reflexively dismiss those who do.

Sure the *Times* runs lots of corrections. Unfortunately, they are usually along the lines of: "Robert L. Jones, who was mentioned in yesterday's story on page A12, should have been identified as Robert S. Jones. We regret the error."

You know when the *Times* will really start to get it right? The day it runs a correction like this: "Robert L. Jones, who we yesterday characterized as a no-good, racist, homophobe, sexist bigot, is in fact none of these things. He is simply a conservative. We regret the error."

A Conversation
with Tim Russert

Watching Tim Russert, you get an idea of what a fair-minded mainstream press might look like. I know he used to work for Mario Cuomo, one of the most liberal Democrats around, as well as for New York's longtime moderate Democratic Senator Pat Moynihan. So I might guess which way he leans politically, but I'd only be guessing. Because watching him on the air, you don't know *what* his personal politics are, since he gives all sides a fair and equal say—and just as important, he challenges all sides with equal skepticism and vigor.

Very simply, Tim Russert tries to be fair, and it shows—which is why, I think, his *Meet the Press* is by far the most popular of the Sunday morning interview shows.

There are probably a lot of reasons Russert stands out from his colleagues in the world of elite journalism, so when he agreed to talk to me for this book, I thought that maybe the place to start was with his background.

GOLDBERG: I think a lot of people have seen a fairness in you that they're not used to seeing on the networks, and I'm wondering how much you think your blue-collar background has to do with it.

RUSSERT: There's no substitute for it, Bernie, believe me. I've worked on garbage trucks. I drove a taxi. I tended bar. I delivered pizzas. I worked with liberals, conservatives, blacks, whites; that's how you grew up in this interesting world, and people were always simply judged in the end on their quality as a person: Did they tell the truth? Did they honor their commitments? Did they show up for work on time?

GOLDBERG: What I learned from my father, who worked in a factory, while I was growing up in the Bronx, was the same thing: You show up to work on time, and if you tell someone you're going to do something, you do it. Those are old-fashioned values.

RUSSERT: My dad said that all the time: People are people; they'll treat you the way you treat them—and I have adhered to that the best I possibly can. And I also believe that going to the schools I did—St. Bonaventure school, Canisius High School, John Carroll University—these are not fashionable, elitist schools. These are schools where you learn to read and write and learn right from wrong. But they would never wave a wand and say, this is the way you must think.

The key to it was always respecting another person's view and never suggesting that anyone had a monopoly on correctness. And that should be the centerpiece to being a journalist. You don't go out there bringing to your profession an attitude that you know what is right for the country or you know what view is the *progressive* one or the *appropriate* one to have.

GOLDBERG: On the other hand, I've worked with network people who literally referred to the audience as white trash. They were talking about people who didn't go to school in the Northeast and sometimes literally did live in trailers.

RUSSERT: They've said it about me: "Russert attended middling schools. Russert admits to being a practicing Catholic.

GOLDBERG: *Admits?* ? ?

RUSSERT: [*laughing*] Right!!! "If he didn't go to Harvard, if he's not Ivy League, how can he be smart?" Bernie, there's not a moment when I'm sitting there on *Meet the Press* when I'm not thinking about my dad. He's in my head; he's in my heart. That's why I ask them straight questions: What are you going to do about that issue? How about this one? Well, that's not what you said about this!

It's the way our dad engaged us—always give the other guy the benefit of the doubt but hear him out. Hear him out. And don't dismiss him and don't brand him as anything. It's not right. I think it's so imperative, particular for those of us who have been *blessed* with these jobs in journalism, to approach things in an open-minded way.

GOLDBERG: Does your blue-collar radar detect an elitism even amongst your colleagues?

RUSSERT: Sure, some. Among politicians, among journalists, it exists.

I am all for having women in the newsroom, and minorities in the newsroom—I'm all for it. It opens up our eyes and gives us different perspectives. But just as well, let's have people with military experience; let's have people from all walks of life, people from the top-echelon schools but also people from junior colleges and the so-called middling schools—that's the rich pageantry of America.

GOLDBERG: It seems to me, Tim, that you're a real proponent of diversity. You believe in it when it comes to race and gender and ethnicity because it's better to have lots of people with different points of view covering the news, and . . .

RUSSERT: . . . and you need cultural and ideological diversity, also. That's central to this. I'm a great believer in racial diversity and gender diversity, but you need cultural diversity, you need ideological diversity. *You need it.*

GOLDBERG: You say we need ideological diversity in the newsroom. But how do you actually do that? How do you get all sorts of people with all sorts of backgrounds and worldviews into the newsroom?

RUSSERT: Take *Meet the Press.* Every person on the *Meet the Press* staff started out as an intern. But I make sure they come from a cross-section of schools. We've had kids from Holy Cross and Fordham, for example.

GOLDBERG: So you go to places where kids might be traditionally liberal, but you also go to places where kids, because of their . . .

RUSSERT: . . . culture . . .

GOLDBERG: . . . because of their culture, might be conservative?

RUSSERT: Absolutely right.

GOLDBERG: When I say that I see a liberal bias in the news, a lot of journalists who live in a world of politics dismiss it. They say, "What are you talking about? We don't go easy on Democrats and tough on Republicans." And I say there's a lot of truth to that. But that's not my point about liberal bias. While there is no conspiracy—*no conspiracy*—there is like-mindedness in too many newsrooms. . . .

RUSSERT: There's a potential *cultural bias.* And I think it's very real and very important to recognize and to deal with. Because of background and training you come to issues with a preconceived notion or a preordained view on subjects like abortion, gun control, campaign finance. I think many journalists growing up in the sixties and the seventies have to be very careful about attitudes toward government, attitudes toward the military, attitudes toward authority. It doesn't mean there's a rightness or a wrongness. It means you have to constantly check yourself. John Chancellor used to say, if your mother says she loves you, check it out.

GOLDBERG: Why the close-mindedness when the subject comes around to media bias? There are a whole bunch of people in the world of journalism and the world of academia who just shut the discussion down. They not only don't believe there's this cultural bias, they think it's not worth talking about.

RUSSERT: That, to me, is totally contrary to who we're supposed to be as journalists. My view was, invite Bernard Goldberg and *Bias* on my [CNBC] show. This is central to who we are. Let's talk about it! If we miss a story, if we got our facts wrong, we would have a postmortem and ask ourselves, where did we go wrong? How can we improve ourselves? So, if there's any suggestion in any way, shape, or form that there's a liberal bias, a cultural bias, let's examine it; that's what we do for a living.

GOLDBERG: When I was on your show we talked, off the air, during a commercial, about the op-ed I wrote in the *Wall Street Journal* back in 1996 about liberal bias in the news, which caused quite a furor. You told me that you actually passed the op-ed around the newsroom in Washington. Do you remember that?

RUSSERT: The first person I talked to that morning was Tom Brokaw, and I said, "Did you see the piece?" and he said, "I sure did." I told him that I was going to give it out down here. I talked to people about it. I said, "We have to engage on this issue. *It is imperative that we talk about this issue.*" If someone suggested there was an antiblack bias, an antigay bias, an anti-American bias, we'd sit up and say, "Let's talk about this; let's tackle it." Well, if there's a liberal bias or a cultural bias we have to sit up and tackle it and discuss it. *We have got to be open to these things.*

GOLDBERG: This willingness to be open goes back to those early days in Buffalo, doesn't it?

RUSSERT: As I say, the people I grew up around had a wonderful way of encouraging, insisting that you understand people, that you give them their say and not be dismissive of any point of view. No one has a monopoly on what is right and what is wrong.

GOLDBERG: I think that piece of advice—"don't be dismissive of people"—while it may sound fairly obvious, just might be the single most important piece of advice you ever received.

RUSSERT: It's so imperative that when you sit around a table and discuss stories that people be there from different perspectives and different life situations. For example, for me a robust conversation is with people who are for abortion rights and people who are *against* abortion rights. It's just central to a journalist that we not adopt a code of correctness that *this* is the *preferred* position on the issue.

When I had [Democratic House Leader] Nancy Pelosi on *Meet the Press,* she said that when Newt Gingrich was Speaker, he was radical and extreme right wing and [House Majority Whip] Tom DeLay is far right, and when I said then the dichotomy is that you would be perceived as far left, she said, "No, no, I'm moderate, I'm centrist."

GOLDBERG: But you see, Tim, in my view that same point can be made about journalists, too. When you get to the big social issues— whether it's race or gender or feminism or gay rights—I think journalists see conservatives correctly as conservative, but they see liberals as middle of the road.

RUSSERT: I think this is the most important challenge confronting journalists: *There is no preferred position.* One cannot be dismissive of one person as extreme and find another acceptable just because of how you define liberal, conservative, or mainstream. To a journalist covering this country there should not be a preferred position on abortion, a preferred position on gay marriage, a preferred position on gun control, a preferred position on campaign finance reform. And you have to work at it and think back to where you came from and keep applying those same standards. It really is *fascinating* to me when you talk to political figures and to some journalists, they'll say the center is *here*—if you are for abortion rights, for gun control, for campaign finance reform, that's a mainstream position; and those opposed to it are on the fringe. And that's just not the way reporters should approach issues.

GOLDBERG: But when you say it's the most important challenge confronting journalists . . .

RUSSERT: It truly is.

GOLDBERG: Is that because you see a problem in that area?

RUSSERT: Whenever we were going through the whole situation with President Clinton on a variety of issues involving his veracity, I would say in the newsroom: What if Richard Nixon had said this? And people would sit up [because they hadn't thought of it that way]. You have to apply a single standard. And the single standard has to be one of objectivity and not in any way, shape, or form demonstrating a preferred position. And if you call Tom DeLay—and I have—the *conservative* Texan, then I call Ms. Pelosi the *liberal* Californian.

GOLDBERG: Speaking of all this, you had Rush Limbaugh on *Meet the Press*. How did you come to that decision?

RUSSERT: He has the most widely listened-to radio program in America, he has done an enormous amount to engage and encourage political discussion around the country; he articulates a political philosophy as well as anyone in the country. To suggest his views are anathema and therefore should not be put on . . .

GOLDBERG: But you have heard from the critics.

RUSSERT: Oh, sure. They want to know, "Why would you have Rush Limbaugh on *Meet the Press*?" I don't *sanction* his political views by having him on. But to suggest that he does not deserve the opportunity to present his views—I mean, *Meet the Press* is a forum for ideas! And to have a censorship for his ideas . . . [*laughs*]

You may disagree with him philosophically, but his demeanor, his presentation was perfectly appropriate for *Meet the Press*. And to suggest otherwise is absurd.

By the way, when I have Ralph Nader on, I say to people, "I didn't hear any complaints there" [*laughs*].

GOLDBERG: Some conservatives complain that when the subject gets around to taxes you tilt to the Left, that you ask too many questions about whether we can afford tax cuts but not enough questions about whether the government is spending too much.

RUSSERT: I guess you can conclude that by watching me question people, that I think deficits matter. I guess if there's a bias, it's that yes, I do think that deficits matter. And you know where that comes from? [*laughing*] It comes from Mom and Dad's kitchen table. We never floated loans.

GOLDBERG: But there are two ways to balance the budget, whether it's around the kitchen table or in Congress. One is by raising revenue. So your father can go out and get a *third* full-time job. Or you can cut out some spending.

RUSSERT: Exactly right. I couldn't agree more. But I question both tax cuts and spending. I was aggressive regarding the cost of the Clinton health care plan. I was very aggressive about the cost of Medicare and Social Security. I constantly say to Democrats, "Can you have it all?"

GOLDBERG: Let's jump to another subject. When you interviewed Vice President Cheney on *Meet the Press,* you wore the red, white, and blue ribbon on your lapel.

RUSSERT: This was September 16, 2001, at Camp David.

GOLDBERG: And you heard from critics about that, too.

RUSSERT: A very good friend of mine died at the World Trade Center, and his family asked if I would, in his memory, wear this ribbon. I never thought for a second about it.

GOLDBERG: And to those who say journalists shouldn't wear red, white, and blue ribbons, that by doing that somehow you're taking the government's side in some debate or another—which I don't frankly see, by the way . . .

RUSSERT: It is imperative that we never suggest that there's a moral equivalency between the United States of America and the terrorists. Period. I'll believe that until the day I die. I have talked about being a journalist—but also being an American. And first and foremost, you're an American. I want a debate about national security, and who defines national security. I understand all that. But in the end, you have to make judgments, and on that day I made a judgment that five days after the most horrific event of my lifetime and of my journalistic career, that for me to say to the country I too am part of this, I too have experienced this gut-wrenching pain and agony, and I too have enormous remorse and sympathy, with not only the people who died in the World Trade Center, the Pentagon, and in the field in Pennsylvania, but all of us—we're in this together; this isn't covering Democrats and Republicans or the Bills versus the Redskins; this is *us.* The Taliban doesn't believe in the First Amendment.

I'm an American and then I'm a journalist.

Barbara Walters, Guardian of Standards

"News used to be considered a public trust. It was and perhaps still is what gives the networks [their] dignity and integrity. It deserved respect, and so, I think, do we."
—20/20 *anchor Barbara Walters, speaking during the furor over*
  ABC's plan to dump Nightline, *March 2002*

"Up until that point that was the . . . best sex I'd ever had. I felt . . . cared for, loved . . . on a sexual level . . . that I had not [had] before with a man. I felt . . . sensuous and sexual in a way I hadn't before."
—*Actress Anne Heche about her relationship with comic Ellen*
  DeGeneres, in a 20/20 interview with Barbara Walters,
  September 2001

A (Black and White) Hollywood Ending

nyone remember Erica Pratt?

My guess is, not too many. I mean, we're constantly being bombarded by supposedly earth-shaking stories that are important only until the next earth-shaking story comes along, which is usually in about ten seconds. Who can keep track of an Erica Pratt, or just about anyone else?

Still, for a brief moment in the summer of 2002, seven-year-old Erica Pratt was a genuine television news star. In July of that year, Erica was playing near her row house in Philadelphia when two men in a junk heap of a car pulled up and snatched her right off the street in broad daylight. They blindfolded her and took her to the dirty basement of an empty house, tied her up with duct tape, and left her there, in the dark, all alone. Then they sent a message that they would kill her unless Erica's family came up with $150,000.

Remember now? If you do, then you may remember how the story ended. How Erica Pratt chewed through the tape, kicked open a basement door, and got to a window, where she screamed until some neighborhood kids heard her and came to the rescue. And if you think back, you just might also remember that beautiful smile on that heroic little girl's face when she was back home safe and sound.

But what you definitely won't remember is that there was an uglier side to this terrific story. And the reason you won't remember is because the networks decided not to tell you.

No one watching any of the three network evening newscasts on July 24, 2002, was aware of a couple of crucial pieces of information: The police were telling reporters they believed that Erica Pratt had been taken by people familiar with her family, and that there may also have been a drug angle.

Erica Pratt came from what we euphemistically call "a dysfunctional family." One uncle had been shot dead after being charged with attempted murder in connection with another shooting. Another uncle had recently survived a murder attempt. Her father was on probation after pleading guilty to charges of drug possession and intent to distribute.

For anyone interested in figuring out what was going on with the little girl's kidnapping, this information—information that reporters covering the case knew the police were focusing on—obviously was crucial. As the *Philadelphia Inquirer* straightforwardly wrote on the morning of July 24, 2002, "Neighbors of the Pratt family said the names and reputations of the two suspects [James Burns, who a year later was found guilty of kidnapping, and Edward Johnson, who pleaded guilty to the same charge] were familiar to residents. Court records show Burns, 28, has repeatedly been arrested on gun charges. Johnson has a string of drug arrests and is on probation. On Monday, the kidnappers, who apparently knew Erica's family, began contacting the girl's grandmother within 20 minutes of dragging her into their car and speeding off. The kidnappers demanded $150,000 ransom. . . . Police said rumors had circulated in the neighborhood that Erica's grandmother had just received a $150,000 insurance payment for the March 23 murder of Erica's uncle. . . . Joseph Pratt Jr., 25, was killed in a barrage of bullets as he sat in a car parked on South 56th Street near Woodland Avenue. Before the killing, he had been involved in drug dealing and a series of serious assaults. At the time of his death, he was facing charges of attempted murder, police said."

The next morning's *Inquirer* elaborated on the same theme: "Late yesterday, investigators were still trying to untangle a web of ties between her suspected abductors and the Pratt family—which has a violent history, including the recent slaying of an uncle of the little girl and another uncle's acquittal in a double murder."

To any news organization interested in honestly reporting the story, as the *Philadelphia Inquirer* was, these details go to the heart of the matter. They go to *the very reason Erica was abducted*. If the random, inexplicable abduction of a small child was "every parent's worst nightmare," as reporters are always telling us, then the specifics of this particular kidnapping would actually have made some parents rest a lot easier. Because what had happened to Erica Pratt would be their worst nightmare only if they lived in a high-crime neighborhood where members of their extended family ran with low-life thugs.

Why, then, did this crucial part of the story go unreported on the evening newscasts? Why was everyone involved so determined to put a sunny Hollywood ending on what was really a much grimmer West Philadelphia story?

In the end, *that* is what is truly of interest in this fleeting story about this remarkable little girl. Because what the network news correspondents did *not* say tells us a lot more than what they *did* say. What they left out of their stories speaks volumes about the attitudes, habits, and calculations the mainstream media bring to all sorts of stories that touch on that most radioactive of issues in America: race.

Now, let's be perfectly honest about this: The bias on race cuts more than one way, meaning that a very different segment of the population—upper-middle-class white people—also often gets a free ride from the media. Reporters, local and national, have done a lot more stories about drugs in poor black neighborhoods than stories about drugs in dorms on college campuses, where most of the users are middle- and upper-middle-class white kids, to use one example. And how many times have you heard a reporter ask the cops why, if they're so interested in ridding our society of illicit drugs, they're not cracking down on yuppies doing drugs in the suburbs?

Try almost never.

The larger truth is that the elite media make a practice of promoting upper-middle-class liberal attitudes and values in their stories—and that means giving preferential treatment both to those they regard as oppressed minorities and (when it comes down to it, even more so) to well-off white people just like themselves.

On the Erica Pratt story, you may recall, there was a context. As summers go, 2002 had not been a good one. It wasn't just the stock market tanking and the economy teetering on the brink of a double-dip recession, or the possibility that Martha Stewart might soon be fashionably decked out in stripes, or even the constant warnings about weapons of mass destruction and the nonstop speculation about another invasion of Iraq. More depressing and more frightening than any of that were the kidnappings of young girls.

You couldn't turn on the television that summer without hearing about another little girl who had been abducted by some monster. It didn't really matter that there wasn't actually an epidemic of child abductions—that in absolute numbers there wasn't any real increase in kidnappings. The barrage of stories about missing kids made it feel that way. A summer earlier it was the shark attack "epidemic" that really wasn't. Television has that effect.

Child abductions seized the nation's attention in early June, when the neighbor accused of killing seven-year-old Danielle van Dam back in February went on trial in a San Diego courtroom. The very next day, fourteen-year-old Elizabeth Smart—blonde, wholesome, and child-model pretty—was taken from her own bed in Salt Lake

City in the middle of the night and for nine long months vanished from the face of the earth. Then, on July 15, we learned of five-year-old Samantha Runnion, who was lured from her Stanton, California, front yard by a man claiming to be looking for a lost dog. This set off a desperate search by thousands of police and volunteers before she was found, murdered by another pathetic loser with a twisted mind. Over and over we endured the painful, almost unwatchable images of the helpless families grieving for their children.

So by the time Erica Pratt came along, America was desperate for some good news on the child abduction front. And network executives were just as desperate to give the nation a story that finally had a happy ending—even if that meant leaving out a few inconvenient details.

Okay, happy endings are a big part of show biz, which, like it or not, is what a lot of television news has become. But there was another reason the networks played the Erica Pratt story the way they did. And that's where race comes in.

For the previous month, ABC, CBS, and NBC News had all been feeling heat from black interest groups. Remember, all the girls we were seeing on the evening news were white. They all lived in nice white neighborhoods—which, frankly, is the main reason the producers and executives who shape the network news gave them such prominent play. They know full well which heartbreaking stories are most likely to draw the middle-class and affluent, overwhelmingly white viewers they crave—the ones who have the most money to spend on products advertised on TV.

This is white media liberalism at its most hypocritical. I spent a lot of years with these people, and you have no idea what major-league phonies they can be. How they will enthusiastically support every item on the liberal agenda . . . until, God forbid, the fallout starts to affect them—or their bottom line. If missing white kids from middle-class families get better ratings than missing black kids from the wrong side of the tracks, hey, just leave those darn black kids out. Segregate them. It's nothing personal of course—certainly not racism. Racism is what *conservatives*—not *liberals*—practice. Everyone knows that. This is just good business.

In the past I have called these media elites "Liberals of Convenience" because of how easily they justify the way they marginalize black people and poor people in their news coverage—and all in the interest of maximizing ratings and otherwise furthering their own careers. But that was way too generous. They are simply hypocrites. No need for embellishment beyond that.

Only this time they found themselves with a problem because, as the black pressure groups were more and more insistently letting the world know, there was another little girl, to whom—a full month earlier!—the same gruesome thing had happened as had happened to Elizabeth Smart. She was a seven-year-old black girl in Milwaukee named Alexis Patterson, who had vanished on May 3, 2002, on her way to school. Yet all this time later, none of the network newscasts had devoted even a single word to her—a fact that became all the more glaring after the massive coverage television started giving the Smart case.

Alexis's cause had been taken up by, among others, the NAACP and the National Association of Black Journalists. Indeed, by mid-June, Alexis had become for many black people in America the very symbol of the media's appalling double standard.

A story in the *Milwaukee Journal Sentinel* on June 15, 2002, began this way:

"Two girls are missing.

"The national media flocked to Salt Lake City to tell the nation about Elizabeth Smart. Why haven't the reporters descended on Milwaukee to tell the nation about Alexis Patterson?

"Two cases, two cities, two different stories."

The missing girl's parents were understandably distraught. "We're not in control of the media," her stepfather said at a news conference sponsored by The National Association of Black Journalists. "And it's basically a white media."

The critics had it right: The media seemed to think a white girl's

life was more important than a black girl's life; the media believed
that the face of a white girl "plays" better on TV than the face of a
black girl; in the media's view, America *cared* more about white girls
than about black girls.

The "basically white media" were under the microscope, a spot
where they put every other institution in America, but one they
themselves will go to almost any length to avoid. A week after the
Journal Sentinel piece, CBS News—in what a friend of mine calls
"self-flagellation mode"—ran a piece that all but acknowledged the
double standard. "Our baby is seven years old," Alexis's stepfather
told the camera. "She's been missing a month and a half and she's not
got a half of the attention [of Elizabeth Smart] and it hurts. You know,
it really hurts."

The very next day, the NBC News "In Depth" segment ran a similar mea culpa. "She [Elizabeth Smart] got more coverage than Alexis
did," the missing girl's stepfather told correspondent Jim Avila. "She's
in everyone's living room; Alexis is not."

So when Erica Pratt came along, she was a godsend in more than
just the obvious way. Yes, America was desperate for some good news
on the child abduction front—and network executives were just as
desperate to give the nation a story that finally had a happy ending.
But not only did Erica's story have a happy ending . . . *she was black,
too!*

And she was about to be in everyone's living room.

"And tonight," announced Tom Brokaw on NBC, "a story of a
daring and resourceful escape at a time of several high-profile abductions of young girls." "From Philadelphia today," enthused
Charles Gibson on ABC, "the story of one very resourceful seven-
year-old girl." "We close tonight with the story of another child abducted just outside her own front door," Dan Rather reported on
CBS, "another child taken no one knew where. But this time, as
CBS's Jim Axelrod reports from Philadelphia, the climax of the story
is nothing less than a great escape."

Axelrod's story on CBS and the ones from Rehema Ellis on NBC and John Yang on ABC were all essentially the same. Each gave the details of the kidnapping and of Erica's brave escape. All were upbeat, even inspirational.

Not one said a thing about drugs.

Having watched the *CBS Evening News* that night and knowing only what Dan Rather and Jim Axelrod told me, I almost fell out of my chair when I turned on *The O'Reilly Factor* on the Fox News Channel just one hour later and heard the following:

"In the Impact segment tonight, seven-year-old Erica Pratt of Philadelphia is a national hero this evening. She was kidnapped in front of a row house but escaped, according to police. However, there are a number of troubling aspects to this case, including an apparent drug connection."

O'Reilly then interviewed a local Philadelphia TV reporter named Dave Huddleston, who said, "Well, it appears from police sources that there is some gang rivalry, some drug trafficking rivalry going on, affiliated with this family. There are police sources that say that Erica's father and uncle ran a drug trafficking operation in West Philadelphia."

What? Why did I have to go to a cable news outfit to hear about this? Why didn't I get those crucial facts from the much bigger "mainstream" television networks?

But, of course, familiar as I am with both the attitudes and the apprehensions of decision-makers from my own twenty-eight years at CBS News, I already had a pretty good idea. I had a whole catalog of examples where politically correct senior producers put concerns about race above their concerns about telling the truth. They were always worried about showing too many black criminals in jail even when the prison was loaded with black criminals. They were worried about showing a few black men looting stores after a hurricane, even though the looting was happening on a Caribbean island where just about everybody, including the cops who arrested them, was black. And now, with Erica Pratt, it was looking like they were going PC again.

For sure, this time part of it was that no one wanted to mess up such a terrific, feel-good story. But I also was sure that no network news executive wanted to run the least risk of being called a racist merely because his reporter told the truth about some of the more unsavory aspects of life in a gritty urban neighborhood where Beaver Cleaver wouldn't have lasted ten minutes.

A day or two later, I called Jim Axelrod, whom I had known for several years and whom I consider an excellent reporter, and put it to him directly: What did he know and when did he know it, and why wasn't the drug angle on the air? I also told him I would be writing about the subject. Jim told me he had no comment.

Next, I had a very brief E-mail exchange with John Yang of ABC News, letting him know I had a few questions about his coverage of the Erica Pratt story. He wrote back a few hours later: "Before committing to do this, I'd like to know what angle you're pursuing."

I e-mailed back: "Did you know about it [the drug connection]? If yes, why was it left out [of your story]?"

After that, I never heard from John Yang again.

Rehema Ellis, the NBC News correspondent, was far more open about the subject, agreeing to talk on the record as long as I made clear she was not speaking for NBC News, just for herself. She offered a spirited explanation of the choices she and her producers made in her story. She told me that she was aware of the possible drug connection, that "it was no secret." Despite that, she said, she and her NBC colleagues felt Erica's escape "was such an extraordinary story, that that was the story we needed to tell. I'm proud that we didn't try to diminish the significance of little Erica's achievement and her courage by talking about the kind of neighborhood she lives in. Because I'll tell you, Bernie, it didn't make a damn bit of difference about the level of courage that this little girl had."

I appreciate the fact that Rehema Ellis had the guts to stand up for herself. And since Erica Pratt is indeed an incredible kid who had done nothing wrong, I understand the impulse not to rain on her parade by dragging some ugly truths into the story. And yes, I know that for network reporters and producers these are not the easiest calls to make. Because I also understand how delicately they must proceed when the subject involves race in America.

It may sound insensitive, but I think the press has—or should have—a higher obligation than protecting the image of a courageous little girl, even if she is black. It's called telling the story, wherever it leads, fairly, honestly, and completely. Sure, it might offend a few good folks if the networks told the whole story. But newspeople offend a few good folks all the time and have never seemed to mind; offending people comes with the territory.

Not that I'm any better than anyone else in this area of racial hypersensitivity. Eleven years earlier, in 1991, I did a story in the very same Philadelphia neighborhood where Erica Pratt now lived, a story about unwed teenage mothers, fifteen-year-old girls with babies. But the powers that be at *48 Hours* wanted to make sure we did the *right kind of story*—one that was upbeat and optimistic despite the oppressive reality of the situation. So instead of dwelling on the destructive behavior of children having children, I was told to do a story about one of the very rare fathers, a teenager himself, who was working at a fast food restaurant and trying to help support the baby. The story was legitimate, as far as it went. But the real story, the one no one in charge wanted to do, was about a neighborhood so dysfunctional that just about every young girl living there was a mother—and virtually none of the boys who got them pregnant were important and meaningful parts of their lives anymore, or the lives of their babies. But I didn't do *that* story. *That* story might have made CBS News look insensitive and racist. And concerns like that trump concerns for solid journalism every day of the week.

"Race is the biggest issue in the world, and we dry-clean this stuff all the time so as not to appear insensitive," is what Jerry Nachman of MSNBC told me. Jerry has been in the business a long, long time, knew Thomas Jefferson personally, and is one of the straightest shooters around. Did race play a part in the way the networks handled the Erica Pratt story? I asked him. Jerry is too good a reporter ever to admit being 100 percent sure of anything in the absence of a smoking gun.

"I think the answer is a definite maybe."

But of course in these situations there is *never* a smoking gun. No network news president has ever written a memo to his staff saying, "Be careful when handling stories involving black people. We don't want to be called racists, after all. And if you happen to cover a story about a little black girl who escaped her kidnappers, make sure you leave out the part about the police suspecting a drug connection *involving her own family.* Not only would that really make us look like the bad guys, it could also cause us big problems involving picketing outside our studios, possibly organized by Jesse Jackson or Al Sharpton."

But anyone who's been in the news business for more than five minutes knows that memos like that aren't necessary. When race is involved, everyone in the newsroom knows how the game is played. I spoke to one former network journalist with more than thirty years in the business (who didn't want his name used), who put it this way:

"No one gets up in the morning saying 'I'm *not* going to be fair, accurate, and balanced in this story.' But there are institutional pressures regarding race that lead us [journalists] to sanitize."

The Pratt kidnapping, he said, took place in "a drug-infested culture where kids are used often times as pawns in the give-and-take." Why, he asked, wasn't that a legitimate part of the story, especially with the police themselves putting out the information? And as he thought back to the night of the Erica Pratt story—with the benefit of long experience covering the news—he told me, "I was suspicious." What he saw, he told me, didn't feel right.

It didn't feel right to Michael Smerconish either, a local Philadelphia guy who does a radio talk show and writes a column for the *Philadelphia News.*

"Are we ready for a candid conversation about the circumstances surrounding the Erica Pratt kidnapping?" he began his column, less than a week after Erica Pratt was safely back home.

"I seriously doubt it.

"I tried on the radio the other night and it only took about ten minutes until a caller used the *R* word to describe me and what I had to say. . . . The *R* word is usually all it takes for most—but not me—to end the discussion. It also explains why we often don't have the tough talks and why nothing ever changes with race relations.

"Erica has been put in harm's way by those around her," Smerconish continued. "Her relatives have not only put themselves at odds with the system, which is their adult decision, but they have placed this promising young girl in the crosshairs of drug violence, a situation over which she has no control.

"They are as much to blame as the men who kidnapped her," he writes. "There. I said it."

Granted, as a columnist, not a reporter, Smerconish gets a lot of leeway. But the point is, the column was based on facts—precisely the ones that network viewers never got to hear, because not only would those facts have screwed up the Hollywood ending, but they would have kept the story from defusing the all-too-legitimate accusations about the networks' preference for stories about little white kids over little black ones. Indeed, had they told it straight, the story might actually have made matters worse for network news executives—bringing down the wrath of black activists and black journalists claiming—*this time falsely*—that while a missing white girl automatically gets sympathetic coverage, a missing black girl brings on an investigation of her family!

But most of all, reporting all the nasty details surrounding the Erica Pratt kidnapping would have done something the media elites never do. It would have challenged their own liberal view of themselves as healers and uniters, as the most decent and caring among us.

We have come a long way in America. Once it was "We shall over-come." Today, far too often, in the hands of a racially frightened, po-litically correct, overwhelmingly white liberal media, it has become "We shall overlook."

Pass the Mashed Potatoes, Please

odfrey Cambridge, a black comedian who was pretty big in the sixties, used to tell a story about being invited, as the token black, to a fancy Manhattan dinner party. When the mashed potatoes got around to him, Cambridge said, he scooped out a big portion *with his hands* and passed the platter—then, in quiet amusement, listened as his sophisticated friends "calmly" whispered to each other, "Don't say anything; *don't say anything!*"

Maybe it really happened, or maybe the story was just part of his act. Either way, Godfrey Cambridge was on to something. Because like most good comics, Cambridge was also part social commentator, and in describing such a crazy scene—a bunch of polite liberals pretending they hadn't just noticed an intelligent black man in an expensive suit acting like the Wild Man of Borneo—he was making a serious point about a kind of condescension, one unique to white liberals, that black people experience all the time.

There are few forces on Earth more powerful than white liberal guilt. It has no known limits. In the hearts and minds of plain old regular liberals, it's bad enough. But in the hands of journalists, white liberal guilt becomes a very dangerous force indeed. Because it stifles all sorts of important *public* discussions on vital issues that might actually help us make some meaningful progress.

And this is especially true when it comes to the subject of race.

Let's face it: Some guilt probably is a good thing, given America's racial history. And let's also acknowledge right up front that for a long time liberals were the ones on the right side of civil rights; that while conservatives hid behind all sorts of sorry excuses to try to block civil rights laws, liberals were fighting the good fight for fairness and full equality under the law.

I was there, as a young reporter for CBS News, at the tail end of the civil rights movement, covering demonstrations all over the South. I saw white police on horseback clubbing unarmed black demonstrators in Atlanta in the early '70s. Years after they made history, I met and talked to and got to admire many of the brave people who had marched from Selma to Montgomery, a march that helped change not just Alabama but America, too. I interviewed John Lewis, one of the most decent men I know, who was savagely beaten on that march and who is now a United States congressman. I interviewed Daddy King, too, the father of Martin Luther King Jr., and I sat in the Ebenezer Baptist Church on Auburn Street in Atlanta, where both Daddy King and his son had preached, and listened to heroic men and women sing "We Shall Overcome"—and I can tell you that anyone who isn't moved by that will not be moved by anything.

But it is this very legacy—this glorious liberal crusade all those years ago, and the Right's monumental moral failure at that historic crossroads—that has created for liberals a terrible bind, because it has left many of them incapable, even today, of aligning themselves with conservatives on *anything* having to do with race.

This is the case even when, deep down, they have this uneasy feeling that their old liberal assumptions are tired and out of date and not really helping anybody anymore. Most of my liberal friends don't seem to have much doubt about other items on the liberal agenda. They don't second-guess themselves about the importance of "choice" or the danger of global warming or the evil of guns. They're rock-solid on those issues. But race is something else altogether.

If you catch them at *just* the right moment, some of my pals on the Left (the more open-minded ones, anyway) will admit to the sneaking suspicion that it may actually be liberals—the "good guys," who fancy themselves smart and cutting-edge and hip on all sorts of hot issues—who have fallen far behind the curve on matters of race. They have this uneasy feeling, I think, that liberalism's endless need to perpetuate the image of blacks-as-victims has come to seem more and more like white *condescension* rather than white decency. I think they know, by now anyway, that in supporting all sorts of racial preferences it's the "good guys," the liberals, who have been violating the very ideals of color-blindness and respect for the individual that were at the very heart of the civil rights movement.

And it must make them very uncomfortable to realize that it's the "bad guys" on the Right, the very same ones who are committed to personal accountability over group entitlements, who are pushing hard for school vouchers and other programs that stress "choice," and who may now be the ones more truly committed to equality and fair play, which is what the civil rights movement has really always been about.

So why, then, won't more liberals come clean? Why won't they be more honest about those doubts and be more open, publicly, to the arguments from the other side? What's the payoff in continuing to deny what to so many of us is so apparent?

Simple. By hanging on to the old party line for dear life—and conveniently to see anyone with contrary views as "racially insensitive" Neanderthals if not out-and-out racists—they get to continue to do what too many liberals enjoy doing best: bask in their own moral superiority.

"Since the sixties, whites have had to prove a negative—that they are *not* racist—in order to establish their human decency where race is concerned," is how the black conservative scholar Shelby Steele so aptly put it in an essay entitled "Liberal Bias and the Zone of Decency."

So how do you prove that you're *not* a bigot if you're white and liberal?

According to Steele, you desperately try always to show "good racial manners," which is part of a bigger concept he calls "deferential liberalism." This is how white liberals inoculate themselves against guilt and criticism. It's how they not only (ostensibly) show respect for black people, but even more important—*way more important!*—it's how they show they are good and decent *themselves*. As Steele observes, it's how they *redeem themselves* from "America's racial shame." "That peculiar, post-sixties deferential liberalism," Steele writes, "has been more interested in redeeming moral authority of whites than in actually helping blacks."

And this is where journalism comes in. On the face of it, the job of the press and television should be to question the most controversial assumptions about race: Is affirmative action good policy? Why are so many black children—far more today than in the old days when racism was all over the place—born out of wedlock? Is white racism mainly responsible for holding black Americans back, or is the real culprit something more complex and dicey, like the dissolution of the black family? At the very least, the media have a responsibility to be fair and give full coverage to responsible contrary views on all sorts of important racial issues. But journalists, even those who secretly harbor doubts about the liberal agenda on race, are almost always liberal themselves, and work for liberal bosses, and work in newsrooms populated by other liberal journalists, which turns those newsrooms into ideological echo chambers, and so they don't spend a lot of time even thinking about challenging the liberal status quo.

John McWhorter, an independent black scholar and author of

Losing the Race: Self-Sabotage in Black America, put it this way in a conversation for this book. "Nowadays, well-intentioned white people worry more than anything else about being considered racist. They consider it their *duty* to bend over as far backward as they can, at least in public, toward the black victim routine. To question that routine for many is to be morally irresponsible—or worse, to risk being tarred as a racist. And this is particularly true in the media, where what you say is so public."

Frankly, if the story of little Erica Pratt were an aberration, it wouldn't even be worth mentioning. The problem is, it isn't an aberration. It's the norm. This "deferential liberalism," this desperate fear of being accused of racism, affects how journalists cover stories every day, all sorts of really important stories with serious consequences in the real world.

Worse, for the most influential mainstream media, liberal guilt isn't just some vague feel-good concept floating around the newsroom; *it has actually become codified as official policy.* The American Society of Newspaper Editors (ASNE), an organization that represents every major paper in the country, is downright obsessed with diversity and affirmative action, concepts the editors apparently don't regard as even mildly controversial. Indeed, based on its public agenda, The American Society of Newspaper Editors might think about changing its name to the American Society of Racial Bean Counters. Take a look at the following, a key sampling of its Web site:

ASNE

"Diversity in Newspaper Newsrooms"
Published: October 09, 2001
Last Updated: April 30, 2002

Newsroom Employment Census
An annual survey of U.S. newspaper newsrooms. We count
the number of journalists, their gender, and race.

Recruiting
ASNE sponsors events and programs to help newspapers
recruit a diverse workforce.

The ASNE/APME/Freedom Forum Fellows Program
A program to induce journalists of color to work at smaller
newspapers.

Time-Out for Accuracy and Diversity
A joint program of ASNE and the Associated Press Managing
Editors to help newsrooms think about diversity.

The ASNE Reporter
A newspaper published during and about the ASNE
convention and put together by a diverse staff of young
people.

And that's only the start of their obsession with diversity. This is
how the American Society of Newspaper Editors' mission statement
concludes:

"By 2025, the minority population of the United States will grow
to an estimated 38 percent; to reach parity, newspapers will need
to increase their percentage of minorities in the newsroom by 229
percent."

There is only one way to do that, of course, and that is to take race
into account whenever a newspaper hires just about anybody. I could
be wrong, but it sounds like the newspaper editors are flirting, dan-
gerously, with the Q word—*quotas*—which, of course, are illegal. So
they talk instead about reaching "parity." But whatever they want to
call it, the question is the same: Is factoring race in, just about every
time they hire somebody, a problem? Not to America's newspaper editors, who practically brag on their Web site that "Minority employment grew 270 percent from 1978 to 1998, while white employment
during the same period increased 17 percent."

In his meticulously documented, award-winning book *Coloring the News, How Crusading for Diversity Has Corrupted American Journalism,* William McGowan describes a "Diversity Summit Meeting" sponsored in part by the very same American Society of Newspaper Editors. "This get-together had the unmistakable air of a tent revival, full of grim jeremiads, stern calls for repentance and holy roller zeal. Diversity has been fast becoming one of the most contentious issues in American society and in American journalism, responsible for polarizing, if not balkanizing more that one newsroom around the country. Yet only one side of the issue was present in the crowd. Speaker after speaker got up to declaim in favor of diversity and to warn of editorial sin and financial doom if this cause was not embraced."

Which might lead a reasonable observer to ask a highly pertinent question: How in the world can a journalist report fairly on affirmative action and racial preferences after the organization for which that journalist works has already taken sides? And not merely taken sides, but declared only one position good and fair and moral? How can he or she even pretend to represent honestly the views of those millions and millions of decent Americans who do *not* think affirmative action is an open-and-shut moral case; who believe, to the contrary and with equal passion, that affirmative action is nothing more than a nicer way of saying "reverse discrimination"?

By the way, in the spring of 2001 a poll came out, sponsored by some pretty heavy hitters: the *Washington Post,* Harvard, and the Kaiser Family Foundation—not exactly a right-wing troika. The poll asked this question about affirmative action and racial preferences: "In order to give minorities more opportunity, do you believe race or ethnicity should be a factor when deciding who is hired, promoted, or admitted to college, or that hiring, promotions, and college admissions should be based strictly on merit and qualifications other than race or ethnicity?"

Of the 1,709 adults surveyed, 5 percent said, "race or ethnicity should be a factor," 3 percent said, "don't know," and 92 percent said, "should be based strictly on merit and qualifications other than race/ethnicity."

But here's the real shocker: Of the 323 African-Americans surveyed, 12 percent said race or ethnicity should be a factor, 2 percent said they didn't know, and *86 percent said hiring, promotions, and college admissions should be based strictly on merit and qualifications other than race/ethnicity.*

Almost nine out of ten blacks rejected racial preferences in that poll, and I had to read about it in a piece by Stuart Taylor in a hard-to-find magazine called the *National Journal.* I watch and read a lot of news, and I don't remember any big splash about the poll. The fact is, I don't remember reading or hearing anything about it in the mainstream media, though I'm sure it popped up someplace, briefly. Why, do you suppose, that is? Could it be because the findings didn't fit the preconceived notions of all those mainstream journalists who have already taken sides on affirmative action?

And what is the endgame, the goal America's diversity-obsessed newspaper editors are trying to achieve?

"We believe that diverse newsrooms cover America's communities better."

Well, for what it's worth, so do I. It's better to have whites and blacks and Hispanics and Asians and men and women and gays and straights covering the news, instead of just straight white males. But it's better *only* if the newsroom really does become more diverse— and doesn't simply *look* more diverse. And since news executives are always preaching the importance of diversity, why then don't they also recruit some solid journalists who are Christian fundamentalists or orthodox Jews or observant Muslims or people who served in the military or members of *any* group, for that matter, that has a different and distinct point of view, the kind that's not generally represented in the newsroom?

But of course, as far as the news media elites are concerned, diversity is only skin-deep. In fact, if we assess diversity using the far more meaningful measure of "diverse points of view," American newsrooms over the years have become markedly *less* diverse. In the bad old days, when newsrooms were almost exclusively white and male (and, of course, that part *did* need correcting), they at least harbored white males of every political stripe. Yet precisely because the ideological baggage so many young "diverse" journalists have brought along with them is so heavy, "diversity" has pushed newsrooms further and further to the left, leaving them less and less tolerant of their dwindling band of fellow journalists (and anyone else) with other points of view.

And as diversity became more entrenched, newsroom caucuses—often highly organized, sometimes more informal, but almost always with a specific and very narrow agenda—began to exert their muscle. In almost every major newsroom today there is the black caucus and the gay caucus and the Hispanic caucus, all trying, to one degree or another, to make sure that their particular group comes out looking the way they want it to look in the news. Too many of the journalists in these lobbies think their job is to "liberate" their people from "oppression" and, most of all, to make sure they don't report anything that might give ammunition to the "enemy"—the enemy being anyone who doesn't buy into their own racial, ethnic, or sexual politics.

Of course, the minority interest groups in individual news organizations only reflect the increasing power of minority interest groups on the national level, which support the same general goals. While the NABJ—the National Association of Black Journalists, which was organized in 1975 and is comprised of about 3,300 blacks in the media—is in some respects a standard-issue professional association, it is also (like the National Association of Hispanic Journalists, the National Lesbian and Gay Journalists Association, and the Asian American Journalists Association) a political pressure group—a watchdog, *with an agenda.* The NABJ not only holds conventions where members can network with one another, but it is constantly on the lookout for coverage it deems offensive to black sensibilities. Occasionally, to be sure—as when the group helped draw attention to the mainstream media's failure to report on Alexis Patterson, the black girl missing in Milwaukee—this is useful; but just as often the PC version of "sensitivity" promoted by the NABJ for the coverage of stories involving race serves to hamper full and honest coverage, its very presence intimidating liberal reporters into ignoring angles that might get them labeled insensitive, or even racist. On affirmative action, for example, the NABJ is about as open-minded and impartial as PETA is on animal rights. Yet it is a measure of the group's growing clout that all sorts of big American media corporations—including the three major broadcast networks and the *New York Times* and *Washington Post*—have publicly aligned themselves with the NABJ, sponsoring its conventions and contributing millions of dollars to the organization.

I know this sounds crazy, but just imagine if a group of honest, decent journalists—not a skinhead in the bunch—formed an organization called "Fair-Minded Journalists Against Affirmative Action As It's Currently Practiced." Would the networks sponsor *their* convention and give *them* money?

Okay, we all know the answer. But let's give this a moment's thought. Why does the idea of such an organization sound so alien? Why does the very notion that ABC, NBC, CBS, and the *New York Times* would even think about giving such a group money and moral support strike us as downright laughable? Well, we know the answer to that one, too. Because inside the big-time, mainstream media bubble, being *against* affirmative action is tantamount to being wrong, close-minded, and, yes, probably racist.

It's not a surprise that trying to challenge such a mentality within such organizations is a difficult and often thankless task. It means taking on not only the status quo but, very likely, individuals and groups in the newsroom who are willing and ready to fight for their agendas—individuals and groups that management, practicing "good racial manners," is always eager not to offend.

I experienced some of this firsthand.

In December 1997, I did a story for the now defunct CBS News program *Public Eye* with Bryant Gumbel about a prominent University of Texas Law School professor named Lino Graglia who had started a mini–World War III on campus by provocatively asserting that the main reason minority students didn't do as well as white kids in school was *not* racism, but that in his view too many black and Hispanic families put a low priority on education. Or as he put it in a speech, "they have a culture that seems not to encourage achievement." As you might imagine, students on campus—and not just black and Hispanic students—compared him to the grand wizard of the Ku Klux Klan. We put them in the story along with the professor himself and some of his law school students and an official from the university, too. The piece, in my humble view, was as objective as can be.

After it aired, a top producer on the program—white and very liberal—came up to me, shaking his head in disbelief over what he considered the incredibly backward things the professor had to say. "Can you *believe* this guy?" he asked. The question was meant to be rhetorical—there was not a scintilla of doubt in his mind that I, like everyone else in the wide world of big-time journalism, shared his contempt for the professor.

Since my old CBS colleague wasn't expecting an answer, I gave him one.

"I could," I replied.

Silence.

He was studying my face for reassurance that I was kidding. "Actually," I added, knowing it was so politically incorrect it would throw him even further, "I agree with him." Okay, I understand that Professor Graglia may have been painting with too broad a brush, but (his bluntness aside) I did agree with his fundamental point: that in order to succeed, kids need encouragement at home; they need their parents to push them and stress the importance of education. I had covered too many stories for CBS News in what we used to call "the ghetto," where that encouragement just didn't exist, where kids were left to fend for themselves after school, where there wasn't a book in the house. Of course, this was true in a lot of white households, too. Unfortunately, it was disproportionately true with minorities.

As I recall, my friend the producer smiled what is colloquially known as a "shit-eating grin" and walked away. I had very little doubt what he would be saying about me as soon as he turned the corner. *"Can you believe this guy?"*

Before that, when I was still a reporter on the *CBS Evening News,* I lined up a story about juvenile house thieves who were driving people nuts in a very nice middle-class neighborhood in Orlando, Florida. Before heading off to Orlando, as a matter of routine, I filled in the senior producer on the details.

"Are the juvenile delinquents black or white?" she asked.

"I don't know," I told her, "I didn't bother to ask. Is that important?"

"They need to be white," she told me, not mincing words and going on to make it clear that was the only way the story would get on the *CBS Evening News.* In case you're wondering, yes, she was also white and also quite liberal.

I called back my contacts in Orlando and delicately asked the race question. When I told the senior producer that the criminal kids were white, she was relieved, and I was allowed to do the story.

Most Americans have no idea what goes on behind the scenes. But just from watching the network news, they can see the extent to which such a mentality dominates the coverage of race. Shelby Steele is only slightly overstating things when he compares it to the way the Soviets used to do things. "They built gulags for anyone who disagreed. The liberal media do the same thing. They put conservatives in it."

John McWhorter is another black iconoclast who has been stung by the blatant unfairness of the coverage he's received. Shut out by most media outlets, he's come to expect to have his views sneered at or misrepresented when he is covered. "The fact is, for many of these people, the black conservative must be shouted down even more loudly than the white conservative," he observes. "People like me and Shelby [Steele] make these people [white liberals] particularly angry, because they like to feel they're down with the black thing, and we kind of confuse them. The solution is to say, here's a black person who's betraying his own cause."

Indeed, he points out, after the appearance in the *Philadelphia Inquirer* of "one of the few profiles of me that was really actually fair, the reporter, a white woman, told me outright that she'd put herself at a certain risk in writing a piece that didn't trash me, by not corralling a bunch of people to talk about what an asshole I am."

Far more characteristic was his treatment at the hands of ABC's Carole Simpson, a black reporter and anchor, who brought a crew to his Berkeley home to do a piece on McWhorter. "She took up a whole morning and afternoon," McWhorter says, "and she was all smiles most of the time. But the minute the camera was on, she became beautifully histrionic. No smiles—she just went at me for about an hour. Finally the cameras are off and suddenly the smile is back and she tells me, 'It's frustrating; I was hoping to get you.' By which she meant, she was hoping to ask me a question where I'd come up short and not be able to answer, and then she'd probably end the segment there with me looking like a jackass. Mysteriously, the segment never aired. Frankly, I think that Carole Simpson, as a black reporter who has to tell the 'right' story, came out there to make me look ridiculous. And when I wouldn't cooperate, they dropped the story. Because she wasn't interested in giving coverage to me and my ideas; she was interested in discrediting me."

Ward Connerly, the black, conservative businessman from California who leads efforts around the country to do away with racial preferences wherever they pop up—in college admissions, in the job market, wherever!—says a lot of minority journalists do in fact put journalism first. But when they join a group like the National Association of Black Journalists, groupthink sets in, which is very unhealthy for the free and open exchange of ideas.

"I've met with many black journalists, of course, and there are some . . . guys who've been very candid with me and confessed they get annoyed at being asked to cover only black and racial issues, and that once they think about what I'm saying, it begins to resonate with them. But as an association, the herd mentality takes over, and they'll never say before an audience what you hear one-on-one."

Because Ward Connerly has been so rude as to stray from the liberal plantation—and make no mistake about it, in the eyes of other minorities and liberal whites, too, this is the most egregious sin any minority member can commit—he is seen by many journalists as a traitor to the cause, never mind that journalists aren't supposed to have causes.

"When I began speaking out against race preferences and asking for some honesty in how the issue was defined in the media," he said in an interview for this book, "the media regarded me as something of a freak. The feeling was, 'How dare this guy betray his people! How dare he speak out against prevailing wisdom!'"

So, there we have the situation in America's newsrooms: black journalists with a racial agenda on the one hand, eager-to-please white journalists practicing "good racial manners" on the other. It's a very powerful—and very destructive—combination.

How destructive?

While I was doing research for this chapter, I decided to highlight some of the more dramatic examples of diversity run amok in recent years, which Bill McGowan outlined in his exhaustively researched book. I gave up before I was halfway through, when my yellow Hi-Liter went dry. The litany of outrages astonished and depressed even me, and as I say, I've been witnessing this sort of thing firsthand for a very long time myself.

I won't bother trying to reproduce McGowan's work here except to say it drives home with particular force the lengths to which liberal journalists will often go, in their zealous and misguided paternalism, to avoid reporting the whole truth in stories about crimes perpetrated by blacks. A lot of important papers routinely fail to reveal the race of a rapist—*who is still at large*—for fear of offending blacks (in and out of the newsroom) and of feeding into racial stereotypes. Never mind that telling their readers everything they can about the suspect, including his race, might actually help find the monster preying on women. That's not important enough, apparently—not in the hands of "deferential" liberal newspeople.

And what about hate crimes—the ones, that is, where the culprits are *black* and the victims are *white?* Well, it seems that some major papers practice "good racial manners" here, too, because even in clear-cut cases of black-on-white hate crimes, they bend over backward to make the assault look like nothing more than a misunderstanding between the races.

In *Coloring The News*, McGowan tells about a string of black-on-white assaults in the Washington, D.C., subway system. In one, a white woman was harassed by a group of black teenagers who shouted, "Let's kill all the white people!" In another, a white woman was threatened with rape by black youths. "Yet the [Washington] *Post*," McGowan writes, "in an obvious bid to minimize the criminal nature of the misconduct, reduced the trouble to a 'clash of two cultures' in which the perceptions and racial stereotypes of the older white passengers were assigned equal weight to the misconduct of the teenagers, which was explained away as youthful rowdiness."

Then again, given today's climate—both in America at large and in American newsrooms—the pressures to play with the truth can be too intense for any liberal to resist. On August 22, 2002, for instance, the *Philadelphia Daily News* ran a front-page crime story—complete with police mug shots—of the suspects wanted by the Philadelphia police for murder. Unfortunately for the paper, not one of the men being sought was white. Of the fifteen suspects shown in the mug shots, all were black or Hispanic or Asian-American.

Before you could say, "Racist," the phones at the paper were ringing off the hook. The callers were angry, not because they claimed the story was false, but because of the impression it might leave. In short order a group calling itself the Coalition for Fair News Coverage was on the case, threatening a public protest over what it called "racially and ethnically insensitive patterns."

So, did the editors responsible for the story defend their work? Did they point out that their story was accurate in every respect? Did they assert that yes, the impression left by the piece may have been unfortunate, but the reality was even more unfortunate, especially since most of the alleged killers victimized their own community?

No. The editors *apologized.* "The front-page photos from last Thursday sent the message to some readers that only black men commit murder," the paper's managing editor, Ellen Foley, wrote in a classically mealy-mouthed mea culpa to readers. "In addition, the stories didn't address a key question: Why are there no white suspects on the loose? That also was a mistake."

In fact, one of Philadelphia's top cops (in a separate news story) did address that very question. Sergeant Bill Britt, second-in-command in the Philadelphia Police Department's homicide fugitive squad, explained it this way: "There are plenty of white people in jail for murder, but those guys are locked up. But people in the inner city, in high-crime areas, they don't want to get involved with the police." In other words, the primary reason so many minority murder suspects remain at large, at least according to the police, is that law-abiding minorities tend not to be as helpful as they might be to the authorities.

Is that really so? If distrust of cops in the black community is really so pervasive that it outweighs even concerns about personal safety and security, that in itself would make a terrific story. What is the police response to that kind of distrust? To what extent is it legitimately the result of law-abiding black citizens' deeply felt sense that cops hassle *anyone* who's black, and how much of it is a product of decades of divisive antiwhite and anticop rhetoric put forth by black activists?

Think it'll ever be written? Don't hold your breath.

Indeed, as McGowan points out, the newsroom double standard

is so powerful that many white liberal journalists ignore a black person spewing racial poison—even when he's a colleague. One black *Los Angeles Times* reporter wrote in his memoir that he was so annoyed at a white fellow reporter who had made a story suggestion he didn't like that he wanted to "grab her by the throat and shake her like a rag doll," and that after an unwelcome editing suggestion by another white colleague, he wanted "to rip his lungs out." At the *Washington Post*, a black reporter brags in his widely praised account of his transformation from the young thug he once was, that as a young man, he found "fucking up white boys made us feel real good inside," adding that even as a successful professional, "sometimes I wanna do that now . . . take one of those white boys where I work and bang his head against a wall or stomp part of him in the ground until all the stress leaves my body."

Even if we grant that this *may be* hyperbole, can anyone even begin to imagine a white reporter writing such words about a black colleague and living, professionally speaking, to tell about it?

When I read things like this, I am saddened not just by the black racism, but even more by the pathetic weakness of so many white liberal journalists, who are no different from those sorry white liberal "sophisticates" at that Manhattan dinner party who didn't want to notice Godfrey Cambridge, a black man, eating with his hands.

How is it liberal, I keep wondering, to tolerate violent racial fantasies just because the ones doing the fantasizing are black? How is it liberal to pretend that violence and bigotry aimed at white people isn't just as despicable as bigotry aimed at blacks? How is it liberal—how is it helpful at all to women—to leave the race out of stories about rapists who are still at large, simply because the suspects are black? How is it liberal, time after time, to be so damn paternalistic toward black people?

As Shelby Steele says, liberal whites "must always imagine blacks outside the framework of individual responsibility." Because, deep down—*and this is the darkest, dirtiest secret of them all*—it is white liberals who think blacks are inferior, incapable of making it in society without the white man's help.

"To me," Steele says, "the untold story is that almost everything in American race relations is about whites."

Racial profiling: Just about everyone knows what those words mean. We've heard a lot about racial profiling in the news.

But the fact is, we've heard so much about racial profiling for so long that most of us don't even realize there's another side of the story.

What we've mainly heard about in recent years are police who stop more black people for speeding down the turnpike than they stop white people. They see a black man driving down the highway and they pull him over. His crime? DWB: driving while black. There is only one explanation for all of this, of course, and that is that the police—not every single cop in the whole country, of course, but way too many—are racists!

Does it ever happen that way? Of course. Is it wrong? Certainly. But is there more to the story than what we routinely get from the big national media? Absolutely!

Heather Mac Donald, a Yale graduate (and a lapsed liberal), is a scholar at the conservative Manhattan Institute, and perhaps the most authoritative voice on racial profiling in the whole country. Too bad we almost never get to hear from her in the big national media. Mac Donald has written extensively about racial profiling (mainly in think tank journals and conservative publications) and has concluded that what you read in the papers and what you see on the news bears little relationship to reality.

In one piece in the *City Journal* titled "The Black Cops You Never Hear About," Mac Donald spoke with African-American police officers in eight U.S. cities—cops who are routinely maligned for simply doing their job but who never get their side out to the public. "Why doesn't the press ask these guys if the police are racist?" is the subheadline on her article.

"Most officers I spoke to reject the racial profiling myth," she writes. "If you're stopped, said these policemen, it's for a reason—you fit a description, or you've done something to raise an officer's suspicion, such as hitch up your waistband in a way that suggests a hidden gun. Statistics that tabulate officer-civilian interactions by race alone grossly distort the reality of policing, complain many black cops."

She quotes one of them, Mark Christian, a lieutenant on the San Antonio police force, as saying, "You have to look at time, place, and situation. You know what goes on at that corner. If someone's hanging out with a known offender, ethnicity is the last thing that comes into play."

But being a black cop, she says, "by no means insulates officers from the racial profiling charge when they arrest a lowlife they've spotted."

She relates a conversation with Carl McLaughlin, a black detective working in Brooklyn, New York, who says he's often told by people he arrests, "You're locking me up because I'm black." To which he responds, "I'm locking you up because you're wrong."

Mac Donald goes on, "The racial profiling myth rests on a willful blindness to reality, say many black cops, like Baltimore police Lieutenant Tony Barksdale. 'We're so afraid to tell the truth. Often the entire neighborhood is black, so of course you're going to be stopping blacks—based on their behavior.' And San Antonio's Lieutenant Christian adds: 'Most crime against blacks is committed by blacks, not Anglos or Hispanics.'"

Why don't we hear about this? Why don't we hear from these black cops on our evening newscasts? Is it because they, too, have sinned by straying from the liberal plantation and are saying "the wrong things"? And for that matter, why don't we hear from Heather Mac Donald in the *New York Times* or on the network evening newscasts that take their cues from the *Times*?

"Very few reporters even get it," Heather Mac Donald says. "They think I'm saying racial profiling is a good thing, which isn't what I'm saying at all. What I'm saying is, we're unfairly condemning the police, because overwhelmingly what they look at is actually not race but behavior. The fact is that blacks and Hispanics are engaged in criminal behavior a lot more than whites—that's why they're being stopped, not because of race. But in the reporting on this, that part of it is never there."

The more hysterical on the Left will call that racism, pure and simple, but even Jesse Jackson knows it's true. Remember that statement he made a while back that caused such a ruckus. "I hate to admit it," Jackson said, "but I have reached a stage in my life that if I am walking down a dark street late at night and I see that the person behind me is white, I subconsciously feel relieved."

Can you imagine if a prominent white man had said that?

After it hit the fan, the Reverend Jackson said he didn't quite mean it that way. But it was too late. He said what he and a lot of other Americans, black and white, know is true. By actually saying it out loud, was Jesse Jackson guilty of racial profiling or of nothing more than politically incorrect common sense?

Speaking of the Reverend Jackson, you may recall that in January 2001 he found himself in the middle of a hugely embarrassing and potentially devastating scandal when it came out that he had fathered a child out of wedlock with a colleague at his Chicago-based nonprofit organization, the Rainbow Coalition. Given the Reverend Jackson's role as America's preeminent civil rights leader, given his status as a role model, and given the sad reality that some 70 percent of black babies are born out of wedlock in this country, it was a story that raised numerous important and troubling questions. Upon its release, black community leaders across the country, especially clergymen, expressed the need to hold Jackson to account.

So which major national newspaper broke the story? The *New York Times*? The *Washington Post*? The *Chicago Tribune*, in the city where Jackson is based?

No, the *National Enquirer.*

Not that the story came as a giant shock to more mainstream journalists. According to Steve Coz, the *Enquirer* editorial director, both Chicago dailies—the *Sun-Times* as well as the *Tribune*—had the Jackson story at the same time his paper did, but didn't release it. No news executive in his right mind would ever confirm that, admitting that he or she chose to sit on such an important story in order not to embarrass a black civil rights leader (or more to the point, bring down on oneself an anticipated charge of racism), but on CNN's *Late Edition*, Clarence Page, an important liberal columnist with the *Chicago Tribune*, a man who had won the Pulitzer Prize, did acknowledge that several mainstream news organizations had known about the story concurrently with the *Enquirer.*

When Bernard Kalb, then a CNN regular on *Reliable Sources*, asked Page directly "Did you hear vibrations of this story in the media community that you work in?" Page was just as direct in his response.

"Yes," he replied.

Page explained that he heard about it from "a source here in Washington initially. Another colleague of mine heard it from a source in Boston. I mean, this story was around in the atmosphere."

And how, when it finally got around to acknowledging it, did the *New York Times* play the Jackson story? Showing impeccably good racial manners and impeccably bad news judgment, the newspaper of record put it on page 21 under a one-column headline.

Let's imagine again—this time that it was not Jesse Jackson, a black civil rights leader, but some conservative politician at the height of his power who had just admitted that he had an affair with a staffer that produced a "love child." What if that politician were, say, Newt Gingrich? Does anyone think the *New York Times* would have buried the story on page 21?

As Rich Lowry of the conservative *National Review* put it on *Reliable Sources,* "For people like myself who are skeptical of the media and think they're biased, this is like a heaven-sent example of a double standard . . . because if he had founded an organization that was called the Christian, rather than the Rainbow, Coalition, he would be practically stoned and drummed from public life."

When Patricia Shipp, the *National Enquirer* reporter who scooped all the big, important mainstream news organizations, was asked by Howard Kurtz, the host of *Reliable Sources,* "Why is this a story?" she said what any honest journalist should: "Reverend Jackson in his public and personal life is a minister who was at one time the spiritual adviser to the President of the United States [Bill Clinton]. So it's important that what he says is also who he is. And so, it made it legitimate for that reason alone."

Her answer was as obvious as it was elegant. Of course it was legitimate news. Any kid in a high school journalism class would recognize that. But, incredibly, to "respectable" journalists, this was a story that was too dangerous to touch.

God knows black people have suffered mightily throughout our history. But in the end, "liberal deference" on racial matters does no one any good—not anyone in the media or anywhere else. It does nothing to bring people of different races and ethnicities together. It polarizes, needlessly.

And for what? So journalists can show what good "racial manners" they have? So they can show how "caring" they are?

It seems never even to occur to those well-intentioned souls on the Left that they may be doing the cause of racial fairness and harmony far more harm than good. If we journalists keep defending diversity—even when it means racial preferences and de facto quotas—all we're doing is feeding the myth that blacks really are inferior, that they can't make it without white folks. And this has an effect, not just on white Americans but on black people, too.

"They keep us in this protest mode," Shelby Steele told me. "We then think that our whole future depends on keeping whites feeling guilty and keeping them on the hook. The more we protest, the more dependent we become, the weaker we become. We're weaker today than we were in the nineteen-fifties."

"If America [and the American media] would be honest," Steele continued, "and would break that dependency, black people would start to find themselves and find out who they really are and what they want to do and they would become competitive with other groups."

And even if journalists aren't worried about any of that, then they ought to be a little more concerned about their own credibility. Why should anyone take the liberal media seriously if they routinely distort the news, if they intentionally leave pertinent facts out of their stories, if they refuse even to cover certain stories at all; if over and over those they do cover are skewed?

"I went to Cincinnati right after last year's riots," Heather Mac Donald said in one of her rare national television appearances (not on ABC, NBC, or CBS, of course—on CNN), discussing the tense and confused racial situation in that city, "and the discourse about the riots had been immediately commandeered by a very radical race politician, Reverend Damon Lynch, who was given authority, both by the city leadership and by the media. Because the media goes always to the angriest black male voice, because they're looking for the story and they're committed to the notion of a perpetual white racism. So we had the *New York Times*; we had the *L.A. Times*; we had the networks; we had CNN going to Cincinnati listening to Lynch. I went to Cincinnati and I found a treasure trove of extraordinary black men who were committed to individual responsibility, to the police, to law and order, and to the notion that everybody has the responsibility to go to school and get educated. Nobody goes to them. . . . We heard Al Sharpton tonight. It was ludicrous. Of course, you felt you had to go to Sharpton. I wish you'd gone to Tom Jones in Cincinnati, who would have said, 'You know what? There's opportunity out there.' Sharpton tells our kids there's no opportunity out there. This is absurd."

Maybe, if the news media at last gave something approaching equal access to other voices—rather than just those of Jesse Jackson and Al Sharpton and the leaders of the NAACP—we could have a more meaningful discussion about race in America. Maybe then we wouldn't remain so inflexible and entrenched on racial matters. Who knows? Maybe if we all opened our minds to different ideas—even when they come from conservative blacks who have wandered off the liberal plantation—we could actually make some progress.

"When decent white people finally stop being scared of getting called racist," as Ward Connerly puts it, "when they say I'm not guilty of a damn thing, I treat everyone the same damn way and getting called names will no longer have any effect on me, then that will be true equality. I had a professor once who said to me, 'Mr. Connerly, the day I can get angry and say you're a son of a bitch without your attaching a racial connotation to it, that is the day we will have all truly overcome.'"

What Liberal Media?
Part 1

The quotations that follow are courtesy of the Media Research Center, which as far as a lot of liberal media elites are concerned is a right-wing outfit outside Washington, D.C., populated by a bunch of conservatives who spend way too much time monitoring way too many television sets and reading way too many newspapers and who get way too excited when they spot even the slightest hint of liberal bias in the news.

Are the elves at MRC conservative? Absolutely! Do they love poking holes in liberal media elites? Sure! But so what? What they put out are actual verbatim quotations that come from journalists themselves. On this, the Media Research Center is meticulous. So, with the understanding that many elite journalists hate them, I offer up this observation, with apologies to Harry Truman: The MRC folks don't give the media hell; they just tell the truth and the media think it's hell.

"Twenty-three percent of the young black men in America are behind bars, on probation, or on parole. As surely as an assembly

line, America turns thousands of innocent black children into cast-offs. It's one of the accomplishments of America's system of apartheid."
—*Harry Smith,* CBS This Morning *commentary, March 2, 1990*

"I found it affirming to see the real thing [South Africa], a place where everything was not only in black and white, but where racists had felt free enough to put it in writing. Americans are so much more subtle with their oppression, always leaving enough wiggle room to question the sanity of the victim, accuse him or her of paranoia."
—Washington Post *reporter Mary Ann French, in a Travel section article, July 10, 1994*

"I think there's a big difference when people told [Haitian President] Father Aristide to sort of moderate his views, they were concerned about people being dragged through the streets, killed. . . . I don't think that is what Newt Gingrich has in mind. I think he's looking at a more scientific, a more civil way of lynching people."
—*National Public Radio reporter Sunni Khalid, on C-SPAN's* Journalists Roundtable, *October 14, 1994*

"If being racist is no longer acceptable, then how come the schools are in such bad shape, and black kids don't get a good education still and the criminal justice system is filled with young black men?"
—*Mara Liasson, on* Fox News Sunday, *November 2, 1997*

"There is a scene [in *Roots*] where kidnapped African Kunta Kinte won't settle down in his chains. 'Want me to give him a stripe or two, boss?' the old slave, Fiddler, asks his Master Reynolds. 'Do as I say, Fiddler,' Reynolds answers. 'That's all I expect from any of my niggers.' 'Oh, I love you, Massa Reynolds,'

Fiddler tells him. And instantly, my mind draws political parallels. Ward Connerly, I think to myself. Armstrong Williams. Shelby Steele. Hyperbole, some might say. I say dead-on. 'Clarence Thomas,' I say to my Cousin Kim. And she just stares at me. She may be a little tender yet for racial metaphors. I see them everywhere."

—Washington Post *reporter Lonnae O'Neal Parker, referring to watching* Roots *with her twenty-year-old cousin, in an August 8, 1999, piece*

"If, during his tenure, President-elect Bush ends up making a couple of more appointments like Justice Thomas to the Supreme Court, I have heard many women and minorities say, 'God help us.'"

—*ABCNews.com on-line column by* World News Tonight Sunday *anchor Carole Simpson, December 17, 2001*

"Hi everyone! I hope someone out there can help me. I'm looking for a young black entrepreneur—under 40, tech savvy, who has started his own dot-com or company—to profile for CNN NewsNight. Since this will be part of a series about race in America, the ideal candidate is someone who struggled or encountered discrimination while looking for jobs or working in the tech sector (also could be someone who became frustrated by the predominantly white male culture) and subsequently decided to strike out on his/her own. Or something along those lines. Could be anywhere in the U.S. If anyone knows of such a person or knows someone who does, please get in touch. Many thanks!"

—*E-mail from a producer for CNN's* NewsNight *looking for a person to illustrate how blacks face discrimination in the high-tech world, April 2002*

Who Stole
Journalism?

L et's take a quiz. Which one of the following statements, all widely reported on radio, television, and in newspapers, do you think is false?

A. The number one cause of birth defects in this country is pregnant women getting beaten by their husbands and boyfriends.

B. One hundred fifty thousand American women die each year by starving themselves, many of them victims of a male-dominated society that forces women to be thin or be rejected.

C. Super Bowl Sunday is the worst day of the year for domestic violence against women.

D. Four out of every ten American women are severely depressed at least once a week.

If you said A, give yourself a gold star. You are correct. A is indeed false.

But don't feel bad if you said B. B is also false.

What about C? False! And D? You got it.

Right. I cheated. Not a true statement in the lot. Which raises another question: How did they get on the news in the first place?

Here's a clue: Even though journalists bristle at the accusation that they're in bed with any particular special interest group, anyone who's been on the inside knows that de facto alliances are formed all the time between journalists and the groups they cover. And of all those alliances, probably none is more powerful or more enduringly cozy than the one between journalists and feminists—feminists like the ones who helped spread every one of the phony stories listed above.

You want to know how bad it is? Most journalists I've spoken to over the years are in such a fog that they don't even think of the National Organization for Women as a liberal special interest group. I know it's hard to believe, but they actually think NOW is a moderate, mainstream organization that represents American women. Pretty simple, huh? The fact is that feminists on the Left have no greater friend, no more sympathetic ally, than those supposedly tough-minded and skeptical media elites who are either feminists themselves or are married to them. I know a few top male producers at CBS who would rather walk barefoot on cut glass while drinking Drano than have to face the Ms. back at home after giving the green light to a story on the excesses of feminism.

This is why stories putting women in the familiar (and entirely too comfortable) role of victim—often of big, bad, powerful men—continue to get such enormous play. The watchdogs in the media happily go along with the special interest groups that perpetuate these tales, because they fit the preconceived notions about women held by feminists inside the newsroom.

The fraudulent stories I cited in my little quiz all ran a long time ago and, like a lot of urban and suburban myths, have since been exposed for the shams they are. So, it would be nice if this were just a nostalgic trip down memory lane to the bad old days. But the fact is, things haven't changed all that much in the years since those phony stories were first put out. Feminists are still at it today, putting out bad information—and their pals in the press continue to report it as honest-to-goodness credible news.

I bring up those concocted stories now because they are what opened my own eyes to how tight this relationship between the media and the liberal feminist establishment truly is. My awakening came back in 1994, while I was reporting a piece for the CBS News program *Eye to Eye,* with Connie Chung. The peg for the story was that feminism—at least the version of feminism we came to know through the mainstream media—was under attack, but not from some angry, dopey guy who was against "women's lib"; this time the bombs were being lobbed by a highly credible woman, who was a feminist herself, just not the kind we normally see and hear on the network news.

Christina Hoff Sommers was a feminist who wouldn't toe the party line, the kind of woman who said things that drove the feminist establishment nuts. In fact, in a book she had just written, called *Who Stole Feminism: How Women Have Betrayed Women,* she had debunked some of feminism's most cherished myths.

The title of her book alone was enough to send her to the gulag.

Christina Hoff Sommers presented a problem for traditional liberal feminists because there was no way they could dismiss her as a right-wing screwball. She didn't have a conservative political agenda. In fact, Christina Hoff Sommers was a well-regarded philosophy professor at Clark University in Worcester, Massachusetts, a classic liberal who was just as concerned about equality and women's rights as any of the other feminists who were regulars in the mainstream media, like Gloria Steinem or (at the time) NOW president Patricia Ireland.

But because, like those "uppity" blacks who strayed from the liberal plantation, Sommers was saying the "wrong" things, she was considered a troublemaker and a turncoat as far as the liberal feminist establishment was concerned.

"You see this?" Connie Chung began her introduction of the piece, looking into the camera as she read off the TelePrompTer in the *Eye to Eye* studio at the CBS News Broadcast Center in Manhattan. "It may look like a book, but it's more like a time bomb. And when it exploded into print, it ignited a storm among women. The author . . . has been called the biggest traitor since Benedict Arnold."

Connie put down *Who Stole Feminism,* and the studio camera turned to me, for my few seconds before the videotaped story began. Looking into the camera, I said, "Let me ask you a question: Do you believe everything you hear on the news?" After a brief pause, I continued: "I'm afraid you're right."

Then, while the viewers saw pictures of women going to work and headlines about women's issues, I narrated: "If you live in America, you can't escape it: all the news about how bad things are for women. It's in the newspapers all the time, and it's on TV. Listen to this shocking statement from Patricia Ireland, [then] the president of the National Organization for Women."

Then we heard Ms. Ireland repeating the familiar line, "In fact, battery to pregnant women is the number one cause of birth defects in this country."

In fact, as the piece was about to make perfectly clear, she was dead wrong.

Next we got to the story about wife- and girlfriend-beating on Super Bowl Sunday, complete with a sound bite from (then) Los Angeles District Attorney Gil Garcetti, who told a news conference, "All I know is, the statistics are there. On Super Bowl Sunday there is a spike. Domestic violence goes up tremendously. Is it because of the drinking and the aggressiveness? I don't know. I don't care. All I know is, it's a fact and we want to stop it."

During my long career at CBS News, I interviewed hundreds of politicians, and there weren't many profiles in courage among them. But Gil Garcetti was a special case. He struck me as one of the shallowest, most pandering pols I had ever met. A staunch feminist, he would say lots of dopey things to impress his liberal southern California friends. But when in January of 1993, a coalition of feminist groups held a news conference in Pasadena, California, the site of that year's Super Bowl game, and Garcetti said that on Super Bowl Sunday, "Domestic violence goes up tremendously . . . All I know is, it's a fact . . . ," the only thing being abused was the truth. Because, despite what he and the other feminists were saying, the Super Bowl was not the Abuse Bowl. There simply was no evidence to back up the allegation.

And here's the big surprise (as if you didn't see it coming): despite the fact that it was not true, the story got play on television and in newspapers all over the country. Thankfully, one reporter was trying to separate fact from fiction. Ken Ringle of the *Washington Post*, "a lone island of professional integrity," as Christina Hoff Sommers described him, had been looking into the story, trying to find out if the Abuse Bowl angle was based on anything solid—or if it was based on anything at all, for that matter. On January 31, the *Post* ran Ringle's exposé, which meticulously unraveled the myth on page one, concluding that the claim—that Super Bowl Sunday was Bloody Sunday for too many women in America—simply was not true. It turns out that feminists anxious to spread the Abuse Bowl story got their "facts" all mixed up—intentionally or otherwise.

As the central character in that *Eye to Eye* report, Christina Hoff Sommers put some feminist noses seriously out of joint that night. What she had done, as she told me, "is blown the whistle on the phony research, the male-bashing," along the way making important points that most Americans had never heard before. Because even though she is intelligent, articulate, and comes off very well on television, hers was not a voice that had gotten much airtime on the networks. Her observations didn't fit those preconceived notions journalists are always so eager to tell you they don't have.

"Right now," she told me, "we are in the grip of a kind of paranoia about masculinity. Many women on the more extreme wing of the feminist movement are getting their way. They're convincing a large number of people that maleness and masculinity are synonymous with violence, cruelty, and savagery. Well, this is a form of gender bigotry. There are some men that are batterers; there are some men who starve women to death, I suppose. But to make that into the norm and to act as though that's the typical American male, this kind of monstrous predator, seems to me to be very unfortunate. But what's amazing is that no one's questioning it."

And that was the key point: No one was even *questioning* it. Reporters who wouldn't accept a single word the NRA or the Christian Coalition said at face value were acting like stenographers for the feminist establishment, copying down whatever its leaders had to say and then passing it along to the American people as gospel.

On the other hand, when I decided to introduce Ms. Sommers and her arguments to the CBS News audience, my bosses sure as hell started questioning *me!*

In my nearly three decades as a correspondent with CBS News, having done thousands of stories, none—not a single one!—got as much scrutiny from my producers as this one. I had done stories about Nixon's dirty tricks and about the Miami Cubans who had broken into McGovern's office at the Watergate; I had done stories about drug smugglers, about international weapons dealers, about killers, about politicians convicted of felonies—but compared to the attention being paid to this piece about phony feminist numbers, they may as well have been about little old ladies trying to get their pet cats out of a tree in the backyard.

I was grilled about every line in the story. Every word was put under the microscope. "How do we know *this* is true?" "How about *that?*" "Why should we believe Sommers?"

Meanwhile, Gloria Steinem, who had steadfastly refused to do an interview with me for the piece, was busy calling Connie Chung, complaining that Sommers was misleading us. We also heard from Patricia Ireland, who protested, as I recall, that, "all this quibbling about statistics is doing women an enormous disservice."

It was clear that the top brass at *Eye to Eye* would have felt a lot better if, instead of this, I had done another of those stories about loony Christian zealots protesting outside abortion clinics. *That* would have fit their preconceived notions. But because I wasn't doing that kind of story, you could almost smell the fear. At the very least, this story, which was putting a stake through the heart of certain beloved feminist assumptions, would be a source of embarrassment at cocktail parties for who knows how long. And what proper member of the media elite needs to feel embarrassed over wine and cheese?

For the record: I have no problem with tough questions getting asked before a story airs. No problem at all. We ought to ask them all the time. But we don't. When the homeless lobby tells us there are millions and millions of homeless on the streets of America who look just like you and me, we put that on, even though it's wrong. When the gay lobby tells us that millions and millions of American heterosexuals who live in the suburbs are about to get AIDS and die, we put that on, even though it's wrong. And when feminists tell us the American living room becomes a killing field on Super Bowl Sunday, we go right ahead and put that on, too.

But now that we were setting the record straight, some of my CBS News colleagues were terrified. It's fascinating, isn't it, that when it comes to certain kinds of stories, they're more comfortable when we get them *wrong* than when we get them *right*.

With Sommers's help, the piece took apart the misinformation, phony statistic by phony statistic. On the beating of pregnant women supposedly being the number one cause of birth defects in America, it turns out that *TIME* magazine got the media ball rolling, quoting a March of Dimes study as its source. The *Boston Globe* then ran the story. So did the *Chicago Tribune,* and so did a lot of other papers. There was just one tiny problem. As Sommers pointed out in our interview, the "study" on which all the stories were based, "didn't exist."

And it didn't even take much checking to find out it didn't exist. All Sommers had to do was call the March of Dimes. We at CBS News called the March of Dimes ourselves, and, sure enough, we were told there was no such study. It didn't exist. It never existed. But making a simple phone call apparently was too much for a lot of reporters. So they just went with the phony story.

To its credit, *TIME* magazine did run a correction. *One year later.*

And how about that incredible statistic about 150,000 women who were starving themselves and dying each year from anorexia?

The real number, according to Sommers, was fewer than a hundred. But even if her number was unrealistically low, because it was based on death certificates, and anorexia (at the survivors' families' request) isn't always listed as the official cause of death, how could journalists, like a bunch of lemmings, have put out that 150,000 number? Shouldn't it have set off all kinds of alarms? Nonjournalist Christina Hoff Sommers had merely done the math and calculated that 150,000 anorexia deaths a year comes out to . . . *3,000 a week!* If that were true, she concluded, given the fact that those "most prone to anorexia are upper middle-class, overachieving white girls . . . in places they congregate, like Wellesley College . . . you would need to have ambulances on hand the way you do at major sports events."

This phony story, it turns out, had been launched when a feminist scholar at Cornell wrote a book and said more than 150,000 women "suffer" from anorexia. "Suffer" somehow became "die," and the horrifying (but false!) number was gobbled up by the media and wound up all over the place, including in textbooks and in best-sellers by two of America's leading feminists—Gloria Steinem and Naomi Wolf.

And what about the survey, conducted by a group called the Commonwealth Fund and passed along to the American people through the mainstream media, that claimed 40 percent of American women are severely depressed at least once a week? This set off a whole round of the sort of women-as-victims stories the media can't resist, even though it had "feminist spin" written all over it. "They asked women a series of questions," Sommers explained, "and a high percentage, over 80 percent, said that they'd felt very good that week, but a small percentage had admitted to having crying spells, or some admitted to having periods where they felt blue. And they added it all up and decided almost half of women are basket cases."

I already knew the answer, but I asked Sommers anyway: If there's so much misleading information out there, why do so many journalists pass it on to the American people? "Probably every magazine or every news organization has someone that's a little carried away with the feminist cause," is how Sommers understated it, "so he or she sees it as an opportunity to do the right thing."

Christina Hoff Sommers never accused journalists of deliberately lying—just of being too eager to believe preposterous numbers that paint women as victims and men as oppressors.

As Connie had suggested in her intro to my piece, to feminists and their media allies Christina Hoff Sommers was a traitor, and the media has its ways of dealing with "traitors." Their favorite tactic, once used with great success by those fun-loving dictators in the old Soviet Union (until the whole house of cards collapsed all over them), is to marginalize the unrepentant culprits, rendering them invisible by not letting them on the air or in the newspaper. But there are other remedies, far nastier remedies that in the end betray not so much the "traitors" of the world, but the tenets of what once were regarded as the very essence of liberalism itself: fair play and open-mindedness.

In the case of Sommers, there were many offenders, but one stands apart from the rest: that bastion of modern liberal values the *New York Times*.

The *Times* might have ignored Sommers's book altogether. They might have made her invisible. But instead, the prestigious Sunday Book Review section critiqued *Who Stole Feminism* and, as you might expect, panned it. The reviewer was a feminist professor at the University of Pennsylvania named Nina Auerbach, who wrote that "Christina Hoff Sommers is a wallflower at feminist conferences. In revenge, she attends them obsessively." The book "is so overwrought and underargued that it is unlikely to amuse or persuade."

That was bad enough. And even though the *New York Times* almost never likes any book that challenges conventional liberal assumptions about feminism, assigning Sommers's book to one of her ideological foes was truly stacking the deck.

But it got worse. Much worse. In print, the *Times* had identified reviewer Auerbach as "the John Welsh Centennial Professor of History and Literature at the University of Pennsylvania." But she also happened to be something more: namely, as the Manhattan Institute's *City Journal,* among others, pointed out, Auerbach was "one of those feminist conference speakers Sommers skewered in the book, not by name, but clearly identifiable to anyone familiar with the event." And the *City Journal* added that Auerbach's vicious review was in fact "just more evidence—indeed, the strongest yet—for Sommers's argument about the cozy relationship between the elite media and the over-the-top feminists it refused to monitor responsibly."

When it came to light that the woman the *Times* picked to review Sommers's book had a personal ax to grind, a storm of protest followed—and not just from conservatives. Howard Kurtz, the media critic at the *Washington Post,* ran a column, the title of which said it all: "Review or Revenge?" And even though Auerbach and Rebecca Sinkler, the editor of the *Times Book Review,* both publicly brushed off the complaints, the *Times* felt compelled to run a few angry letters to the editor.

"The *New York Times* should not assign books to partisan reviewers who are too ideologically or emotionally involved with the subject matter to give an objective opinion," one of them said. "When I read Ms. Auerbach's hatchet job," another reader complained, "I was appalled by the personal attacks against Ms. Sommers. Instead of reasoned disagreement, Ms. Auerbach delivered a vindictive tantrum."

But then, incredibly, it got even cheesier. It came to light that Sinkler, the *Book Review* editor, was not exactly a disinterested party herself. She had once been a student of—you got it—Nina Auerbach!

Soon afterward, for whatever reason, Sinkler left the *Book Review.* "If the *Times* bias on feminist matters had long been obvious to anyone who cared to see," as the *City Journal* observed, "rarely had it been quite so glaringly overt."

But were any lessons learned? Did the obvious dangers of the cozy relationship between feminist activists and the elite media Sommers exposed way back in 1994 make even the slightest dent in the way issues of importance to feminists got covered?

Not a chance.

"The media still fail to make distinctions between the kind of feminism that is about equality versus the kind that is about being a victim and about male-bashing," as Sommers told me in late 2002. "To a lot of people in the establishment women's movement and in the media, women are from Venus and men are from Hell."

No matter how much reporters scoff at the notion that they have gotten way too close to the feminists they cover, no matter how much they think this is just one more example of right-wing paranoia, the facts tell a different story.

Among the most glaring examples in recent years of journalists ditching their skepticism to take at face value even the most outrageously implausible information put out by the women's movement was the coverage in the late 1990s on the procedure known by the pro-choice side as "late-term abortion" and by the pro-life side as "partial-birth abortion." For years, the feminist line was, as Kate Michelman of the National Abortion and Reproductive Rights League (NARAL) put it, that this was "a rarely performed abortion procedure used late in pregnancy to protect women's lives or health or in case of grave fetal abnormalities." President Clinton, appearing on the White House lawn with abortion rights activists and a number of women who had undergone the procedure, repeated those words almost verbatim. And the media (which had largely ignored abortion practitioner Martin Haskell's estimate to the American Medical Association that "probably 20 percent are for genetic reasons and the other 80 percent are purely elective") predictably fell into line and repeated the activists' claim that there were no more than a few hundred such abortions performed in the United States each year and that the procedure was overwhelmingly employed to save the mother's life, and that it was painless to the "fetus."

It took a local reporter named Ruth Padawer, who worked at the *Record* in northern New Jersey—not exactly a newspaper of national importance like the *New York Times* or *Washington Post*—to report that, in fact, based on her investigation, "In New Jersey alone at least 1,500 partial birth abortions are performed each year—three times the supposed national rate. Moreover, doctors say, only a 'minuscule amount' are for medical reasons."

Not long after Padawer broke that story, there was more evidence of how duplicitous militant feminists had been on the issue—and how eagerly gullible their friends in the media had been—when abortion rights advocate Ron Fitzsimmons, the executive director of the National Coalition of Abortion Providers in Alexandria, Virginia, admitted on *Nightline* that "I lied through my teeth" when he said the procedure was rarely used and most often to save the life of the mother.

And it's not just how the press mishandles late-term, or partial-birth, abortion stories. It's how the media covers—or doesn't cover—abortion in general. In 1990, David Shaw of the *Los Angeles Times* did a twelve-thousand word, four-part series on that very subject, and he pretty much concluded that the culture of the American newsroom is so overwhelmingly pro-choice that the media have a tough time covering the story fairly. So how did the media deal with Shaw's report? They didn't. As John Leo wrote in *U.S. News & World Report* in March 2002, "This apparently explosive report provoked no self-examination, no panel discussions. . . . Privately, lots of reporters and editors said it was true, and a few articles appeared. But in general, journalists reacted as if the Shaw report had never happened."

John Leo also tells us that he was on the advisory board of the *Columbia Journalism Review,* a magazine that reports on the media, and that he tried to get *CJR* to examine Shaw's findings. "No dice," Leo writes. "Everyone was determined to look the other way. I cannot think of a major newspaper series that got less attention. The reason, I think, was obvious: Feminists in the newsroom would not stand for this issue to be aired. So it wasn't."

So much for fair-minded, impartial journalists checking their biases at the door before walking into the newsroom.

Which brings us to Dan Rather.

On January 22, 2001, right after George W. Bush became president, Rather went on the air and said, "This was President Bush's first day at the office and he did something to quickly please the right flank of his party: He reinstituted an antiabortion policy that had been in place during his father's term and the Reagan presidency but was lifted during the Clinton years."

On January 22, 1993, when Bill Clinton had just taken office, Rather said this about the new president and abortion: "Today, with the stroke of a pen, President Clinton delivered on his campaign promise to cancel several antiabortion regulations of the Reagan-Bush years."

Let's see: When George Bush takes action on abortion he's doing something to "quickly please the right flank of his party." When Bill Clinton takes action on abortion he's not doing something to please the *left* flank of his party; rather, he's delivering "on his campaign promise." One is pandering while the other is simply keeping his word.

You see how bias works?

Yet every bit as fraudulent—and arguably at least as damaging—has been the campaign launched by mainstream feminists and disseminated by their amen chorus in the media to establish that the lives of even little boys and girls need to be reshaped according to feminist doctrine. The chief idea in this campaign—one repeated so often in the press that by now most people (and worse, most schools) simply accept it as fact—is that in our so-called male-dominated culture, girls regularly get the short end of the stick in school. Over and over during the past decade we've heard about an epidemic of sexual harassment in our junior high and high schools; we've heard about girls not getting a fair shot in athletics; above all, we've heard about smart and capable girls, desperate not to be seen by boys as threatening, and scorned by teachers who expect girls to be prim instead of assertive, "losing their voice" and their ambition when they hit adolescence.

Taking the lead in pushing these notions has been the American Association of University Women; despite its august-sounding title, it is one of the hardest-core feminist groups going. Among the AAUW's "studies," enthusiastically and uncritically reported by the national media, was a report entitled, "How Schools Shortchange Girls." It generated an avalanche of media reports on the "crisis" that eventually led to passage of the federal gender Equity Education Act, which categorized girls as an "underserved population" and mandated millions of dollars in research to remedy the situation. A second wave of media frenzy was set off by an AAUW poll of students in grades eight through eleven, *proving*, incredible as it sounds, that 85 percent of girls said they experienced sexual harassment in school, with 65 percent saying they had been sexually touched or grabbed. While any rational soul would seriously question such numbers—since they seem to reflect some parallel universe invisible to the naked eye—to the feminists and their media friends, this was another call to action. "The message," as syndicated columnist Ellen Goodman put it, "is that sexual harassment is not simply widespread, it's virtually a universal experience in the school."

Once again, common sense went out the window. As it turned out, the feminist notion that adolescent boys were running roughshod over girls was not merely way off, it was the *opposite* of reality. In fact, by almost every important statistical measure, it is not American girls who are being ill served by our schools and by society at large, but American boys. They get poorer grades across the board, are far less involved in extracurricular activities, drop out far more often, go on to college and graduate school in smaller and smaller numbers. In fact, this genuine crisis—the one that shows that boys really are at risk in an increasingly girl-centered culture—has been almost completely ignored by the media.

One particularly telling fact: though journalists frequently repeated the feminist-generated statistic that girls *attempt* suicide more than boys, what almost never gets reported is that boys *succeed* three times more often.

My friend Asa Baber, in fact, made that very point in his "Men" column in *Playboy* in March 2003. "I was watching a cable news network," he writes, [and] the crawl at the bottom of the screen printed out details of the tragedy of girls' lives. 'Girls are twice as likely to attempt suicide as boys are,' it said. I waited. The sentence was repeated several times later without any follow-up. And I fumed, because the fact is that while girls attempt suicide more often than boys, they actually kill themselves much less often than boys. What kind of news operation would edit statistics in that fashion? One that is eager to cull sympathy for girls and ignore the deadly facts about boys. . . ."

The cable news network, for the record, was CNN.

Baber was one of the only journalists in America who had been on the case for years, often writing about how boys suffer in our culture. And then, in 2000, Christina Hoff Sommers joined the battle when she came out with another groundbreaking book, *The War Against Boys,* in which she documented the many problems—including the deadly problem of suicide—that plague boys in America. And how did the media greet this effort to set the record straight? Was there a rampant alarm or a call for a national campaign to help boys, like the one instituted earlier on behalf of girls?

Don't be silly.

Even though this new information is, very slowly, at least starting to stimulate some discussion of the issue, after years and years of being fed the feminist line via television and the daily press, there's little question that most Americans—even now—believe it is girls who remain at far greater risk. As for Sommers herself, when she and her ideas get covered at all, she's usually described as a "conservative," which is the media's way of saying that anything she says should be viewed with extreme skepticism. Amazingly, when the *New York Times Book Review* critiqued *The War Against Boys,* history actually repeated itself: The *Times* gave it for review to another ideological foe, this time a colleague of the very woman Sommers cites in the book as being chiefly responsible for turning the educational establishment against boys. Once again readers of the *Times Book Review* section had to point out that this was the journalistic equivalent of a hit job. "Dare we hope that a book like Christina Hoff Sommers's *War Against Boys* might be given full and fair treatment?" as one demanded in a published letter. "Apparently not."

As Sommers herself observes, if the media elites never seem to get it, it's because they don't want to get it. "It's just part of the etiquette of journalism to take a very positive attitude towards the women's movement. They think if you criticize feminism, you're criticizing what they take to be respectable, honorable, and true."

Okay. Christina Sommers is one thing—a longtime renegade who took on the old-girls network. But what's even more revealing is how quickly the media will turn on longtime *friends*—when they get a little too independent in their thinking.

Exhibit A is Tammy Bruce, once a high-ranking official of one of the most liberal political lobbies in North America—the National Organization for Women. As president of the Los Angeles chapter of NOW in the 1990s, Bruce enjoyed huge clout with the media. "During my seven years as president of Los Angeles NOW," as she described in her book, *The New Thought Police: Inside the Left's Assault on Free Speech and Free Minds,* "I worked constantly with journalists to ensure that stories making the newspapers and the radio and television news shows were sympathetic to our issues."

Not that this was exactly heavy lifting, given the alliance between journalists and feminists. During the Clarence Thomas confirmation hearings, for instance, Bruce tells about one day riding in her car and listening to the news on the radio when a story came on saying that

"12 percent of women admitted to sexually harassing men in their office." This would never do, as far as the president of NOW L.A. was concerned, so she called the newsman and "told him that the *real* story was that 88 percent of women *did not* engage in sexual harassment at the office." In the very next news segment, she writes, "the reporter actually apologized and delivered the *real* story (that is, my version of it)."

She admits the on-air apology surprised even her, but the general willingness of the media to go along with the accepted feminist position was just par for the course. After all, to them, feminists like Tammy Bruce weren't so much pitching a liberal agenda as they were pitching a reasonable and sensible agenda, one that every feminist in the newsroom, female or male—which is to say, just about *everyone* in the newsroom—already agreed with.

It was always easy, she says, to get meetings with members of the editorial boards of important newspapers, which gave her the opportunity to influence not just their editorials but legislation as well. On top of that, she was always being asked by reporters to help them find "experts" to quote in their stories—experts who, of course, would tell NOW's side of the story. "With the media's complicity, I knew I could move any issue and make it work."

But then Tammy Bruce made a big mistake. She began saying the "wrong" things. She began challenging some of NOW's positions. And that's when she found out how tolerant the tolerant Left really is. And it's when she found out how fickle her old pals in the media could be. In a flash, Tammy Bruce became Tammy Who?

It started with O. J.

As far as Tammy Bruce was concerned, the O. J. Simpson story was as clear-cut as could be: A battered woman finally was killed by her batterer. The fact that O. J. was a famous black man meant nothing to her. But it mattered to blacks, both on the street and in the civil rights establishment. So when Bruce organized rallies and a march against Simpson—both during his trial and after the not-guilty verdict—and when she told the *Los Angeles Times* that the message about domestic violence was a "needed break from all that talk of racism," she became a target, not just of many blacks, but also of Patricia Ireland, the president of NOW.

In *The New Thought Police,* Bruce describes a phone conversation with a furious female official of the NAACP who said, "I don't know if you understand the damage you're doing to the black community with your vendetta against O. J. Simpson. . . . He's a role model for the black community. . . . He's important to the black male . . . you're condemning young black men with your crusade."

Soon after, NOW president Ireland held a news conference apologizing "to people of color" and calling Tammy Bruce's statements "racially insensitive."

"I guess I should be grateful," Tammy Bruce has said, "that they didn't call me an out-and-out racist, the favored accusation of the thought police."

The next issue Bruce got "wrong" involved President Bill Clinton.

As she saw it, the many accusations of sexual misconduct involving Bill Clinton—everything from exposing himself in a hotel room to fondling a woman (in the White House) who desperately needed a job, to rape (when he was attorney general of Arkansas)—were very serious matters, especially for feminists who supposedly were dedicated to protecting women's interests. Yet, the liberal feminist establishment was practically giving him a free pass.

Bruce was hardly alone on this one, of course; a lot of Americans thought NOW and other leading feminist organizations were selling out, for one and only one reason: Bill Clinton supported their agenda, especially their agenda on abortion. Bruce, for her part, believed such a double standard was reprehensible. "In a *New York Times* op-ed piece," she writes, "Gloria Steinem set the pathetic tone for the 'feminist' . . . elite's response to the revelation of Bill Clinton's sexual scandals. She characterized his encounter with Paula Jones, during which he exposed himself and asked for a blow job, as a 'clumsy sexual pass.' Gosh, I imagine Clarence Thomas and Bob Packwood would have loved to have the sexual-harassment allegations against them characterized as such, but no. They were Republicans. As part of the Democratic Party elite, Steinem was exhibiting her commitment to her boss, not to feminism."

It makes sense that Tammy Bruce, as a dissident feminist, might have shaky relations with the NOW establishment. But what surprised her was how quickly, after she broke with NOW, her once warm and cuddly relationship with the media also went sour. "I found out," as she puts it in *The New Thought Police,* "what it's like trying to get your message out when you're on the 'wrong' side of an issue."

Call me crazy, but wouldn't you think that someone who describes herself as a gun-owning, pro-choice, pro–death penalty, openly lesbian liberal might make good copy? Wouldn't you think that a former president of a the Los Angeles chapter of NOW, a woman who had been in a battle royal with the feminist elite, would still be "hot" as far as the media was concerned? I mean, don't they love a good fight? Well, no—not in Tammy Bruce's case, anyway. And so, when her book came out in 2001, not one major mainstream newspaper (except the *Denver Post*) reviewed it. The media elites shunned her the same way the feminist elites shunned her. That's how the alliance—the one that journalists claim doesn't exist—actually works.

And the Nobel Prize for Hillary-Gushing Goes To . . .

O n the other hand, there are certain individuals whom feminists can never get enough of, or write about too enthusiastically, or whose faults they are more eager to airbrush away.

Let's pick one. How about, oh . . . Hillary Clinton.

It's gotten to the point for a lot of us that anytime we get too close to certain kinds of Hillary coverage, we feel the need to take insulin, the stories being so sugary they actually induce the onset of diabetes.

Read on, but if you think you're getting light-headed, put this book down and take a short break before continuing.

Here's Carole Simpson, the ABC News anchor, in an on-line commentary about Hillary joining the Senate: Hillary Clinton has "finally come into her own, free at last to be smart, outspoken, independent, and provocative—all qualities she had been forced as First Lady to hide under a bushel. Still, she was voted one of America's most admired women. Just wait. You ain't seen nothin' yet."

And how about this from no-nonsense *60 Minutes* reporter Lesley

Stahl, as quoted in the *Philadelphia Inquirer* in December 1999: "I'm endlessly fascinated by her. She's so smart. Virtually every time I've seen her perform, she has knocked my socks off."

And there's this from former *TIME* reporter Nina Burleigh—probably best known for her elegant and charming comment that, "I would be happy to give him [President Clinton] a blow job just to thank him for keeping abortion legal"—on the wife of the guy she would be happy to blow: "It was hard in the summer of 1992 for a young woman to stay objective and not become enchanted by the promise of Hillary. I had spent my formative professional years undercover in the dark age of Reagan-Bush. Those were the days when women were not allowed to wear pants in the White House. Anita Hill had just been whomped. Antiabortion judges were packing the Supreme Court. And here was a woman who had kept her own name! . . . I'll be voting for her just to make sure Trent Lott doesn't get another foot soldier for his holy war."

And finally . . . in June 2003, there was *the* book. Barbara Walters got the exclusive on Hillary's *Living History,* the first interview with the author, which even some liberals acknowledged looked more like an hour-long infomercial than a production of a serious news organization. Let's put it this way: After watching that interview on ABC no one was going to confuse Ms. Walters with Bill O'Reilly or Chris Matthews or Tim Russert or Mike Wallace—or *any* real journalist for that matter. Watching the Walters interview, I kept waiting for her to ask a really inconvenient question—just one—that might make Hillary squirm. How did she manage to turn a thousand-dollar investment in cattle futures into a hundred-thousand-dollar profit—a matter more pertinent than ever in the era of Enron and Martha Stewart? What did she say to her husband before he issued the infamous pardons in the closing days of his administration? Did she have any regrets about the role she played in Travelgate? When did she first hear that an Arkansas woman, Juanita Broaddrick, was claiming she was once raped by a state attorney general named Bill Clinton—and how did she react?

But let's be fair: Polite and deferential as she was, Babs did indeed ask a few good questions. And she certainly was no softer on Hillary than the many other network correspondents who did stories about the book and came off sounding more like PR agents for Simon and Schuster than the tough, hard-nosed journalists they like to think they are.

Still, Nina Burleigh, Carole Simpson, and even my ex-colleague Lesley Stahl all take a backseat when it comes to painting Hillary's toenails. They are all runners-up in the "How May I Serve You, My Queen?" Sweepstakes. Because none of them—not even *Newsweek* contributing editor Eleanor "Rodham" Clift—can rival Margaret Carlson, who does commentary for *TIME* magazine (and is a regular on CNN's *Capital Gang*) for sheer devotion to Ms. Hillary. If they gave out Nobel Prizes for Hillary-gushing, Margaret Carlson would be on her way to Stockholm.

Margaret has written that Ms. Clinton "is the disciplined, duty-bound Methodist, carrying her favorite Scriptures around in her briefcase and holding herself and others to a high standard."

Margaret has also written that Hillary is "the icon of American womanhood; she is the medium through which the remaining anxieties over feminism are being played out. Perhaps in addition to the other items on her agenda, Hillary Clinton will define for women that magical spot where the important work of the world and love and children and an inner life all come together. Like Ginger Rogers, she will do everything her partner does, only backward and in high heels. . . ."

And on the new Clinton home in Washington, Margaret Carlson offers this: "Secluded and quietly elegant, it has a spectacular garden in the back, with a pool tucked in amid hundred-year-old trees. . . . Hillary wanted an instant Washington salon, as grand as her health care plan, with as many rooms as her ambition."

Never mind how many rooms her ambition has. Here's a thought you could fit in Hillary's closet: Margaret Carlson has actually said that she thinks her reporting is "down the middle" when it comes to Ms. Clinton.

By the way, just in case you're thinking that *TIME* magazine is this generous with all prominent political women, throw some cold water on your face and get back in touch with reality. On Marilyn Quayle, wife of the conservative then vice president (and slyly, on Nancy Reagan, both at the same time), Margaret's colleague, Priscilla Painton, wrote: Mrs. Quayle "would make Americans long for Nancy Reagan—taffetas, tyrannies and all." Painton called Mrs. Quayle a "watchdog of a wife with an ambition as long as her enemies list." Of course that description would *never* fit Hillary Clinton.

Another Margaret colleague at *TIME*, Michael Duffy, wrote that "Marilyn Quayle can seem hard, intolerant, and combative. . . . Ever since a *Washington Post* series on her husband last winter depicted her as a power-mad spouse who once kicked to shreds a framed picture of her husband playing golf, Mrs. Quayle has been trying to soften her Cruella De Vil nature."

Speaking of Cruella De Vil . . . during the Florida vote fiasco of 2000, *TIME* magazine ran a composite picture matching up the body of Cruella De Vil . . . with the head of Katherine Harris, the Republican Florida secretary of state who liberals thought was rigging the election for George W. Bush. About this time, our old friend Margaret Carlson chimed in with this little shot: "Harris, often compared to Cruella De Vil, snatching ballots rather than puppies, was briefly the most powerful woman on the planet."

Wait a minute! I thought feminists like Margaret adored powerful women. Isn't that supposedly why they're so gaga over Hillary? Or maybe it's just powerful *liberal* women they like, even as they swear to you that they're "down the middle" in their coverage.

All of this raises two crucial questions: So what? And, who cares? Well, if it were just a matter of feminist journalists gushing over a feminist heroine, no one would care; it would merely be good, sugary, coma-inducing entertainment. And who's against *that?* But of course, Carole Simpson and Lesley Stahl and Nina Burleigh and Margaret Carlson and countless others like them supposedly have a job to do. They're supposed to cover her.

In fact, we saw exactly how *unrelenting* reporters were with

Hillary Clinton when she ran for political office in what was supposed to be the capital of tough-minded, no-holds-barred political media—New York.

Hillary and her defenders are forever pointing out that over the years no First Lady in history ever endured such tough questioning on so many issues, and there is something to that. On the other hand, no First Lady in history ever did so many things that merited such tough questioning—and the truth is, when it comes to the kinds of scandals like those generated by the Clintons, reporters will always set aside their personal political preferences, at least for a while. Most reporters I know would crawl over their aunt Tilly if there were a potentially big enough headline on the other side . . . or a few minutes on the evening news.

But the media showed their true color (think blue, as in the blue of the electoral map) during Hillary's Senate campaign. Suddenly, in her presence, the baying pack of hounds turned into lapdogs. Hillary sailed through the campaign virtually without facing any tough questions at all.

"What's particularly striking," said Michael Kelly, the insightful editor and columnist who tragically died way too young covering the war in Iraq, "is that she got such a complete pass on the old scandal issues. Generally speaking, fairly or unfairly, when somebody's running in a big campaign, particularly a first campaign, the press will make a big to-do about reporting old scandals. And that just didn't happen. There was none of the knee-jerk press reaction of 'let's rehash the Tyson's Commodities thing' or the health care debacle or the disappearing files or her support of various left-related causes or groups which would have been unpopular with certain voting groups. Those issues were just not raised."

"The media was disgracefully quiescent in her campaign," ex–Clinton pollster Dick Morris told me. "They let her get away without doing any hardball interviews, except for one or two with Gabe Pressman [the dean of New York City television reporters]. They let her do softball segments on the network morning shows right in the middle of the election. When she was asked tough questions about Whitewater or FBI files or any of the other scandals, she waved them off saying, 'I'm not going to talk about that. It's already been investigated and talked to death.' She never had to elaborate."

Morris added that Hillary was allowed to get away with using "Secret Service to keep the media at bay during rallies, a technique she refined as First Lady," and that the press generally applied "the same First Lady rules they formulated for the likes of Mamie Eisenhower and Lady Bird Johnson to Hillary while she was running. . . . Since she became a senator, she continues her inaccessibility. She never goes on talk shows like Fox or MSNBC or CNN. When she did go on Fox, she insisted on an interview only with Alan Combs [the liberal] and not with Sean Hannity [the conservative]."

All of this makes you wonder: What can we expect when Hillary goes, as everyone knows she will, for the Big Prize?

I, for one, can't help thinking back on Hillary's appearance before the assembled media heavyweights at the 2001 convention of the American Society of Newspaper Editors. After Hillary's speech, a woman named Wanda Lloyd of the Freedom Forum, an organization set up by the Gannet newspaper chain as a "nonpartisan" group dealing with media issues, stood up and asked Hillary this hard-hitting, nonpartisan question: "You and I have something in common," she said, "in that we are both mothers of college-age daughters, and as professional women we are role models for our daughters and lots of young women around the country, and my question is, what are the chances that you will become the ultimate role model for Chelsea Clinton and Shelby Lloyd and all the young ladies who wonder when we'll have our first female president?"

Of course, when Hillary does take the leap and makes a run for the White House, reporters wouldn't dare toss her softballs like that, would they? Surely, at that point, they'll have to start treating Mrs. Clinton just the way they treat any other controversial, highly partisan politician—the way, say, they used to treat Newt Gingrich.

Won't they?

Speaking of Sports and a Lot More with Bob Costas

L egend has it that the late Howard Cosell once said to Irving Rudd, the sports publicist, "Irving, I'm my own worst enemy." To which Rudd replied, "Not as long as I'm alive, Howard."

Bob Costas reminds me a lot of Cosell. Like Cosell, Costas is smart. And like Cosell, he has courage. Here's the one thing that's different: To the best of my knowledge no one ever held a contest in a bar, the winner getting to throw bricks at a television screen when *Bob Costas's* face popped up.

Why talk to Costas, or any sports journalist, about bias in the news? Because we Americans take our sports very seriously. We are more passionate about sports than almost anything else in our culture. It's true that sports are often just fun and games, but sometimes—at some very important times—sports are a lot more than that.

"Sports have often been the stage on which social issues have played themselves out in a vivid way that brought the issue to a head to a large portion of America that would not have confronted it otherwise," is how Bob Costas put it in a conversation we had late one night in a Manhattan restaurant.

GOLDBERG: I think it's pretty obvious that political correctness has infected the general culture, as well as a lot of journalism. But I think a lot of people would be surprised by how much it's touched the world of sports journalism.

COSTAS: The first thing I would say is that sports journalism, in most areas of the broadcast media at least, barely exists. There are notable exceptions, of course, but most coverage, apart from the games themselves, is either hype, maudlin sentimentality, or the kind of hot-button stuff that sports radio at its worst represents. But, when real issues come up, one of the things at play is political correctness. It affects both how real issues are addressed and how they are not addressed. And it can be frustrating for someone like me, who over the years would certainly have identified with what would be called the liberal point of view on issues of race and gender.

GOLDBERG: Give me an example.

COSTAS: Well, one example is the issue of the Masters. The idea that there is moral equivalency between the exclusion of women at a golf club and the exclusion of blacks, as some have argued, is an affront to both morality and to intellect. Look, we know that legally a private club like Augusta has the right to establish its membership policies. Of course, that doesn't protect it from public disapproval or moral outrage, and their policies can be affected by those reactions. There is also a valid argument that Augusta is a quasi-public club because the Masters is such a high-profile event, and therefore the private club argument isn't so convincing. Then there is the notion that the issue here isn't golf—it's business. Since many powerful business leaders belong to clubs like Augusta, it can be argued that excluding women from their ranks is part of the glass ceiling for women in business. So there is a good case to be made, and on balance I find it persuasive. Augusta would be well advised to admit women, but it is not a cut-and-dried moral issue like exclusion based on race. To inflate its importance by putting it that way is an attempt to frighten people into line.

If you cast political correctness aside, and we talk about the reality of the world, it's entirely possible for a mother or father to believe that their daughter should have no less opportunity or ambition than their son, but to recognize that it is part of human nature that some men and some women will prefer male- or female-only situations some of the time, and this is perfectly acceptable. Have we become so politically correct that we won't allow for even that small occasional variance in people's behavior and personal choices? I can't imagine any circumstances in which it would be morally acceptable for any group to say they prefer that their ranks not include people based on race. However, there are women's clubs, women's schools, women's and men's organizations of various kinds. Why? Because there are *differences* between the genders. If there weren't, you would have no Title IX debate; you'd just have one basketball team at your university, one golf tour, one team or league in every sport, and let everybody come out and play, and fill the rosters with whoever is good enough. That's absurd, but so, too, is the idea that all claims made in the name of gender equity have moral standing.

As a matter of my personal sensibility and comfort, I would not belong to an all-male club, but as a matter of principle, I have always refused to even set foot on any golf course—even as a guest—without first being assured that black members and guests were welcome. They are both valid issues, but morally one is truly black-and-white. The other has shades of gray.

GOLDBERG: But you understand that there are people at the *New York Times,* for example, who would say you just don't get it. The *Times* has run about ninety-five stories and editorials about the controversy at the Masters.

COSTAS: I think it's pretty obvious that the *Times* made this issue a crusade. They are obsessed with this out of all proportion to its importance, and it was very embarrassing for a highly respected paper like the *Times* to quash two columns that took issue with the paper's editorial stance [that women should be admitted to the golf club]. The *Times* said one of those columns didn't meet the paper's standards of logic. It seems quite a coincidence that maybe the only column that writer has ever written that didn't meet their standards of logic also happens not to meet the paper's overall position on this issue.

GOLDBERG: The *New York Times* has criticized Tiger Woods for not taking a stand on women at Augusta. The *Times* even editorialized that he should boycott the Masters. Fair?

COSTAS: I think it is unfair. It's true that whatever Tiger Woods does has some kind of impact. If he doesn't play, the ratings fall. But, if he was exactly the same golfer, with all of the same achievements, and was also white, the *Times* wouldn't ask him to do it. It's true that black athletes sometimes have been at the forefront of social change. But I don't think the issues that Jackie Robinson fought for or that Arthur Ashe fought for can be equated with women at Augusta. The issue just doesn't rise to the same level of moral concern and clarity. So, why should Tiger put a portion of his career on the line for it?

Here's another thought. What if a superstar athlete, extremely accomplished, popular, thoughtful, and articulate, was a principled and outspoken conservative who used his or her position to advocate ideas not regarded as "progressive"? Would that attitude be widely hailed as gutsy and principled, or would that person be told to just shut up and play? I wonder.

GOLDBERG: I don't, but let's move on. How does political correctness play into the debate about Title IX?

COSTAS: Title IX has been a great thing. Its effects are overwhelmingly positive. I think I was the first person to dub the 1996 Olympics "The Title IX Olympics," because we saw a generation of greater opportunity and emphasis on women's sports come to fruition in Atlanta. There are many Olympic and college sports in which I would personally rather watch women than men compete.

I want more coverage of women's sports. I want girls and boys both to appreciate the Connecticut and Tennessee women's basketball teams, and a great athlete like Anika Sorenstam on the LPGA tour. My daughter is thirteen, and she has already participated in at least a half-dozen organized sports. A generation before, my sister participated in none. This is a true revolution, and I want this momentum to continue. But I also have nothing against commonsense reforms. In practice, Title IX has to some extent become a quota system, and there have been significant unintended consequences—the elimination of hundreds of men's sports programs around the country being one of them. Surely some tweaking could be done to address that inequity without undermining Title IX's basic intent. But Title IX zealots act as if any commonsense adjustment is tantamount to an assault on women's sports itself. This is what can sometimes happen when you're on the right side of an issue in the beginning. Because of the major battles you fought and rightly won, everything seems like a crusade, and you start to believe that your position is forever unassailable, no matter how circumstances change.

So, if you have the temerity to suggest that Title IX, great as it has been, is not beyond review and reform, you run the risk of being labeled a reactionary who is somehow hostile to the women's sports movement. This is political correctness as a debating weapon, but it does little to elevate the debate itself.

GOLDBERG: Gender is a pretty sensitive issue, but nothing in America is as sensitive as race. Do you agree with those who say the media seem a lot more comfortable doing a story about a black athlete who is a victim of racism than doing a story about a black athlete who engages in what many would consider punk behavior?

COSTAS: First of all, any time a black athlete is victimized, discriminated against, unfairly criticized, or denied credit, those have always been legitimate stories, and we absolutely have to remain vigilant about them. And, no matter how ridiculous the excesses of political correctness can sometimes be, this nation's history of racism and the racism that remains are real, and much more signif-icant. Still, in sports as elsewhere, political correctness often keeps us from discussing things forthrightly and getting at all aspects of the truth. To your point, those of us who came out of the generation when civil rights was the defining moral issue are just more com-fortable decrying white racism than we are decrying black misbe-havior. Since a large percentage of participants in American sports are black, a large percentage of the miscreants are black. Crass, of-fensive, and even criminal behavior is often soft-pedaled for fear that someone will appear racially insensitive. To me, this turns everything on its head. How can you on the one hand admire, as I do, the dignity and high purpose of Arthur Ashe, or Bill Russell, or Tommy Smith, or John Carlos; how can you admire the courage and sacrifice of Muhammad Ali; how can you admire all those things, and then on the other hand not be appalled by the vulgarity, self-absorption, and public buffoonery of people with little sense of what it means to be a member of a team, or for that matter, a re-sponsible adult?

Yet, behavior and attitudes that were once universally rejected are now excused by some because they say it is an expression of cul-ture.

GOLDBERG: There are those, including some in journalism, who think it's okay to criticize the showboating of a white player like [New York Giants] Jeremy Shockey, but if you do the same with a black ath-lete like [San Francisco 49ers] Terrell Owens, it's because you don't understand black people.

COSTAS: And truth be told, there are also some who see the white guy as passionate and the black guy as hot-dogging. But if you ask me I think both attitudes are screwy. Look, when [former New York Jets defensive end] Mark Gastineau did his "sack dance," I thought he was a jerk. When Jeremy Shockey acts as he does, I find that behavior of-fensive. It's exactly the same behavior I find crass and offensive when evidenced by Warren Sapp [of the Tampa Bay Buccaneers], or whomever. I like what the columnist Clarence Page wrote: "It does not compliment me as an African-American to see black athletes or officials held to a lower standard of behavior than their white counterparts."

GOLDBERG: Of course, that's how it ought to be. But when the subject gets around to race, it seems that some sports journalists hesitate. Do they think twice before jumping into those waters?

COSTAS: Yes.

GOLDBERG: Because . . .

COSTAS: Because you don't want to run the risk of a gratuitous accusation of racism, which can come to anyone no matter what his track record is. The fact is there are some people who take pleasure in hurling that accusation.

GOLDBERG: So even in the world of sports journalism . . .

COSTAS: . . . They worry and with good reason, because it is a very serious accusation, and when it has validity it carries great moral weight, as it should. But it's thrown around promiscuously. It's used as a tool to silence or divert debate on interesting and legitimate subjects, and knowingly or not, people who use it promiscuously reduce its meaning and its impact. It becomes trivialized when it's simply used as a scare tactic to diminish debate. How often have we heard people say, "That was a good point Chris Rock just made, and only Chris Rock could make it"?

GOLDBERG: Because he's black.

COSTAS: Right, not because the point would be any less legitimate if a white person made it—the point is legitimate—but only Chris Rock and a few others can make it.

Let's compare the cases of [former Atlanta Braves pitcher] John Rocker and Allen Iverson. John Rocker, from all I can see, is an idiot, or at least he was at that young stage in his life. But there couldn't be an easier target. So Rocker causes an uproar [with his comments about "queers with AIDS" and a teammate who is a "fat monkey" and about his distaste for Asian woman drivers, immigrants, and welfare mothers], and understandably so; he's become a pariah; he's booed everywhere. But let's face it, there couldn't be an easier target than

John Rocker, with his cartoonish views, and everybody this side of David Duke's immediate family rejects them out of hand. Just about everybody gets it. His comments and attitudes deserve rebuke but have no real standing. Whose behavior should really be of more concern—someone like John Rocker, or Allen Iverson, who has so much appeal to youngsters, black and white?

Now, I understand that appeal. Iverson is not only a good player, but he embodies many classic athletic virtues—David versus Goliath, toughness, daring, originality, verve—many things that people would embrace. But Allen Iverson also releases—or plans to release before the disapproval makes him reconsider—a rap album that talks about bitches and ho's and makes all kinds of homophobic remarks; this from a character who is regarded as cool and cutting-edge, and therefore has much more sway with young Americans—*black and white*—than a bozo like John Rocker ever will. And for all his talent, Iverson is a guy who a few seasons ago showed up late for practices or games forty-seven times. This I'm told by his African-American general manager, Billy King.

The 76ers management strikes me as being very tolerant and forward-looking. Yet, they were this close to trading Iverson because they were fed up with it. Do you think Bob Gibson, or Jim Brown, or Oscar Robertson would accept that kind of stuff from a teammate? Yet, some black pundits as well as some members of the establishment press position it this way: Anyone who disapproves of Allen Iverson, even if they stipulate his positive qualities, is either racist or insufficiently sensitive to a young black man who is just "keepin' it real." To which I say, "Bullshit." Why are punks and gangsta poseurs more authentically black than those who carry themselves with dignity and respect? How warped and maybe even racist is that idea?

GOLDBERG: So what is that really about?

COSTAS: It's about political correctness and it's about race as a weapon. And it's especially distressing to people—not just black people, but to white people like myself—who have been inspired by and

whose heroes were black cultural figures, not just in sports, but in
jazz, in literature. The truth of the matter is that many black pop culture figures today are such demeaning caricatures of black men that
if they were invented by white racists, everyone, black and white,
would call for their heads, and I would be first in line. You could
hardly create more damning images of young black men, and in many
cases their supplicant black women, than you can see and hear every
day in hip hop-videos and elsewhere. This from a culture, in the
grandest sense, that gives you John Coltrane, and Miles Davis, and
Duke Ellington, and Louis Armstrong, and Ella Fitzgerald, and Sarah
Vaughn, and scores of others. Look around. The whole culture is
dumbed down and degraded. Still, it saddens me to see so many black
sports figures contributing to the trash when historically, black athletes and entertainers have so often stood for something so much better.

I'm for cutting almost everyone slack. Short of homicide I'll cut
you slack. If a kid's in his twenties he has a lot of time to improve
whatever's wrong with his life, and I wish him well. And I'm certainly sympathetic to the idea that people, black or white, who come
from difficult and trying backgrounds have to work their way
through it. And sports is the one area in life where every performer
comes to prominence before he comes to maturity. You know, guys
don't become CEOs when they're twenty-two years old. But this
idea that a tough background is a "Get Out of Jail Free" card in the
court of public opinion for everything—what does that say of the
majority of African-American athletes, who came from the same or
similar backgrounds and who obey the law, respect the game, respect their teammates and opponents, show up on time, and don't
act like fools?

GOLDBERG: I once heard you make the point that those of us who
cared deeply about civil rights at the height of the movement in the
sixties didn't respect blackness per se; we respected fair play and justice that blacks were connected to.

COSTAS: That's right. Justice, truth, decency are higher values than race. The reason we're moved by the black experience in America more so than [by] the experience of any other group—not exclusively, but more so—is that their history is connected to the battle for truth and justice and decency. But blackness in and of itself is not a value that trumps all others. Justice trumps all others. Truth trumps all others. Decent behavior trumps all others. Decent, honest behavior should be respected—always. Bad behavior can be forgiven, but it can't be justified. It is illogical to admire the courage, intelligence, and dignity of significant black athletes past and present, as I do, and then not disapprove of punk behavior, which is everywhere in sports. And I mean everywhere. Example: last year's Harlem Little Leaguers. Now, I've been a supporter of the Harlem RBI program for years. They work to revitalize baseball in the inner cities. How do you not root for these kids? It's a great story. But then, at the Little League World Series [in 2002], a number of their players start showboating and getting into an in-your-face thing. You'd prefer not to see that anywhere, *but in Little League?* The Harlem coaches deserve credit for putting a stop to it, but not before a chorus of voices informed us that the kids were just reflecting attitudes and behaviors that are perfectly acceptable coming from their backgrounds. And anyone who had a problem with it was just expressing a cultural bias. Gimme a break! I want to love these kids. I want to root for them. But why should I excuse or overlook stuff for which, if my own kid did it and I was the coach, I'd take him out of the game on the spot?

GOLDBERG: We've been talking about a kind of sensitivity that doesn't lend itself to a vigorous debate on some of the most important issues of our time. . . .

COSTAS: Right.

GOLDBERG: So, how do you deal with that?

COSTAS: The problem on television is that almost everything is reduced to sound bites or quick segments and has to be drawn in primary colors. And it's risky, even if you feel some of these points are worthwhile. In the back of your mind you're thinking: Why run the risk of making them in a half-assed fashion or in some way that invites misinterpretation? I would never venture into these areas unless I felt I had all the time necessary to make my point as clearly as possible.

GOLDBERG: Otherwise . . .

COSTAS: Otherwise, it's just a fool's game.

What Liberal Media?
Part 2

"He went along with having an openly gay congressman address the convention last night, yet Bush opposes hate crimes legislation, gay marriage, and gay adoption."
—*ABC's Dean Reynolds, on* World News Tonight, *August 2, 2000*

"The [GOP] platform is, again, very strongly pro-life and rejects abortion rights, and the platform specifically comes out against gay unions, and against legal protections based on sexual preferences. So is this really an open, compassionate, tolerant party?"
—*Charles Gibson to Lynne Cheney, on ABC's* Good Morning America, *August 16, 2000*

"Since September 11, the word 'terrorist' has come to mean someone who is radical, Islamic, and foreign. But many believe we have as much to fear from a homegrown group of antiabortion crusaders."
—*Reporter Jami Floyd, on ABC's* 20/20 *November 28, 2001*

Ann Curry: "Today House Democrats are poised to pick Congresswoman Nancy Pelosi as Minority Leader. The California Democrat would be the first woman ever elected a party leader in Congress. It is now 7:07 A.M. You are now up to date from the news desk. Let's now turn back to Matt, Katie, and Al."

Katie Couric: "Is it okay to say, 'You go, girl!'?"
—*NBC's* Today *show, November 14, 2002*

Original Sin

ne day in the summer of 2002, I got a call from a producer I once met at CNN. I don't know this woman especially well, but when she contacted me she was upset—upset the way a young, idealistic, honest journalist gets upset when she knows the media is distorting the news. She had read *Bias,* she said, and called me because she thought I would understand. The problem, as she explained it, was with the way her own network was covering a very big story—a story that was being delicately called "the abusive priests scandal."

Over and over, as she told me, her colleagues insisted on calling the sexual molestations of teenage boys and young men "pedophilia," which, in the common understanding of the term, it did not seem to be. Pedophilia is a *mental disorder* involving the sexual molestation of very young children. This was overwhelmingly the molestation of boys in their early to midteens.

To some, this may seem like one of those distinctions without a difference. After all, if kids are being sexually molested by grownups, it's horrible. Who cares how old the kids are? And who cares if the media calls it *pedophilia* or anything else?

The answer is, it matters a lot. Because this story goes to one of the deep, dark secrets of the gay subculture: that a certain, small percentage of gay men are attracted to teenage boys—and to the extent that there is a stigma on that attraction within the gay community, it has never been a particularly severe one.

So when reporters call those who commit these awful acts pedophiles, they're pretty much saying, "These are sick people; they have a mental disorder and we need to understand that"—which is a lot different from "They're grown gay men who like to have sex with teenage boys."

"It's not pedophilia," she said, emphasizing that this wasn't some insignificant word game, that mental disorders were one thing but what was in fact going on in the church was quite another. "Sure, there were a couple of high-profile cases in the very beginning that were about pedophiles, a couple of men who raped eight-year-old boys. But that was completely different." What it was overwhelmingly about, she added, "was gay priests molesting fifteen- and sixteen-year-old boys. Those are the facts, and they are indisputable. It's just amazing how people around here are not getting it."

Or, more accurately, since she and I are both journalists concerned with accuracy, *choosing* not to get it.

Her point wasn't antigay in the least. She understood that the overwhelming majority of gays don't molest teenage boys. But since almost all of the priests involved in the scandal were in fact gay, and since almost all of their prey were adolescent boys, then "our stories," she said, "should ask the question: Why is that, and could that be causing the molestation of these kids? And if so, then what do we need to do about it? Do we need to get rid of gays in the priesthood? I don't know. Maybe so."

But these are not the kinds of questions top producers at CNN, who suffer from the same politically correct virus that has infected so many other journalists, wanted to raise. Instead of saying something that might appear antigay, they, and much of the media, focused not just on the entirely legitimate angle of the cover-ups by senior church officials but on the bogus issue of pedophilia, in the process diverting attention from what the CNN producer saw as significant questions about the secret culture of gays in the priesthood and whether that culture fosters an environment where this kind of molestation happens.

But she also knew this was not happening by accident. The last thing in the world the gay lobby wanted was a bunch of stories on national television and in newspapers around the country about "gay priests" sexually abusing adolescent boys. That's why it was peddling the "pedophilia" angle to reporters. And it's why so many reporters were more than willing to oblige—even if it meant getting the story wrong. But why did they so readily jettison the objectivity and skepticism that are supposed to be part of the job?

Because when you see your main role as being "decent" and "compassionate" rather than telling the whole truth, it's a very short leap from "reporter" to "patsy." But also because in a liberal media world, where taking the approved position often trumps getting it right, journalistic accountability loses all meaning.

Quite simply, when it comes to gay issues, once again ideological journalism routinely fails the public—tilting the news of highly complex issues mainly to one side almost as a matter of course. Once again, as with stories involving race or gender, narrow-interest pressure groups both inside and outside the newsroom are accorded special deference and respect. And, yes, once again it is liberal sympathizers, in this case straight ones, who help enforce the code, branding those who dissent from the approved liberal position as morally flawed.

Of course, in this case the most frequently used bludgeon is the word "homophobic." Though this is another word that means pretty much whatever the user wants it to mean, these days it gets tossed around in the press with reckless abandon. A quick check of the database LexisNexis reveals that in the months of September and October 2002 alone, it appeared 486 times in stories in the major news outlets. Like "racist" and "sexist," it is a word calculated not to encourage dialogue but to choke it off. When it comes to controversial gay-related issues, "homophobe" is the last refuge of the intellectually bankrupt liberal.

For what it's worth, I'm about as libertarian on gay rights as you can get. I don't care what people do in the privacy of their bedrooms, or in any other room of their house, for that matter. I'm completely open to arguments for gay marriage and even gay parenting. In fact, as I write this, I've just returned from reporting a piece for HBO's *Real Sports* about a former NFL football player who was coming out of the closet and who, with his partner, had adopted two Samoan kids. For most Americans, me included, gay adoption is a complex issue. But it was as clear as can be that the kids were in a good home and that the two gay men loved those kids very much. I know this isn't the only choice, but do I think they're better off with two daddies than with heterosexual parents who, for whatever reason, don't want them? Yes, I do. Do I think they're better off with two gay men than being shuttled from one foster home to another? Yes, again.

That, of course, probably won't spare me from being labeled a bigot. That's how lobbies reflexively characterize anyone who so much as sees the other side of the issue. Because, yes, I also understand the concerns of religious people who think gay marriage should never be made legal; that marriage is a union between a man and a woman—period! And I understand why some people will say that every effort should be made to place kids with heterosexual couples before putting them with two mommies or two daddies. I don't think someone is a homophobe just because he or she thinks that way—or, for that matter, honestly disagrees with some of the other items on the gay agenda.

More to the point, as it pertains to journalism, I think those people deserve a full, fair, and equal hearing. The fact is, the gay agenda demands a fundamental shift in the way we've thought about sex and morals for a very, very long time. It literally seeks to wipe away several thousand years of social and religious tradition. So it would be crazy for us *not* to have a free and open debate about its consequences. Yet what we most often see instead in the media is the sort of name-calling that wouldn't be tolerated on a playground. Even traditionalist religious leaders and respected conservative social commentators regularly get called bigots for doing nothing more than upholding the tenets of their faith.

The most notorious case like that was the gay activist attack on Dr. Laura Schlessinger. Groups like the Human Rights Campaign, the National Gay Lesbian Task Force, and especially the Gay and Lesbian Alliance Against Defamation (GLAAD) first put Dr. Laura in their crosshairs in the late 1990s for what they perceived as her anti-gay remarks. Dr. Laura had told her 18 million or so radio listeners that homosexuality represented "deviant sexual behavior." As an orthodox Jew she said what many religious people have said: that she was against gay marriage and against gay adoption. So are a lot of people, even those who haven't set foot inside a church or synagogue. Nonetheless, because of her high profile, that made Laura a target.

But the thing that in their eyes turned her into Public Enemy Number One, The Great Satan, was when Laura—who is not only a huge presence in the world of talk radio, but in the fall of 2000 was also about to begin a syndicated television program—said that homosexuality is "a biological error." That was about a 10 on the Richter scale as far as many gays were concerned. And that's when GLAAD and the others declared full-scale war, setting out not only to get Laura Schlessinger's upcoming TV show canceled before it even went on the air, but also to permanently brand her views as unacceptable in the marketplace of ideas. The sentiment against Schlessinger eventually became so venomous, it prompted death threats (from still unknown sources) and forced her to cancel charity events.

Now, let's be perfectly clear about one very important point: GLAAD and the other gay rights groups have every right to their positions on Dr. Laura—and anybody or anything else. If conservative groups can lobby the networks to take certain shows off the air that they find offensive, liberal groups like GLAAD can do the exact same thing (even though I think a little more open-mindedness *on both sides* would be a good idea). My beef is mainly with the press, which early on took sides in this controversy, portraying the gay activists as being with the angels, and the traditionalist, conservative Schlessinger as bigoted and intolerant.

For instance, look at her treatment in *Newsweek*. At the height of the controversy, the magazine ran a piece applauding the increased acceptance of gays by mainstream America. However, it noted solemnly, ". . . this tide of good news describes only half of the paradox. Last week California passed Proposition 22, becoming the 31st state to pass a new law banning same-sex marriages (Colorado will soon become the 32nd). These are key losses in what has become one of the most contentious fronts of the gay-rights movement. Against the protest of gay groups, Paramount TV announced an upcoming show of Dr. Laura Schlessinger, whose radio broadcasts reach 20 million listeners, and who has called homosexuality a 'biological error' and gay sex 'deviant.' Hate crimes like the murder of Matthew Shepard and Pfc. Barry Winchell, beaten to death in his bunk at Fort Campbell, Ky., last July, shatter the most deeply cherished notions of security."

How's that for objective, fair-minded reporting? Dr. Laura's views are part of the bad news, coming right before the horrific murders of two young gay men.

Indeed, the media—especially the entertainment media, which packs a lot of clout with TV executives and advertisers—turned out to be the activists' most valuable allies in this fight, which eventually led to sponsors like Proctor & Gamble, which was to be the show's first major advertiser, dropping out before it ever hit the airwaves, citing the controversy as the reason. Day after day Laura was portrayed by the press exactly as GLAAD wanted her to be: as a narrow-minded, hate-filled bigot—someone who, as gossip columnist and entertainment reporter Liz Smith put it, "is ridiculous" and would soon "dissolve like the Wicked Witch of the West."

Never mind that Dr. Laura's views were being grievously misrepresented and taken out of context by GLAAD itself. Never mind that she issued a statement saying, "I never intended to hurt anyone or contribute in any way to an atmosphere of hate or intolerance. Regrettably, some of the words I've used have hurt some people, and I am sorry for that." Never mind that she went on to say, "I regularly remind my listeners that we are all made in G-d's image and, therefore, we should treat one another with love and kindness."

Never mind, for that matter, that there were plenty of readers and viewers out there who not only supported Dr. Laura but would see the tactics of GLAAD (an organization described by the conservative *Weekly Standard* as "the jackboot division of the gay community") as way over the top and the real villain of the piece. It was, after all, Joan Garry, the group's executive director, who straightforwardly offered, "If she [Dr. Laura] can't be controlled, she must be stopped."

So much for that core liberal belief—the one about how I may not agree with what you say but will defend to the death your right to say it.

Can you imagine what the media's reaction would have been if some prominent conservative had said of GLAAD, *"If those homosexuals can't be controlled, they must be stopped"*? It would have generated—rightly!—a hundred indignant Trent Lott–like editorials demanding that the pathetic Neanderthal, homophobic bigot be drummed right out of the human race.

Never mind that, too. The press coverage could hardly have been more relentlessly one-sided.

One of those who piled on to attack Dr. Laura in 2000 was the influential editor in chief of *Variety,* Peter Bart, who characterized her in print as a right-wing ideologue who made Gary Bauer look like a "liberal weirdo." Interestingly enough, almost exactly a year later, in a profile of Bart in *Los Angeles* magazine, Bart himself was quoted as having made some pretty despicable antigay remarks of his own, complaining that "I'm not hiring any more fags because they get sick and die." As a result, Bart was suspended for three weeks and forced to undergo "diversity training." But even more interesting, GLAAD—highly selective in its targets—issued not one word of censure, and the episode received only fleeting coverage in the press.

Can you imagine if Dr. Laura had said *that?*

This was all too much even for a handful of people on the opposite side of the political spectrum from Laura. William Raspberry wrote in the *Washington Post*: "Is the talk-show host a bigot for calling homosexuality 'deviant'? Or is she simply a person whose view of the matter may be different—even ignorantly different—from that of GLAAD? . . . It worries me that what used to be mere difference of opinion is often recast as bigotry. Isn't that the same as punishing people for who they are and what they believe? Isn't that bigotry?"

And as longtime civil libertarian Harvey Silverglate put it: "If the respect for free speech erodes, theirs will be the first to go. The number of folks in this country who would rather shut up GLAAD far exceeds the number of folks who want to shut up Laura Schlessinger."

Like the other minority newsroom organizations, the National Lesbian and Gay Journalists Association has many fine journalists in its ranks, and there's not much question that groups concerned with fairness and civil rights have helped make our country a better place. It wasn't so long ago that homosexuals were subject to onerous laws, routinely harassed by cops, and, yes, derided in the newspapers.

Still, as far as I'm concerned, there should be no place for such groups in today's newsroom—not if the object is accuracy and fairness to *all* sides. The problem is, like other newsroom lobbies, by definition the NLGJA represents a constituency—and that constituency is not the public at large. The National Lesbian and Gay Journalists Association has an agenda, which is to make sure that gay-related stories are reported with what it regards as the appropriate slant and the necessary sensitivity. No matter how well intentioned, it cannot be objective enough. Can anyone imagine the howl if the NLGJA stood instead for the National Law-Abiding Gun-Loving Journalists Association, whose goal was to ensure that gun owners' perspectives were prominently featured in every story about firearms?

But this very obvious problem doesn't even register with the media elites. To the contrary, in recent years a Who's Who of media heavies have appeared at the NLGJA convention, their mere presence representing a show of support. Among them: Peter Jennings, Dan Rather, Tom Brokaw, Katie Couric, Linda Ellerbee, and CBS News President Andrew Heyward.

In addition to its other functions, which include the mentoring of young gay journalists and giving awards for "excellence in the coverage of issues concerning the lesbian, gay, bisexual and transgender communities," the NLGJA recently put out a stylebook to help journalists cover gay and lesbian issues. The book defines certain terms and explains how they should and should not be used. Sounds pretty innocent, right? Well, it's not that clear-cut. Words, after all, are the tools of journalism's craft; how they are used determines everything.

The NLGJA stylebook is already in widespread use in newsrooms around the country. Here are a few samples: "Avoid 'AIDS sufferer' and 'AIDS victim,'" it instructs, the thinking being that it is important to convey the message that those with AIDS are living normal, productive lives. "Use 'People with AIDS' or . . . 'AIDS patients.'"

The stylebook also contains this entry: "Fag, faggot: Originally a pejorative term for a gay male, it is now being reclaimed by some gay men. Caution: still extremely offensive when used as an epithet." Same with "queer": "Originally a pejorative term for gay, now being reclaimed by some gay men, lesbians, bisexuals and transgender people as a self-affirming umbrella term. Still extremely offensive when used as an epithet."

I'm not sure we need that in a journalism stylebook, but okay. Maybe *some* reporter *someplace* in America, who has been living alone in the desert for way too long, was thinking of writing a story and calling a gay man a "faggot" or a "queer" but after reading the stylebook decided against it. Who knows?

And then there's this: "Heterosexism: presumption that hetero-sexuality is universal and/or superior to homosexuality."

When I asked a rather sophisticated pal of mine, whom no one in his right mind would call a homophobe, what he thought of the "het-erosexism" entry, he said, "The problem is, it seems designed to pathologize a point of view that most ordinary and perfectly decent people hold: namely, that it is preferable to be straight rather than gay. If the term 'heterosexism' becomes as commonplace as 'racism' or 'sexism,' merely holding that belief will start to be taken as evidence of bigotry."

The stylebook also instructs reporters not to use the term "special rights" when writing about gay issues, defining "special rights" as a "politically charged term used by opponents of civil rights for gay people. Avoid. Gay civil rights, equal rights or gay rights are alternatives."

But if fairness is their first priority, what journalists—gay or straight—must acknowledge is that not everybody who opposes the term "special rights" is an "opponent of civil rights for gay people"—with all the negative implications that go along with the term. There are many who believe that adequate safeguards for gay people are already on the books, and who assert that specifically singling gays out for protection would mean they would indeed enjoy "special rights" beyond those of nongay citizens—that, for instance, an employer would no longer be able to fire a gay employee even for just and reasonable cause, for fear of being charged with antigay bigotry.

In fact, the issue of the potential abuse of "gay rights" legislation was on the front pages of New York's tabloids early in 2003 when Leona Helmsley, the reviled "Queen of Mean" of New York real estate, was sued by a gay man she had fired as the manager of one of her hotels. Citing New York's antidiscrimination statue, he claimed she had dumped him because he was gay, and wanted $40 million in damages. Helmsley claimed he was a bad employee, who had lied on his résumé and then held wild parties for his leather-fetish friends *at the hotel*—and now was looking for the big payoff.

The jury ended up siding with him—$11.175 million worth, an award later reduced to $554,000. Helmsley was planning to appeal the verdict. The gay former employee was also planning to appeal— the court's decision to reduce his monetary damages.

But the particulars of the case aside, to anyone following the proceedings it certainly seemed apparent that abuse in this area of the law was possible, maybe even inevitable. The charge of discrimination is a powerful weapon. And when it is made unjustly, how, realistically, is an employer or landlord supposed to fight it?

But even if fears of such abuse are hogwash, shouldn't they be met with argument rather than by decreeing that certain language be declared inadmissible? Think of some comparable definitions that might appear in a stylebook put out by the National Law-Abiding Gun-Loving Journalists Association: "Gun Lobby: term used as a pejorative by Second Amendment opponents to characterize those promoting civil rights protections for hunters and sportsmen. Avoid."

Name one news executive—running a mainstream newsroom *anywhere* in the United States of America—who would ever tolerate that.

Or how about the Million Moms organization, which put together the famous antigun Million Moms March? Try this definition in the hypothetical stylebook: "Million Moms: an organization purportedly made up of ordinary women concerned with gun violence against children, but actually led by experienced political operatives seeking to ban guns outright. The term 'million' is inaccurate; actual membership is indeterminate but certainly far lower. Refer to it as the 'so-called Million Moms' organization. Statements by its spokespeople should be viewed with skepticism."

You think the president of any of the network news divisions would let that kind of stylebook within a million miles of his newsroom?

And as you proceed in the (real) NLGJA stylebook past the definitions, you come to a handy little section called "Contact Information for Gay and Lesbian Organizations." This is a long list of groups journalists can call to get information regarding stories that involve gays and gay issues. There's the American Civil Liberties Union's National Lesbian and Gay Rights Project. There's ACT UP. There's the Gay and Lesbian Victory Fund, and there's the Institute for Gay and Lesbian Strategic Studies. There's the National Center for Lesbian Rights, the National Gay and Lesbian Task Force, and there's the Gay and Lesbian Alliance Against Defamation, GLAAD. There are dozens of other contacts, and there is no question that these groups can indeed provide reporters with valuable information for their stories. And, yes, I understand why a gay *activist group* would provide the names of friendly sources. But the gay journalists association is supposed to be, fundamentally, an association of . . . *journalists.* So where is the list of organizations and individuals to provide "other" points of view and opinions regarding gay- and lesbian-related issues? Where is the Family Research Council or the Alliance for Marriage? Where is the Orthodox Jewish Congregations of America, or Evangelicals for Social Action, or the Ethics and Religious Liberty Commission of the Southern Baptist Convention?

For that matter, where is Dr. Laura Schlessinger?

Somewhere along the line too many otherwise smart liberals became entirely too illiberal. And that goes for liberal journalists, too. On gay issues, for example, they now revert to name-calling at the drop of a hat in order to shore up their own close-mindedness and orthodoxy. They don't give credence to the "other side," because deep down, I suspect, they don't think there is another side. Not a legitimate one, anyway. Which leads us to our old pal, *New York Times* columnist Frank Rich, who attacks just about anyone who raises questions about any aspect of the gay agenda even more rabidly than he does other ideological foes. In Rich's work, the vicious accusation "homophobic," "homophobia," or "homophobe" turns up so often (*forty* times as of this writing!) it's almost laughable. He refers to the "homophobic Traditional Values Coalition" and "the homophobic right," to "a homophobic, Dobson-endorsed candidate" and "homophobic jurors," to "homophobic rhetoric" and "homophobic lyrics."

Though few can match Rich for sheer poisonous vitriol, his narrow and angry characterization of those who challenge the gay rights agenda as moral thugs is just about the norm in elite newsrooms. And it goes a long way to explaining why, in the years since the AIDS story was botched in the 1980s—when the media scared the hell out of everybody by falsely reporting, day in and day out, that heterosexual Americans would soon be dropping dead all over the place from AIDS, just as gay men and junkies were already dropping dead—coverage of every other controversial gay-related story has been just as slanted.

Look at how the topic of gay parenting and adoption has been covered. In the past few years, two of the most prominent women in television journalism, Barbara Walters and Diane Sawyer, have done specials on the subject, and both have been roughly as balanced as Iraqi television's coverage of Saddam Hussein's reelection.

Both the Walters and Sawyer stories packed enormous emotional wallop, as they were intended to. And both were virtual advertisements for the pro–gay-family side. I have the transcripts of both shows before me now. I also have a story on the same subject from the gay magazine *The Advocate,* and—surprise!—all make basically the same point in the same way. Featuring loving, happy families in which the parents happen to be gay, they remind us that the very existence of these loving happy families and thousands like them is threatened by ignorance and prejudice and homophobic legal and social service systems.

The Sawyer special, two hours' worth, was originally broadcast on ABC's *Primetime Thursday* on March 14, 2002, and opens with a chaotic scene of five energetic kids in a typical American home. Then Diane's voice comes in: "Their days are a controlled explosion of activity, all managed by Roger Croteau, and the man they call Dad, Steven Lofton. . . . Two washers and dryers, churning all the time. A frenzy of doing dishes, Dustbusting, skiing, snowboarding, water aerobics."

Steven Lofton is the hero of the piece, a gay man who's done wonders with his foster kids—kids the state of Florida will not allow him to adopt because of his sexual orientation. He comes across as a wonderfully sympathetic guy, as he probably is, and the home he and his partner have made for the kids looks stable and inviting. Also playing a major role in the broadcast is Rosie O'Donnell—in fact, this is where she first came out as a gay parent herself—and by the end you get the idea that anyone who isn't with these people on this hardly deserves to be called human.

Oh, sure, during the two hours, Sawyer gives those who question the wisdom of gay adoption the mandatory few moments of screen time. Passing mention is made of studies that show a greater likelihood of domestic violence between gay male partners, and of higher levels of drug use and promiscuity. But such concerns are quickly put to rest by the California psychologist described as the leading authority in the field, who reassures viewers that such excesses are far less likely to apply to gay *parents:* "They're the low end of HIV infection; they're on the low end of multiple sexual partners. They're on the low end of substance abuse. They're on the low end of violence."

"And," points out Sawyer, the psychologist's "report shows that the households with the *least* violence are not heterosexual households but lesbian couples."

The special ends with Steven Lofton putting his kids to bed. "It's a real safe feeling," he says, "when everyone's home, secure and safe, and we're ready to start it again."

As you might imagine, Diane Sawyer and her ABC News program drove conservatives nuts. As syndicated columnist Cal Thomas wrote, "There are credible scientific, legal and religious arguments against gay adoptions. ABC didn't present them because if they had, Rosie O'Donnell would not have appeared on *Primetime Thursday*. This was journalism at its worst but propaganda at its best . . . Will ABC follow these youngsters into maturity and report any negative consequences of their childhood experience? Not likely." "Even the

title of the show"—'Rosie's Story: For the Sake of the Children'—
"sounded like propaganda," he wrote.

Who can deny that Cal Thomas, no matter how conservative he
may be, has a legitimate point? It makes you wonder why in the world
journalists give conservatives that kind of ammunition. Why not do a
more balanced report? Isn't that what journalism is supposed to be
about?

And it's more of the same with Barbara Walters, who has actually
done a number of broadcasts on the subject of gay adoption. Maybe
the most heavy-handed was the *20/20* segment that first aired March
9, 2001, called "The Children Speak," in which a number of children
describe what it is like to have a homosexual couple for parents.

The segment shows us two sets of parents, one a lesbian couple
(since split up, we're informed) with a girl and a boy, and one pair of
gay men with two little girls. And how are the kids doing with these
parents? Are you kidding? Straight moms and dads pray for children
as loving and secure as these kids. The two little girls, especially, are
amazingly adorable, as pretty and precocious as those you'll find in
any commercial. As Barbara tells us, "They have a big circle of
friends, always seem busy, and they do well in school. They're even
learning Chinese, and already speak Spanish and French fluently."

Which is more than I can say for . . . *everyone I know!*

Five months later, on August 3, that segment was rebroadcast.
Partly this was because it was the summer and, as Barbara described
it, it was "our most provocative story of this season." But partly, too,
as Barbara herself indirectly tells us, there was a new political point
that needed to be made. It seems that a lot of attention had been paid
recently to a study that made gay activists and their liberal supporters
very unhappy and gave new ammunition to their traditionalist opponents. The study said that kids of gay parents were more likely to engage in gay sex themselves.

"Now, about that controversial new report we mentioned earlier
on children raised by same-sex parents," Walters says, back in the
studio as the segment ends, "California researchers reviewed many

studies and found that in fact, these children are different, in some ways, from children with straight parents. They say they are less likely to accept stereotypes about men and women. They are more tolerant of differences, and the finding that stirred the greatest controversy: Yes, they are more likely to experiment with a same-sex relationship. But—and this is important—they are not any more likely to be gay than children of heterosexuals."

What if, instead of liberal reporters and producers, *somehow, some way,* it were conservative journalists who were in charge? And what if their stories tilted just as heavily to how *wrong* gay adoption is and how difficult life is for children with gay parents? What if those hypothetically conservative journalists at ABC News devoted most of their program to attractive, likable people of faith, who explained that gay "unions" and gay adoptions violate a moral code that has been in place for thousands of years? What if they gave short shrift to the mandatory "other side"—the side of the gay parents who say their kids are happy and well adjusted? Would the gay lobby and gay journalists and straight liberal journalists and reasonable people in general regard *any of this* as fair play?

Why should it always take turning the tables this way to see how obvious and how blatant the bias is?

Or maybe Diane and Barbara should just tell it like it is and say, "We live in Manhattan. All of our friends are sophisticated and just about all of them are liberal, to one degree or another. And here in Manhattan—crossroads of the universe—we don't think this subject of gay adoptions is all that controversial. So we're going to put on a program with pretty much only one side. Sit back and enjoy the show."

At least it would be honest.

In important ways the church/molestation story that broke in 2002 harked back to the fight a couple of years earlier between the Boy Scouts and gay activists.

In January 2000, when the Supreme Court ruled that as a private organization the Scouts could exclude gay scoutmasters, almost across the board the media played it as a victory for narrow-minded bigots. For months James Dale, the gay man who had sued the Scouts, had been lionized as a civil rights hero, an Eagle Scout with the guts to stand up for the very principles of integrity and fair play that the Scouts themselves had walked away from. "For twelve years, they thought I was great," as he put it in an adoring *Dateline NBC* profile. "But when they found out one small piece of who I am, then I wasn't good enough anymore. And that's wrong."

I don't for a moment question that James Dale was a terrific scoutmaster and would have continued to be one; or that the overwhelming majority of other gay scoutmasters would also perform admirably. And I'm certainly open to the idea that the Boy Scouts should consider judging scoutmasters individually, instead of making blanket assumptions based on sexual orientation.

Still, the whole media discussion was basically dishonest from the start because it all but left out what the issue was really about: the concern that allowing gay scoutmasters to supervise overnights of teenage boys would at least increase the odds of boys being molested. The militant gay position, routinely echoed by the elite media, is that statistically gay men are no more likely to molest minors than are straight men, and in fact some studies say *even less so.* Then again, other studies (which you hear a lot less about in the media) say exactly the opposite—and so, frankly, does common sense. At the very least, many reasonable people can hardly be faulted for simply having doubts about sending their sons on an overnight with someone whose stated sexual preference is for males. Let's face it—if anyone even dared suggest a young, unmarried, straight man spend the night in the woods with a troop of Girl Scouts, the heads of feminists and their liberal supporters would start spinning like the kid's in *The Exorcist.*

In any case, in early 2002, the howls of protest abruptly stopped—just around the time the Catholic priest scandals broke. All at once the Boy Scouts didn't look so vicious and narrow-minded, after all. All at once their caution looked pretty smart. The world had discovered, as *National Review* editor Rich Lowry wrote, that "the Boy Scouts' policy is informed by a simple, commonsensical insight: Homosexual men shouldn't be put in proximity, in often isolated circumstances, to dozens of boys."

But as Lowry also rightly observed, this continued to be "the great unmentionable in the crush of media coverage about the Church's agony, partly because its logical consequence is too painful for liberals to contemplate. . . ."

What, in brief, liberals could not face was that the Catholic Church scandal was not about *heterosexual* deviant priests preying on teenage girls, nor was it about mentally ill heterosexual priests sexually abusing very young children—pedophilia—*it was about gay priests molesting adolescent boys.*

For gay activists, this was a potential public relations disaster of unprecedented proportions, and they went to work. GLAAD began issuing bulletins and alerts almost daily, seeking to steer the direction of media coverage and encourage journalists not to stray too far from the approved line that the scandal was indeed about pedophilia, and that it had come about because of the see-no-evil policies of that despised enemy of gay rights, the Catholic Church. That's what the scandal was about, they insisted—the Catholic Church and its heinous cover-up of pedophilia.

"The increasing number of allegations and cases of sexual abuse of children and minors by Catholic priests has engulfed the Church in controversy and is being discussed daily in newspapers, magazines and on talk radio programs and cable news outlets," began one such alert on April 19, 2002. "The Gay & Lesbian Alliance Against Defamation (GLAAD) and the Human Rights Campaign (HRC) have received numerous reports from throughout the country about commentators and spokespeople linking homosexuality to pedophilia and sexual abuse of minors. In some cases increasingly inflammatory rhetoric is being used to characterize this as a 'homosexual problem.'"

The alert goes on to describe measures supporters are urged to take to "debunk the myth that gay men and lesbians are more likely to engage in sexual abuse of children and minors." Most notably: "If you hear a news outlet, talk program or spokesperson try to make a connection between homosexuality and pedophilia or charge that gay men are inclined toward sexual abuse of minors . . . inform the reporter, editor or host of the distinction between healthy adult sexual orientations—gay, straight or bisexual—and any tendency to sexually abuse minors. Since it began reaching out to journalists on this issue earlier in the year, GLAAD has found that reporters who may not be conscious of this distinction are receptive to information that debunks this long-perpetuated myth."

As it turns out, GLAAD had no need to worry. Reporters overwhelmingly did what the gay activists wanted. When I ran a Nexis search to find out the number of stories in which the networks used the term *pedophile priests* as opposed to *gay* or *homosexual priests* in their coverage of the scandal, the results were stunning:

"Pedophile priests"	"Gay priests"	"Homosexual priests"
CBS: 57 references	3 references	5 references
NBC: 31	5	2
ABC: 30	4	3

Why is this so important? Why—as many liberals might ask—*shouldn't* reporters go out of their way to keep the vast majority of decent gay men from being unjustly stigmatized by the ghastly actions of a relative handful?

First of all, because they are journalists, not social workers or therapists, so their job is to tell the truth. Second, because the truth *matters*.

In fact, in this case it matters even more than it usually does. As columnist Betsy Hart smartly observed, "if one is going to root out a problem, one has to have a clear understanding of what and where the problem is." It is a harrowing thing to have to say, but in the coverage of this issue, political correctness took precedence even over the welfare of adolescent kids.

Which brings us back to the CNN producer, a talented, principled journalist still young and idealistic enough to be surprised by what she saw happening. "One day at a meeting," she was telling me, "I brought this up, how it [the gay angle] is part of the story we need to be reporting. And what I heard is, 'We don't want to go there; we'll be seen as bashing homosexuals,' and *that* is what's horrific." She paused. "I mean, girls aren't being raped; boys are. And you have to start with that and ask, what's going on here? That's our job in the media. Instead what you get is, 'We can't do that. This is a group we have to protect.' We're so politically correct, we're so scared to say anything negative about a group that supposedly needs our protection."

I wish I could have offered her more comforting words. But the truth is, she's right. As Walter Cronkite used to say, in today's media culture "that's the way it is."

And Now, the
Rest of the Story . . .

A student at the Appalachian School of Law in Grundy, Virginia, who has just been told he will be suspended for failing grades, storms through the campus, clutching a handgun.

As terrorized students run for their lives, they hear him say, "Come get me, come get me." But before anyone can get him, the student, a forty-two-year old immigrant from Nigeria, goes on a shooting spree, killing the dean, a professor, and a fellow student.

He also shoots and wounds three other students—one in the abdomen, one in the throat, and another in the chest.

Finally, as the *Washington Post* reports, "Three students pounced on the gunman and held him until help arrived." Later in the story, the *Post* says, "The students then tackled the gunman."

John Roberts at CBS News reported the story the very same way: "Three people were killed . . . before students tackled the suspect."

At NBC News, Kevin Tibbles said the students "overpowered the gunman and held him until police could arrive."

The bloody incident happened on January 16, 2002, and was picked up by news organizations all over the country, almost all of which covered the story the way the *Washington Post* and the networks did. Which means virtually all of them left out one tiny, little fact.

Two of the students who "pounced on" and "tackled" and "overpowered" the gunman, also had guns.

They had them in their cars, and when they heard the gunshots and learned what was happening, they got their guns and used them to help subdue the killer who had just shot up the campus.

One might think this was an important element that should have been reported in the story. An honest mistake? You decide. Soon after the law school rampage, criminologist and scholar John Lott ran a LexisNexis search on the story and came up with this: Only 4 of 208 news reports that he found mentioned that the rescuers had guns. James Eaves-Johnson did his own Nexis search for the *Daily Iowan* (at the University of Iowa) and found that just two of eighty-eight stories reported that guns were used to subdue the killer. A third search conducted by Eaves-Johnson, this time using a database called Westnews, which specializes in news about the law, turned up 112 stories on the subject—and again only two mentioned that the gunman was subdued by students using guns themselves.

None of this sounded like it made any sense. Yes, I'm a critic of how big news organizations slant the news, but even I couldn't believe these numbers. All of them struck me as so incredible that I finally decided to run my own Nexis search. I sampled one hundred news sources, which included the major TV outlets and most every big city daily in the country. And what I found stunned me. Sure enough, only a few papers in the whole country reported that the rescuers had guns. I counted a grand total of six out of a hundred. Six! (Giving credit where it's due, the papers were the *New York Times*, the *Richmond Times-Dispatch*, the *Lexington Herald-Leader*, the *Charlotte Observer*, the *Asheville Citizen-Times*, and the *Roanoke Times and World News*.)

Ah, but it gets worse. Many of those newspapers that failed to report the whole story then seized upon the horror at the Appalachian School of Law to editorialize once again against handguns.

No matter whose count you use, the fact could not be more clear: Only a tiny handful of reporters in the entire country were willing to report an essential part of the story: that it wasn't just the killer who used a gun on campus that day, but two of the rescuers, too.

In America, there are pro-gun people and antigun people. The pro-gun people love everything about guns. They love to touch guns and fondle guns and smell guns, and mostly they love to have guns close by. Guns give them peace of mind.

To tell you the truth, I'm not one of those people. I don't like to touch guns or smell them or feel them. I grew up in the Bronx. I played basketball and baseball. Those were my sports. Not hunting. In fact, the only animals I ever got close to were at the Bronx Zoo, and they don't let you hunt any of them. So, unlike kids who grew up with guns in rural America, I never got close to a gun early on—and it carried over to my adult life. But I'll tell you this: It would be just fine with me if everyone on my block now had a gun or two at home, just to discourage criminals from even thinking about preying on the neighborhood. I wouldn't even care if they sat out on their lawns brandishing their guns alongside homemade signs reading, "Attention bad guys: If you're thinking that someone's gonna get hurt around here, you're right—and it's gonna be you!"

But here's an important point: While I'm not exactly comfortable around guns myself, I am not *anti*gun.

The antigun people don't like anything about guns. Guns do not give them peace of mind. Just the opposite. And the vast majority of mainstream media people—certainly those who work in the biggest, most important newsrooms in the country—fall into this antigun category. To a lot of them, guns are destructive and evil. Period. In fact, they think there *are* no credible arguments on the other side, just the irrational rants of all those crazy "gun nuts."

A poll in the *Los Angeles Times* once showed that while 50 percent of Americans are for tougher gun controls, 78 percent of journalists favor stricter gun laws. Bob Herbert of the *New York Times* spoke for a bunch of those antigun journalists when he wrote that "Gun violence in America is as common as the sunrise. The truth is, we are addicted to gun violence. We celebrate it, romanticize it, eroticize it."

Okay, maybe for some losers, having a big gun at home is a substitute for having a small something else, but that doesn't give the media elite some kind of 007 license to kill certain inconvenient facts that don't mesh with their particular biases. After all those years on the inside, I am more than a little familiar with how the big-time media operate; I know how biased they can be when it comes to certain issues. Still, even I found the coverage of the shootout at the Appalachian School of Law absolutely astounding. I mean, only a handful of news stories pick up on such an important fact—that the students who stopped the killing spree used their own handguns to do it!

Not long ago I was talking to a pro-gun person, a very bright guy, who said he often asks people a simple question: "When was the last time you watched the national evening news and heard a story about someone using a gun to save a life?" "Most people," he went on, "can't think of a single case."

Actually, I told him, I did just such a story myself, not for the evening news, but for *48 Hours* at CBS. It was about a young woman who lived in rural North Carolina, whose father had just given her a gun for self-protection. Late one night, she went to a deserted post office to pick up her mail from her lock box and was ambushed by a man with a gun, who forced her into her car and demanded that she drive away with him. At this point, fearing she would not be alive when the sun came up, the young woman pulled out her own brand-new gun and stuck it in the gunman's face, which not only took him by surprise but also apparently scared the hell out of him, because he jumped out of the car and fled.

The producer I worked with—whose views on a whole range of subjects I'd put in the Barbra Streisand category—was practically in a state of depression. "We should never have done the story," he told me some time later in full mea culpa mode.

"Why not?" I asked him, naively not having a clue where he was going.

"Because it gave the impression that this [defensive use of guns] was far more common that it really is."

I remember saying something like, "How do we know how common or uncommon it is?" I knew he had no idea, no facts to marshal, just knee-jerk antigun biases. Living as he does in a well-to-do community in Westchester County outside New York City, where most people have never shot a gun and almost everyone is as liberal on guns as they are on everything else, my pal the liberal producer *knew* because . . . well, because *he just knew.*

In fact, there have been many studies that indicate the use of guns *to prevent violence* may be quite common. In 1995, for example, Dr. Gary Kleck, a criminologist at Florida State University, found that Americans use guns defensively 2.5 million times a year. They almost never actually fire the gun; its presence alone is enough to scare off a criminal. But this isn't the sort of data you're likely to see mentioned in the mainstream press. And its absence stands in marked contrast to the attention generated in 2000 by the publication of *Arming America: The Origins of a National Gun Culture,* a fiercely antigun book by Michael Bellesiles of Emory University. Bellesiles claimed that a review of probate records dating back to the Colonial era proved that gun ownership in early America was far less common than believed—suggesting, therefore, that the Second Amendment was intended to protect not individual rights but only organized militias.

The book was widely hailed in the press for its important groundbreaking research. A front-page review in the *New York Times Book Review,* for instance, gushed that *Arming America* "has dispelled the darkness" in the debate on guns in America. "Furiously researched," is how the *Rocky Mountain News* put it, right there in the heart of gun country, adding that "Bellesiles has performed heroically in plumbing the depths of our history."

"Thinking people who deplore Americans' addiction to gun violence have been waiting a long time for this information," said Stewart Udall, the Democratic former secretary of the interior. "Michael A. Bellesiles," he went on, "has uncovered dramatic historical truths that shatter the 'Ten Commandments' promulgated by the National Rifle Association."

In no time at all the book received the Bancroft Award, the most prestigious prize given for historical research in the United States.

There was only one problem—some of *Arming America's* most provocative claims were completely unsupported.

Conservatives and Second Amendment activists quickly discovered that the probate records Bellesiles cited had been grossly misrepresented—or didn't exist at all. For an inexcusably long time, liberals in the media and elsewhere resisted these findings, but the evidence against Bellesiles was overwhelming, and in the end he was discredited. In October 2002, after an Emory University panel of independent scholars accused him of "unprofessional and misleading work" that "does move into the realm of falsification," he resigned in disgrace from Emory, calling the university's findings against him "just plain unfair." Two months later, the Bancroft Prize was rescinded.

The real question is, why was he so readily believed in the first place? His claim that few early Americans owned guns should have seemed ludicrous on the face of it. There were all those letters and diaries of the era that had so many gun references; there was the art and literature of the time; there was work by other scholars about guns in colonial America. But none of that sounded the alarm. Because, as in all the other issues involving core liberal beliefs, the eagerness to believe overcame all skepticism and reason—with journalists leading the way.

All of which brings us back to the way the media handled the story about the shootout at the Appalachian School of Law in Grundy, Virginia, and what seems to be the only plausible reason so much of the media left out the salient fact that the students who finally helped subdue the gunman also had guns. If they had reported that, it would lend support to an argument liberal media elites detest, namely, that having guns around sometimes actually does some good. That maybe, to put it bluntly, in some instances more guns really do mean less crime.

I have always argued that there is no formal media conspiracy—*because there is no need for one.* The real problem, I have said, is liberal groupthink—the idea that if everyone at all the right Manhattan cocktail parties thinks guns should be banned, there's nothing more to be said on the subject. Being against guns becomes the noncontroversial, reasonable, civilized position. End of discussion.

But the Appalachian Law School shootout raised groupthink to a whole new category of duplicity. This was *group lying.* Because there's no way the media's failure to tell the whole story can be written off as an honest mistake.

On February 7, 2003, I spoke to one of the students who used his gun that day to end the violence. Tracy Bridges told me he spoke to about a hundred reporters about what happened at the law school, and told every one of them that he and another student had gone to their cars to get their guns to try to stop the killer.

"It was kind of shocking [to learn that they didn't use the gun angle]. At first I thought maybe they didn't hear the whole story, but then after you read about it time after time it becomes obvious why they left it out."

And why was that? I asked him.

"I believe they didn't want to put out an image that a gun was actually used in defense to help someone out. They definitely did not want to put a story out that a handgun was used for some good. I've collected handguns for a number of years, and the short time I've been on this earth [he's twenty-seven] I've never read a story where they've put a favorable light on someone using a handgun. I only read the negatives. And I just *know* there have to be good stories out there, but I haven't read one."

For the record: there are conflicting reports on precisely how the episode at the law school ended that day. Not everyone tells it exactly the way Tracy Bridges does. Another student, J. Todd Ross, told me that since the killer had already put his gun down and since he had been tackled to the ground moments before Bridges arrived, Bridges and the other student who rushed to the scene with their guns drawn didn't really do very much to subdue the gunman. There was a lot of confusion at the scene so it's understandable that different people remember the incident differently. But however it ended—whether the students with guns played a major or a minor role that day—isn't it still a vital part of the story to report they did indeed have guns and that, however belatedly, did indeed at least help to subdue the gunman?

This time the bias was as bad as it looked, and then some. On this one, as much as on any story I've encountered, the media gave their critics all the ammo (pardon the expression) necessary to make the case that Big Journalism was more interested in promoting an agenda than in promoting the truth.

So much for the responsibility to present as many sides of the debate as possible. So much for the responsibility of seeking to fully inform the American people on this vital issue. There are millions of Americans out there who never hear anything but arguments against gun ownership. Do you think the gun debate in America would be different today if even some of these stories got news coverage?

Yet in failing the public, once again reporters also fail themselves. Because there are great stories on this subject just waiting to be told—if only they would tell them. And not only small, riveting stories like the one about the rescuers at the Appalachian School of Law, but larger stories of potentially great significance to society at large.

Take what happened in Great Britain and what it might mean on this side of the pond.

In 1997 Great Britain banned handguns. The government didn't simply ban the future sale of handguns; honest, law-abiding citizens who had guns in their homes actually had to turn them in. As you might expect, this event was hailed by the American media as an exercise in sanity, the sort that we Americans would do well to emulate.

"The echo of the shots that killed sixteen children in Dunblane, Scotland, last March is still being heard across Britain," is how CBS's Mark Phillips opened his piece on the gun ban. "Today, after an official inquiry into the shootings, the British government is expected to announce a virtual ban on all privately held handguns. Only small-bore target pistols held by gun clubs will be exempt. And for the father of one of the murdered children, the ban is welcome, if too late."

Then we heard from Duncan McLennan, who said, "We are not going to become a gun culture. We're not going to follow the Americans down that road. We are British; there is no place in our society for handguns."

And over the years since the ban went into effect, there has been a lot more of the same, with statistics on British crime regularly held up to show us Americans that we need to follow Britain's more enlightened example.

Here, for instance, is Ted Koppel, on a *Nightline* broadcast entitled, "Guns: An American Way of Life and of Death," which aired on August 10, 1999:

"I'd just like to have you have a little context, something that suggests that it doesn't have to be this way. In 1996, handguns were used to murder two people in New Zealand, 15 in Japan, 30 in Great Britain, 106 in Canada, 213 in Germany, and 9,390 here in the United States. And those, mind you, are just the murders involving the use of handguns . . ."

And here's a May 24, 2000, story in the *New York Times*: "In general, crime rates in Britain are much lower than they are in the United States, a phenomenon largely attributed to the strict laws that ban handguns. . . ."

Now, don't get me wrong. No one in his right mind can possibly excuse the level of gun violence in this country. The statistics are staggering and, in many ways, a source of national shame. The question is whether banning guns, as they have in Britain, really is the answer.

And now, as Paul Harvey might put it, we have the rest of the story—the part we almost never get from our mainstream media: *In the years since guns were banned, violent crime in Britain has exploded to epidemic proportions.*

To be sure, connecting the dots between crime and its causes can be a complicated matter. There are social and economic factors at play. But surely the ban on handguns has been a significant factor in Britain's exploding crime rate; most informed observers agree on that. And you know that bumper sticker that drives antigun people nuts, the one that says, "If you outlaw guns, only outlaws will have guns"? Well, isn't that true?

According to a December 2001 report in London's *Evening Standard,* armed crime in Britain was "rocketing," with banned handguns the weapon of choice. In fact, "in the two years following the 1997 handgun ban, the use of handguns in crime rose by 40 percent, and the upward trend has only continued. From April to November 2001, the number of people robbed at gunpoint in London rose 53 percent."

Those numbers come from an article called "Gun Control's Twisted Outcome," by Joyce Lee Malcolm, a history professor at Bentley College and a senior adviser to the MIT Security Studies Program. It appeared in the November 2002 edition of *Reason* magazine and gives some indication of what this unprecedented rise in crime has meant in human terms. "Over the course of a few days in the summer of 2001, gun-toting men burst into an English court and freed two defendants; a shooting outside a London nightclub left five women and three men wounded; and two men were machinegunned to death in a residential neighborhood of north London. And on New Year's Day this year [2002] a 19-year-old girl walking on a main street in east London was shot in the head by a thief who wanted her mobile phone."

By the end of 2002, Britain's crime rates actually exceeded those in the United States for robbery, assault, and burglary, and the gaps were closing in the rates of murder and rape. The streets of London are now measurably less secure than those of New York and most other major American cities.

I am most definitely not in the business of promoting the gun lobby. The NRA can do whatever it wants with those statistics. I am, however, in the journalism business, and so I keep wondering: Why haven't we seen this story all over the big, national American media? Wouldn't this story about the unintended real life-and-death consequences of Britain's ban on handguns be a natural, especially for television, given all those gruesome pictures of dead bodies lying in pools of blood on the sidewalk, and distraught relatives weeping—images that TV can't seem to get enough of?

If a smart talking head were needed, they could go right to Joyce Lee Malcolm and her chilling conclusion in the *Reason* magazine piece: "The English government has effectively abolished the right of Englishmen, confirmed in their 1689 Bill of Rights, to 'have arms for their defence,' insisting upon monopoly of force it can succeed in imposing only on law-abiding citizens. It has come perilously close to depriving its people of the ability to protect themselves at all, and the result is a more, not less, dangerous society."

Well, actually we have seen a few passing mentions in the American media on the gun ban and its apparent consequences, though you'd have to search pretty hard to find them. In fact, not counting opinion pieces, I could find only one story devoted entirely to the gun ban out of all the papers in the United States. That was in *USA Today*, on August 6, 2001, in a story by reporter Ellen Hale, which told it absolutely straight. The headline read, "British Fear Rise of 'Gun Culture,'" and the story presented both the pro- and antigun positions, not hesitating along the way to describe the mayhem—drugs, gang warfare, and gun violence—that in recent years has become the norm in certain once-peaceful English neighborhoods. Guns, Hale wrote, are "increasingly the weapon of choice of criminals across Britain. In a study released late last month, researchers found that the criminal use of handguns in Britain had increased by almost 40% in three years, to 3,685 incidents from 2,648 . . . The increase in firearm crime has critics questioning whether gun-control laws here, among the world's strictest, have been misguided."

Now, compare that to the story on the very same subject that appeared on *The CBS Evening News* in the summer of 1999. Dan Rather introduced the piece, saying, "This summer, thousands of Americans will travel to Britain, expecting a civilized island free from crime and ugliness, and, in many ways, it is that. But now, like the U.S., the U.K. has a crime problem, and believe it or not, except for murder, theirs is worse than ours. Tom Fenton is on assignment in London tonight."

Then my former colleague Tom Fenton, a solid and smart reporter, came on and began his piece, accurately describing the extent of the problem: "At first sight, England is a green and pleasant land. But in reality, it is one of the most violent urban societies in the Western world. The violence of British soccer fans is the most familiar, but that's only the tip of the iceberg. The streets and shopping malls of Britain are a battleground."

It was a great beginning. But in the entire rest of the piece—trust me, friends, you will find this almost impossible to believe—Tom Fenton never once mentioned . . . *the ban on handguns in Britain.* Not a word about it. No indication whatsoever that the "battleground" Fenton was describing may have, in some way, come about, at least in part, as a result of the ban on handguns; no hint that Tom even grasped that maybe, just maybe, the ban might have emboldened criminals to turn "the streets and shopping malls of Britain [into] a battleground."

In fact, Fenton's story turned out to be yet another *anti*gun story, with an English doctor speculating at the end of the piece that England would see real "mayhem" if guns were added to the mix.

Nowhere in the story did Fenton say to the good doctor, *But this mayhem you fear is already evident—and things have only gotten worse since the ban on handguns became the law of the land.*

This failure to mention the ban in a story about crime in England is as misleading and deplorable as all those stories on the shooting in Virginia, which conveniently left out the fact that the rescuers also had guns. What if at least part of the problem, in Great Britain anyway, is that guns have been taken *out of the mix?* What if part of the problem is that the "dopey" slogan has turned into a gruesome reality: that now that they've outlawed guns, only outlaws do indeed have guns?

Isn't any of this even worth considering?

What Liberal Media?
Part 3

"My fear is that Mr. Gingrich, given his history, may increase what I see as a new mean-spiritedness in this country. . . . I would like to think that the American people care about poor people, about sick people, about homeless people, and about poor children. I am shocked by the new mean-spiritedness."
—*Carole Simpson, in an America Online auditorium session, January 5, 1995*

"The new Republican majority in Congress took a big step today on its legislative agenda to demolish or damage government aid programs, many of them designed to help children and the poor."
—*Dan Rather, on* The CBS Evening News, *March 16, 1995*

"There are 60 million Catholics in America, and for many of them he also speaks with the voice of a conservative crank when he stonewalls on abortion, birth control, married priests, women priests and so on."

—Washington Post *reporter Henry Allen, referring to Pope John Paul II, October 2, 1995*

"TV viewers saw a well-orchestrated image of a moderated Republican Party, portraying itself as pro-woman, pro-minorities, and pro-tolerance. This is in sharp contrast to the delegates on the floor, sixty percent of whom self-identified as conservative Christians."

—*Bonnie Erbe, NBC Radio News/Westwood One reporter, hosting* To the Contrary *on PBS, August 16, 1996*

"See George. See George Learn Foreign Policy"

—Newsweek *headline over story on President Bush's upcoming trip to Europe, June 18, 2001*

"I can't think of anyone more qualified to write another book about Ronald Reagan. The question is, do we need another book about Ronald Reagan?"

—*Katie Couric's first question to former* Washington Post *reporter and Reagan biographer Lou Cannon on NBC's* Today, *November 26, 2001*

"We have an attorney general that is, I don't know, how would you describe him, demented? We have an attorney general who doesn't seem to understand the law."

—The New Yorker *writer Seymour Hersh, to the Chicago Headliner Club, May 2, 2002*

Charles Gibson: "My wife has a sign on her office wall and it says, 'Won't it be a great day when the Air Force has to hold bake sales to get a new bomber and the schools have all the money they need?'"

Diane Sawyer: "I love your wife! I love her for many reasons. Love that sign."

—Good Morning America, *October 2, 2002. Gibson's wife runs an all-girls private school in New York City.*

Actually, I Don't Have an Opinion on That

I could never understand the Swiss. Or more to the point, I could never understand their warped view of neutrality.

Take World War II. The Swiss could support the Nazis and their storm trooper pals on the one hand, or they could go with the forces of freedom and democracy on the other. Let's see, the Swiss weighed: Nazis on one hand, freedom on the other. Nazis? Freedom? And in the end, the Swiss just couldn't decide. "Actually," they said, "we don't have an opinion on that."

So what should we make of David Westin, the president of ABC News, when he uttered those very words—*"Actually, I don't have an opinion on that"*—just six weeks after America was attacked on September 11, 2001?

That's when David Westin had traveled about fifty blocks north to the Columbia University Graduate School of Journalism in Manhattan to speak about the First Amendment, one of those subjects journalists love to talk about—mostly because it makes them feel noble. Westin talked a while but said nothing memorable. And then came the question-and-answer session.

"Do you believe the Pentagon was a legitimate military target, even if [using a hijacked jetliner] was not?" one of the students asked.

Two hundred innocent Americans, who literally didn't know what hit them, went up in flames at the Pentagon on September 11, and here was a student at the most prestigious journalism school in all of America, wanting to know if David Westin, the president of ABC News, believed "the Pentagon was a legitimate military target."

Only a college student at an elite university could ask a question so appallingly offensive. But it was nothing compared to David Westin's answer.

"The Pentagon as a legitimate target?" Westin repeated, contemplating the question. Then, after he had contemplated long enough, he continued: "Actually, I don't have an opinion on that."

And why, exactly, didn't the president of ABC News have an opinion on an issue that was so clear-cut to just about everyone else in the United States of America?

"It's important I not have an opinion on that as I sit here in my capacity [as president of ABC News] right now. . . . Our job is to determine what is, not what ought to be. . . . I can say the Pentagon got hit. I can say this is what their position is, this is what our position is, but for me to take a position this was right or wrong—I mean, that's perhaps for me in my private life; perhaps it's for me dealing with my loved ones; perhaps it's for my minister at church. But as a journalist I feel strongly that's something that I should not be taking a position on. I'm supposed to figure out what is and what is not, not what ought to be."

Let those words sink in. David Westin said it would be journalistically improper to take a position on whether the attack on the Pentagon *"was right or wrong."* Let it sink in.

I wonder if David Westin would be so Swiss if someone had asked what he thought about what those vicious white bigots in Texas did to James Byrd, dragging him to his death from the back of a pickup truck?

Would David Westin, president of ABC News, say, *"Actually, I don't have an opinion on that"*?

Or what if someone had asked him, "What do you think about those monsters in Wyoming who beat Matthew Shephard because he was gay and left him tied to a fence post to die?"

Would David Westin respond that *"As a journalist I feel strongly that's something that I should not be taking a position on"*?

And if someone wanted to know, "Do you think, Mr. Weston, that maybe the Taliban have a point when they say that girls shouldn't be educated?"

Would he respond that *"Our job is to determine what is, not what ought to be"*?

Fat chance.

Why, then, is it okay to be so appallingly neutral, just six weeks after September 11, when a student asks, "Do you believe the Pentagon was a legitimate military target?"

Why is that question different from the others? Why, when faced with the mass murder of his own countrymen, can't David Westin simply say whether in his humble opinion "this was right or wrong"?

True enough, journalists have no business taking sides on controversial issues, the kind that are hotly debated in homes and in offices and on TV and radio talk shows, arousing honest passions on both sides. That's what this entire book is about, for God's sake! But please tell me, what is so controversial about this one question that David Westin could not bring himself to answer? Are there two legitimate sides to the question?

Well, yes, maybe there are, if you're a certain kind of liberal. In fact, one such liberal recently sent me an E-mail about September 11, reflecting a point of view, he assures me, that he's heard from "smart reasonable people—non-sociopaths, non-Bellevue residents," as he put it. What followed is so fascinating—and, for me, so repulsive—that I will share it at some length: "Mr. Goldberg," he writes (explaining what those justifying 9/11 would say), "picture yourself living on some dung heap in some third world nation. All around you the people you love are dying—from disease, malnutrition, hard labor, etc. Stretching back to your great-grandparents' era, everyone in your family has been trying to improve conditions, but the controlling powers don't listen. And the reason no one listens is that the game is rigged. Multinationals and governments in league with these multinationals depend on you and yours living on your dung heap so others can live the good life. You've got two choices: eat more dung and prepare for your early grave, or resist. The catch is, the only weapon you can use to resist is terrorism. Which do you choose?

"On the one hand, one looks at say, a child on that plane that slammed into the field in Pennsylvania and says, 'How can it ever be right for that innocent child to die?' On the other hand, one looks at a situation of permanent misery for say, a Palestinian child living in a Gaza refugee camp and says, 'How can it ever be right for this child to never know anything but hellish poverty and sadness her entire life?'

"These two views are almost impossible to reconcile, and yet one suspects—I suspect at least—that's it's good to have both points of view represented. It's good to have people saying, 'Hey, I don't care what your beef is, it is never, ever right to kill an innocent human being.' But it's also good to have someone saying, 'Maybe we should ask ourselves why 20 people are willing to give their lives to destroy a piece of America, why they hate us so much. Maybe we've been too self-absorbed. Maybe we need to pay closer attention to what's been going on 'over there.' Maybe we need to get proactive and see if we can improve these people's lives."

That's it—the E-mail an intelligent, sophisticated liberal sent me, reflecting the view, he says, held by "smart reasonable people." Boiled down to its essence, this is the message: "Hey, maybe the terrorists have something of a point. Maybe America is also responsible for September 11. Maybe both sides are right and both sides are wrong."

According to such logic, would it also be reasonable to wonder if in some way the Jews brought the Holocaust on themselves? The

Nazis certainly thought so—and who are we to question the legitimacy of their point of view?

In decent circles, this is called "moral equivalence"—and at its heart, it could not be more immoral.

One might say that those who make such arguments are on the fringe, that they make up only a tiny fraction of Americans. Well, they may be fringe, but they are the fringe that help shape our popular culture. Manhattan and Hollywood are full of such people—people who disseminate ideas in the worlds of books and entertainment and, yes, in journalism, too.

Is this what David Westin was so concerned about—that some of the "smart reasonable people" in his circle might believe the Pentagon was in fact a legitimate military target? Is that why he was so reluctant to share his views with the journalism students at Columbia?

I do not know David Westin personally. But I assume he loves America just as much as I or anyone else in this country does. Nor am I suggesting that his sorry performance at Columbia is an example of liberal bias. It is not, at least not in the usual sense, since it doesn't fall into the category of slanting the news. But the reason this episode matters, the reason I raise it even though it happened a while back, is that it reflects an *attitude* that is all too pervasive in American newsrooms.

It is an attitude uneasy with overt expressions of patriotism—an attitude that starts with the assumption that America can never be wholly in the right. This was an attitude completely out of sync with America after September 11. But totally in sync with the elites the David Westins of the world actually broadcast the news for, namely, their smart, hip, sophisticated liberal friends, the ones they go to cocktail and dinner parties with in Manhattan and Georgetown and Beverly Hills—and when they take a break for some R and R, in the Hamptons and Martha's Vineyard. In these places it has long been understood that nothing is quite so narrow-minded or provincial as flag-waving. That's the sort of thing left to *ordinary* Americans, those conformists who live in fly-over country and follow stock car races and don't read the *New Yorker* and have probably never even tried sushi.

And while patriotism was surging all across America in the weeks after the terrorist attacks, we kept getting hints of how uncomfortable it made the elite press feel. The managing editor of the British news service Reuters went so far as not to let his reporters use the word "terrorist" at all. "One man's terrorist is another man's freedom fighter," is how he infamously put it.

And as the war in Afghanistan was getting under way, there came repeated, ominous warnings in the American media of an impending "quagmire." In fact, the pundits kept saying it almost to the day the Taliban collapsed and the Afghans emerged from their homes and took to the streets to celebrate their liberation.

But most of all we heard over and over about the threat of anti-Arab bias. To be sure there was some of this, including the savage murder in Arizona of a man from India who was wearing a turban and was thought, by some violent, nasty idiot, to be an Arab. But what was truly remarkable, in light of the intensity of the passions stirred by September 11, and in light of the fact that this is a very big country with nearly 300 million people living in it, was how *little* hostility was directed at those of Middle Eastern descent. Still, the press, as self-appointed watchdogs against the supposed ills of patriotism, managed to keep up the drumbeat.

So more than anything else, I think, it is this liberal attitude that explains David Westin at Columbia. The poor guy, confronted with the question about whether the Pentagon was a legitimate military target, just didn't want to look like a hayseed. He didn't want to come off like one of those hopelessly ordinary Americans who would have simply stared, dumbfounded, at the student who asked it.

But if Westin had answered the question about the attack on the Pentagon—if he had been more in tune with ordinary Americans and their penchant for clear thinking—how would that have jeopardized his precious journalistic standards, which, by the way, he didn't seem to care all that much about when, on his watch, Barbara Walters and Diane Sawyer did those blatantly one-sided programs about gay adoption and gay parenting?

And if David Westin is so concerned about the purity of television journalism, then maybe he ought to start watching his own network news magazines, where he would see his high-priced stars—with Mr. Westin's very own blessings—selling serious journalism down the river with an endless stream of mind-numbing interviews with the red-hot celebrity of the moment, the likes of Justin Timberlake and Leonardo DiCaprio and J. Lo and Kate Hudson and Lisa Marie Presley and even Eminem's mother.

This corruption of serious news apparently doesn't trouble David Westin. But coming out and unequivocally saying, "No, the Pentagon obviously was *not* a legitimate military target," somehow would tarnish him; somehow it would turn this man who is a shameless cheerleader for crap on television into something far, far worse in his mind—a shameless cheerleader for America.

When Terry Smith, on the Lehrer *NewsHour,* asked Geneva Overholser, formerly of the *Washington Post* and currently a member of the faculty of the well-respected University of Missouri journalism school, what she thought of Westin's comment, she said, "Well, it was certainly made inelegantly."

David Westin's only mistake, in Ms. Overholser's view, was that of inelegance. Because she made absolutely clear that she saw his point. "We can't afford to be a propaganda arm for the Taliban," she said, "nor can we afford to be a propaganda arm for the American government. . . . Skepticism is patriotism for a journalist."

But, of course, that is a straw man. Reasonable people were not asking Westin to pick up his pom-poms and put on a short skirt and cheer for American foreign policy. Nor were they asking him to jettison his skepticism. But certain issues, it seems to me, are clear-cut. Certain issues do not have two sides. In a society built on shared understandings about decency and morality there are certain acts civilized people simply cannot in good conscience regard with anything but unmitigated horror, revulsion, and anger. Dragging a black man to his death is one of them. Killing a gay man for being gay is another. And, yes, mass murder by terrorists is a third.

Why, then, couldn't David Westin, in his capacity as president of ABC News, bring himself to flatly condemn the slaughter of his countrymen at the Pentagon on September 11, 2001? Why did he give so pathetic a nonanswer, dressed up as principle no less?

Maybe, in the end, David Westin's only crime was being too "sophisticated" to say, *"I'm a journalist, but I'm also an American. What those bastards did to our fellow Americans, they did to every single one of us. Was the Pentagon a legitimate military target? If that unfortunate question even needs an answer, here it is: No, it most definitely was not!"*

How would that outburst of nonobjectivity have compromised David Westin's neutrality?

You Can't Make
This Stuff Up

"If she had lived, Mary Jo Kopechne would be 62 years old. Through his tireless work as a legislator, Edward Kennedy would have brought comfort to her in her old age."
—*Charles Pierce, in a* Boston Globe Magazine *profile of Senator Kennedy, January 5, 2003*

Welcome to the Gulag

When Stephen F. Hayes, a young journalist at the conservative *Weekly Standard,* heard about what David Westin had said at the Columbia School of Journalism, he was as disgusted as just about everyone else.

But Stephen Hayes found something else almost as hard to take—the fact that of all those elite journalists-in-training sitting in the journalism school's World Room, listening to the ABC news president firsthand, *not one found anything newsworthy in what he said.*

"It's really pretty amazing. Here you had a room full of two hundred journalism students, and none of them even recognized as news that the head of ABC can't say whether or not the attack on the Pentagon was appropriate."

And of course, he's right. That day at the Columbia School of Journalism, David Westin may as well have been talking to a bunch of deaf-mutes, or maybe Albanian pig farmers, for all the attention his comments generated. It wasn't until four days later, on October 27,

2001, no thanks to Columbia's journalism students, that the news finally got out.

That's when C-SPAN, which had recorded the lecture, broadcast Westin's speech and the question-and-answer session that followed. Two days after that, on October 29, the conservative Media Research Center picked up Westin's remarks and put them out on the MRC Web site. Then the right-leaning *New York Post* picked up the story, and so did Matt Drudge and Rush Limbaugh and a bunch of newspapers around the country. And suddenly a great many *ordinary* people were saying what none of the *elite* people who heard him had noticed: that his words were asinine and deeply offensive.

It took roughly another day for David Westin to buckle.

At Columbia, he had presented himself as a man of principle, boldly defending the best interests of journalism. Now that the heat had been turned way up, David Westin had a change of heart and mind.

"I was wrong," his mea culpa flatly stated, which came in the form of a written statement. "I gave an answer to journalism students to illustrate the broad, academic principle that all journalists should draw a firm line between what they know and what their personal opinion might be. Upon reflection, I realized that my answer did not address the specifics of September 11. Under any interpretation, the attack on the Pentagon was criminal and entirely without justification."

That's nice.

At one time or another every one of us has said or done something stupid. So I truly would like to believe that David Westin simply saw the light. But I don't. He is not a careless man, prone to imprudent public observations. Before he became president of ABC News, he was a corporate lawyer by trade. And he had served as clerk to a justice of the United States Supreme Court. David Westin knew what he was saying at Columbia. That he retracted his remarks only after they began circulating among the *common* folks—the ones who just might boycott ABC News—shows that, like so many television news executives, he has far more agility than backbone.

That Westin acknowledged, for whatever reason, he had made a mistake is, in the end, a good thing. But what about those journalism students, the ones who apparently neither were shocked by Westin's remarks nor thought they were especially newsworthy? Disgusted as he was by their nonreaction—not to mention the silence of their professors—Stephen Hayes cannot say he was surprised in the least.

That's because he himself had graduated from the Columbia J-School, as it's called, only a few years before, in 1999. And so he knew that although Columbia is by far the most prestigious school of journalism in the country, having produced a virtual Who's Who of big-time journalists—from former *New York Times* executive editor Joe Lelyveld (who was brought back as interim executive editor after Howell Raines resigned), *Newsweek* editor in chief Rick Smith, and *Nightline* executive producer Tom Bettag to *60 Minutes* correspondent Steve Kroft, CNN's Myron Kandel, and the *Washington Post* columnist Howard Kurtz—it is also an intellectual gulag. And as a handful of "dissidents" who end up within its walls will tell you, challenging politically correct assumptions is not only *not* encouraged, it is sometimes actually punished.

Entering the school in the fall of '98, Hayes soon saw what passes, at the dawn of the twenty-first century, for a topflight journalism education in this country. As he tells it, of the more than two hundred students in his class, there were two—*two!*—who would publicly admit to being right of center. "I knew the school would be left-wing," he says, "but I really didn't anticipate the ferocity of the bias."

In fact, Stephen Hayes speculates that it may have been the environment in the room where David Westin was speaking, "this sort of free-floating, everything-on-the-Left-is-good feeling," that caused the ABC News president to feel safe enough to be so honest. "He probably was comfortable saying things there he'd never have said otherwise, just because it fit the prevailing mood."

"One of my first classes was in ethics, and it was immediately clear how far left the professors were," Hayes says. "It was the presumptions they made, the questions they asked. In that class, the left-wing social position was considered the ethical position. For instance, it was assumed you couldn't possibly have any respect for [the pre-September 11] Rudy Giuliani—he was considered so far right, he couldn't even be taken seriously."

If anything, the faculty was even further out in far left field—that is, even more out of sync with the world at large—than the student body.

"Let's just say the other conservative student and I had to kind of bond for protection," Hayes says, laughing. But he quickly adds that it wasn't funny at the time. In the second semester of the one-year program, one of his professors became so furious when he tried to make a point that the professor shut him up with this put-down in front of the whole class: "Mr. Hayes, if you think you have a point, you don't!" In what class did this happen? you may ask. Was it a class devoted to covering affirmative action or some other hot-button issue? Was it in the course of a heated discussion on abortion or religion?

Think again, naive reader. It was a class on . . . *sportswriting.*

"We were discussing the coverage of men's and women's sports, and I was trying to make the point that men and women are different in certain ways, that they have different strengths and abilities, and that this was just common sense. It totally infuriated him." He laughs. "The thing is, I had actually backed out of another class to get into the sportswriting class because I was so tired of being attacked for my politics.

"It was just inescapable.

"Sportswriting class met on Monday evenings," Hayes continues, "and afterward a handful of us would always go out for beers at the Amsterdam Grill across the street. *That's* where we would finally have the open, freewheeling discussions we should have had in the classroom. As far as I'm concerned, far more learning took place at the Amsterdam Grill over a couple of pitchers of beer than ever took place at Columbia. All told, the pitchers of beer probably cost me a couple of hundred bucks, while between housing and tuition I was spending in the neighborhood of fifty thousand to go to Columbia."

But if anything, his friend Stacey Pressman had it even worse. Now a producer at ESPN, she says she entered Columbia with an equal passion for politics and sports. "But I had such a miserable experience at the J-School, I decided to recuse myself from political journalism entirely. I still can't believe how I was treated at that place. I mean, can you imagine being persecuted for believing in the free market?" She laughs. "I swear, if I hadn't met Steve, I don't know if I'd even have graduated."

Her initial trial by fire also came early in the year, at the hands of a feminist professor who sent out the following E-mail to all the students in her class:

Dear All,

For those of you not in my office yesterday, this week's assignment is a story about sexism, one that you find on your beat. It can be the subject of a lawsuit or someone who's filed a complaint with the Human Rights Commission. It can be a profile of a business where women believe there's discrimination based on gender. It can be about the problems of daycare and childcare that make it difficult and/or expensive for women to work. It can be a lifestyle problem in which women feel trapped at home while the men are not. It can be about maids, especially maids from foreign countries. It can be about sexual harassment. These are only suggestions. You are free to write about any subject you find on your beat in which the problem is fundamentally one of sexism.

Stacey says she was prepared to do the assignment, but she also sent the teacher an E-mail—a polite one, she says—telling her that the assignment was "loaded" and that she didn't agree with her assumptions. In response, she says, the professor "freaked." In the face-to-face meeting that followed, Stacey pointed out that " 'by sending us out to do stories on sexism and racism, that in itself was a bias; you've already reached a conclusion before I even do the story.' That made her even angrier. She told me—and I quote—'You make me not want to teach.' Then she said, 'You will have a nine-hundred-word essay on my desk Monday morning on what sexism is.' I just looked at her and said, 'I don't think so. You can't penalize me and give me extra work just for disagreeing with you.' Next thing I hear, she brings my name up at a faculty meeting and tells the entire faculty she has an insubordinate student—which didn't exactly endear me to the rest of the faculty."

Stacey laughs before putting the final punctuation point to the story: "Welcome to journalism."

The amazing thing to me is that Stacey Pressman sounds like she has all the tools to be a first-rate journalist. As she herself puts it, "Isn't journalism *supposed* to be about skepticism?"

"It's a school full of the Stepford students," she concludes. "That's how they want it. God forbid you challenge them, or rock the boat—you're gonna get it. Supposedly, they believe in the Socratic method of give-and-take and free and open dialogue. But what they really practice is the *autocratic* method: If you think you have a point, forget it; you don't. End of discussion."

But not to worry, the Columbia School of Journalism is undergoing a makeover, the goal of which is to transform it into an even better, more relevant twenty-first-century institution of higher learning. What could possibly be wrong with that—especially when you consider that, as they say, as goes Columbia, so goes journalism education in this country?

In 2002, the new president of Columbia University announced

that he was ordering up an exhaustive reassessment of the school and its "mission." The president appointed a blue ribbon committee full of famous journalists to study the matter.

Wait, on second thought, *keep* worrying. In fact, this may be a good time to start panicking. Because the new president of Columbia, Lee Bollinger, may well be the most liberal major college president in America, and in his earlier job as president of the University of Michigan, he instituted the most aggressive affirmative action program anywhere.

So who was on President Bollinger's blue ribbon panel? Mostly committed liberals and leftists: There was columnist Anna Quindlen, an ideological liberal who, if her work is any indication, is incapable of taking a conservative idea seriously; and there was former SDS radical-turned-academic Todd Gitlin; and there was also Victor Navasky, J-School professor and former editor of *The Nation*, the most left-wing political magazine going.

Who was *not* on the blue ribbon panel? William F. Buckley was not, and neither was William Kristol, the publisher of the *Weekly Standard*—both very smart men and highly regarded in the field of opinion journalism. Nor was Brit Hume of Fox News on the panel. Neither was Dorothy Rabinowitz, the critic-at-large at the *Wall Street Journal*, nor Paul Gigot, the *Journal* editorial page editor—both Pulitzer Prize winners, and both, of course, conservative.

In fact, while there were lots of unmistakable liberals, among the twenty-nine people on the list there wasn't even one clearly identifiable conservative. Didn't anyone concerned with the "mission" of the Columbia School of Journalism care even a little about that point of view?

Once upon a time the best schools in America had no use for black people. Now they have no use for conservatives, whom they also see as intellectually and morally inferior. They love diversity, these academic elites, but have no passion for a diversity of ideas. And that is precisely why the new president of Columbia didn't go out of his way to find even a few token journalists from the Right to put on his blue ribbon committee, and it's why no one at Columbia's journalism school is losing any sleep over the fact that there is hardly a shred of diversity of thought among the students in the school, either.

So let's look at the issues the panel thought were important to consider in order to make Columbia Journalism an even better place to study. Well, they discussed whether the faculty should include more academics or mainly working journalists.

Okay.

And they considered whether it made sense to expand Columbia's program from one year to two.

And they had very smart conversations about whether journalism schools should offer courses in philosophy and statistics.

Fine.

But let's take a stab at what these liberal thinkers did not take up. That's right, for all the ballyhoo about this blue ribbon panel and its "mission," there was nothing about the single journalistic issue tens of millions of ordinary Americans care about more than any other: liberal bias.

And when the Columbia panel had completed its work, and in April 2003 a brand new J-school dean was named to begin instituting some of its recommendations, the nod—big surprise—went to a member of the club: Nicholas Lemann, a guy from Harvard and the *New Yorker*, a guy with a professional pedigree as staunchly liberal as Bollinger's own.

But when you think about it, it all makes sense. No one at the Columbia School of Journalism thinks there is a liberal bias problem in the media, so why put it on the agenda?

"There's just this *huge* blind spot about what's wrong with the place," as Steve Hayes puts it. "I mean, I think it's great they could get Victor Navasky to run their magazine program. I may disagree with ninety-nine percent of what he says, but he's had a long history in political journalism. But why would it never even occur to them to ask William F. Buckley?"

"I used to joke with my friends I was going to Columbia in part to launder myself, so I could be respectable enough to get a job at a mainstream publication. But after getting all that ideology crammed down my throat, I wouldn't even think of ever working in a mainstream newsroom—assuming someone with my politics could even get a job." He pauses. "I guess in that sense, at least, J-School taught me what I needed to know."

That's Entertainment!

Match the angry celebrity with the offensive quotation:

A. "I despise him [President George W. Bush]. I despise his administration and everything they stand for. . . . To my mind the election was stolen by George Bush and we have been suffering ever since under this man's leadership."

B. "I find George Bush and Dick Cheney frightening. . . . Donald Rumsfeld and John Ashcroft frightening . . . poison in the water, salmonella in the food, carbon dioxide in the air and toxic waste in the ground that polluters no longer have to pay to clean up— the taxpayers do."

C. "This is a racist and imperialistic war. The warmongers who stole the White House (you call them 'hawks,' but I would never disparage such a fine bird) have hijacked a nation's grief and turned it into a perpetual war on any nonwhite country they choose to describe as terrorist."

D. "We live on an island. A giant big fucking island. We don't understand that people actually get mad at us. We still think of ourselves in terms of WW2. It's not uncommon for us to say to
France, 'Hey, you'd still be speaking German if it wasn't for us.'
The problem is the world has changed, and our involvement in
these tiny little places is different than it was in 1941. It was a
lot clearer then. We were attacked."

E. "Iraqis, I think, feel that if we drove smaller cars, maybe we
wouldn't have to kill them for their oil."

F. "Yes, he's [George W. Bush] a racist."

G. "Let us find a way to resist fundamentalism that leads to violence.
Fundamentalism of all kinds, in al-Qaeda and within our government. And what is our fundamentalism? Cloaked in patriotism
and our doctrine of spreading democracy throughout the world,
our fundamentalism is business."

H. "The reason that the World Trade Center got hit is because there
are a lot of people living in abject poverty out there who don't
have any hope for a better life. . . . . I think they [the nineteen hi-
jackers] were brave at the very least."

I. President Bush is a "sad figure: not too well educated [who is]
leading the country towards fascism [even though] he wouldn't
understand the word fascism anyway."

J. "This present government in America I just find disgusting, the
idea that George Bush could run a baseball team successfully—
he can't even speak! I just find him an embarrassment. . . .
When I see an American flag flying, it's a joke."

1. Woody Harrelson, in the *London Guardian*, October 17, 2002

2. Susan Sarandon, Washington, D.C., rally, October 26, 2002

3. Jessica Lange, news conference, September 25, 2002

4. CNN founder Ted Turner, Brown University, February 11, 2002

5. George Clooney, in the *London Observer,* January 20, 2002

6. Danny Glover, in Brazil's *Isto E* magazine, February 2003

7. Barbra Streisand, Democratic fund-raiser, September 29, 2002

8. Bill Maher, on *Larry King Live,* November 1, 2002

9. Robert Altman, film director, in the *London Times,* January 22, 2002

10. Larry Hagman, to a reporter in Berlin, February 20, 2003

Answers:
1-C, 2-G, 3-A, 4-H, 5-D, 6-F, 7-B, 8-E, 9-J, 10-I

Congratulations to everyone who matched all the angry celebrities to their offensive quotations. But most of all, thanks to all the entertainment elites for their scintillating observations.

Liberal Bias?
Never Mind!

Maybe I shouldn't have called this book *Arrogance*. That only gets them angry. And if they get too angry, they'll *never* take me back.

To be honest, there are times when I miss my old pals from network television news. I miss how those well-educated, sophisticated correspondents, who would sell their children into prostitution if it meant getting more airtime, still root for each other—to get hit by a bus. I miss how much fun it is to be told you said something that offended the anchorman and that he's very, very upset and that he's in his big office pouting and may never, ever talk to you again. I really miss being told by Ivy League–educated executives that we need to do more "dog kills baby" stories because that's what those pathetic idiots out there in the double-wides tune in for. And once in a while I even miss those great secret conversations no one is ever supposed to learn about, where liberal producers tell you that no one in "our" audience gives a crap about black people so let's not do stories about them.

Those were the good old days.

So I start thinking: What would I have to do to get back into their good graces?

Easy! Instead of calling this book *Arrogance,* I could have entitled it *I Got It All Wrong: A Media Culpa by Bernard Goldberg.*

Man, oh, man, if I had done that, you'd see me all over network television. Mike Wallace and Leslie Stahl, neither of whom would even consider doing a story on *Bias* for *60 Minutes,* because it would have offended Dan Rather, would be killing each other to line me up for a segment on how I finally saw the light and confessed that they had been right all along, that there really is absolutely no liberal bias in the news. And, of course, I'd have to respond to their probing questions by looking contrite and admitting the error of my ways, and appealing for understanding and forgiveness. I'd have to admit that I wrote *Bias* after being shamelessly seduced by the rich and powerful moguls of corporate America who despise the media, which they mistakenly (I now realize) think are liberal, and who wanted to make me the poster guy for their right-wing conspiracy.

And that would be just the beginning of my grand media tour.

Katie Couric, during her adoring twenty-five-minute chat with me on the *Today* show, would ask me for a date. No can do, Katie, I'd have to say; I'm married, and besides, I'm going out with Diane Sawyer, who is setting up a fifty-five minute piece about me for *Primetime,* which she assures me will be even bigger than her really hard-hitting interview with J. Lo. Unless, that is, Barbara Walters talks me into doing her two-hour special, which they're going to call "Bias in the Media? What Bias in the Media?"

It's a tough call, but I might just have to go with Babs.

Even Dan Rather, who has said he would "never" forgive me for spilling the beans about bias in the news, would do a piece about the new book. "Tonight, a story about a guy I'm tighter with than rusted lug nuts on a '57 Chevy. A guy who I once wouldn't touch with an eleven-foot pole, which is the pole I reserve for people I wouldn't touch with a ten-foot pole. But now, this guy is my bud for life. His name is Bernie Goldberg, and in this *Eye on America* segment, which will take up tonight's entire evening newscast, Bernie will tell you what I've been saying for a mighty long time now but you just wouldn't listen: That only right-wing nut-jobs think we slant the news around here. Bernie wrote a brand-new book called *I Got It All Wrong*, which he got *all right*—right as rain, as a matter of fact, on a porcupine's ass in July."

But I can't do it. The truth is, if I were going to call this book something else, it would be *They're Not Only Arrogant, They're Also Two-Faced and Delusional.*

These are people who operate by a double standard that gives even double standards a bad name! No matter how they cast it or try to dodge the issue, to most in the big-time media, a liberal is, by definition, a good guy, someone who is decent and compassionate. A conservative, on the other hand, by definition is a selfish, mean-spirited moral slug.

There are many cases in point. But for an especially clear-cut one, let's just turn to the media treatment of David Brock.

If you're a conservative, you might recall that David Brock was once a figure celebrated on the Right. As a reporter for the right-wing *American Spectator* in the early '90s, he wrote a best-selling book called *The Real Anita Hill,* which furiously attacked the credibility of Clarence Thomas's accuser. He followed this up with reports on the Clintons in Arkansas, which led to the emergence of one Paula Jones, thus setting in motion the events that would lead to the impeachment of Bill Clinton.

Back then, when David Brock was an unapologetic right-winger, the media hated him. For all the controversy generated by his work, he couldn't get arrested by the elite press. Mainstream journalists would rather have had dinner with lepers in a hepatitis ward than go anywhere near this creep who could not be trusted to tell the truth. He'd have to shoot someone—preferably himself—before they'd put him on the news.

In fact, when he was promoting his blockbuster Anita Hill book in 1993, the only time he made it onto CNN was as a punching bag for Michael Kinsley on *Crossfire.* And when he made his one and only network appearance, on the *Today* show, it was not to talk about his book, but to be confronted by an angry, accusatory Charles Ogletree of Harvard—one of Anita Hill's closest allies.

As Brock told *TV Guide* at the time, "If the book were called *The Real Clarence Thomas,* do you think for a minute they'd put on a Thomas supporter for balance?"

But then, in the media's view of things, David Brock wised up. He had a change of heart—and politics. He publicly apologized to Anita Hill and the Clintons for all the trouble he'd caused them. And in due course he wrote a book denouncing his former conservative political allies, called *Blinded by the Right.*

Andrew Sullivan, former editor of the *New Republic,* probably got Brock just about right when he said that there are "those who see politics as an arena for personal warfare more than political debate . . . Alas, this has always been what David Brock has been about. He once did it from the Right. Now he's doing it from the Left. The only difference is that now . . . it's more respectable in the mainstream media."

And that's putting it mildly!

Conservatives hated David Brock when he crossed over to the other side. They called him "a pathetic little man," and that was the nicest thing they had to say about him. I, on the other hand, have absolutely no interest in David Brock's conversion from right-wing hatchet man to left-wing hatchet man. The subject doesn't even vaguely interest me.

On the other hand, the *media's* conversion fascinates me.

All of a sudden, the once-reviled Brock was a good guy—for many, an out-and-out hero. What Brock's about-face had done, said *Newsweek* editor Jonathan Alter in his role as an NBC News analyst, is "illuminate some larger facts about our times. I think when historians look back on all this, they're going to be less concerned about all the legal details of who said what to whom when, and more concerned about the way we drove this truck into the muck. And if David Brock, who helped drive the truck into the muck, wants to help push it out now, great."

Many other liberal commentators struck the same theme. The august *New York Times* gave Brock's anticonservative confessional a major send-off in its Sunday *Magazine.* But even more striking was the way Brock was now treated on television. For a few weeks there, it was impossible to turn on the tube without seeing Brock, alternately asking forgiveness from his new liberal friends and attacking his old conservative ones. David Brock, the right-winger who once was poison as far as the mainstream media were concerned, had become one popular guy now that he was bashing conservatives.

He again did *Crossfire* on CNN. But this time CNN also had him on *Reliable Sources,* and *American Morning with Paula Zahn,* and *NewsNight with Aaron Brown,* and *Wolf Blitzer Reports.*

But the most breathtaking moment in the media about-face on David Brock may have been his March 14, 2002, appearance on the *Today* show. This time, Brock appeared alone. This time, the *Today* producers didn't think they needed to pair him with someone from the other side, someone who might challenge him. This time David Brock was just an author with something important to say. This time he wasn't a "controversial" figure who required "balance." This time . . . Well, why don't we just look at Matt Lauer's introduction.

"His specialty was character assassination, and throughout the nineteen-nineties he made a living as a right-wing hatchet man. But after years of lies and, some would say, malicious journalism, this Washington insider wants to clear his conscience. In his new book, *Blinded by the Right,* best-selling author and ex-conservative David Brock exposes how he says the GOP tried to destroy the Clinton presidency through a series of well-plotted smear campaigns."

That was the moment, right there on the NBC News *Today* show, that David Brock officially was rehabilitated. He was no longer scum. Now that he was taking on the Right, he was respectable.

Gee, Matt, to think once upon a time poor David Brock had been so misguided as to actually think there was a liberal bias in the media!

Something like that can give a guy pause. I'm only human, and the perks that come with being on the media's side are obviously pretty tempting. And it would be so easy: All I have to do is confess that I was wrong, that there is not now and never has been a problem of liberal bias in the media, and—presto!—I'm back in the club.

This is something I definitely need to think about.

I just did.

No thanks.

Quagmire!

On April 9, 2003, as jubilant, liberated Iraqis stomped on what used to be a twenty-foot-tall statue of Saddam Hussein, a statue that just moments earlier had been ripped down from its perch in downtown Baghdad, Alessandra Stanley of the *New York Times* was embedded in Manhattan, watching the event unfold on television. But somehow she missed the story.

This is how Ms. Stanley began her "TV Watch" piece the next day in the *Times*:

"A dismayed hush fell over Firdos Square in Baghdad yesterday as a United States marine pulled an America flag over the head of Saddam Hussein's statue like a gallows hood.

"The sight also silenced news anchors and many viewers: the tableau of conquest was exactly the image most likely to offend the Muslim world. And it was exactly the image that the administration had most wanted to avoid in its campaign to portray the fall of Baghdad as a popular insurrection."

So now, thanks to Ms. Stanley's television review in the *New York*

Times, we know that it is possible for a reporter to get the facts right and still manage to get the story wrong.

The toppling of the statue was riveting television. Maybe it wasn't the Berlin Wall coming down, but Baghdad didn't have a wall. They had Saddam. And now that he was gone the locals seemed to be genuinely happy. But instead of focusing on the jubilation, she chose to concentrate on the "dismayed hush" that "silenced news anchors," and the image of "a gallows hood." Reporters are always picking and choosing what to emphasize and what to minimize, and on this day Ms. Stanley chose to accentuate the negative, or at least what she and her editors at the *Times* considered to be the negative.

The fact is, the American flag was up there on Saddam's doomed head only briefly before it was taken down (and the *Times* TV review also noted that). At no time was this show of enthusiasm by a young marine, who had made his way across a dangerous desert and was now, understandably, caught up in the celebration, an official statement of U.S. policy. Any fair person would understand that *at its absolute worst* this was a momentary lapse on the part of a proud and happy marine.

Big deal!

But a big deal is exactly what the liberal elites in and out of the media made of "the flag incident." They smelled blood, or more accurately, they smelled the possibility of embarrassment—for the government of the United States of America and its president, George W. Bush. And so they fretted over this tiny episode as if it were a war crime. They saw it as a sign of American imperialism and pontificated on its devastating effects on the Arab street, never bothering to point out that this Arab street we hear so much about thinks suicide bombers who kill children in pizza restaurants are "martyrs" and considers all sorts of other murderous lunatics in their midst genuine heroes. But now the *Times* was fretting that "the tableau of conquest was exactly the image most likely to offend the Muslim world."

The fact is, I was fretting about something else entirely. My concern was with the relentless and grinding pessimism that was coming out of the media elites almost every day since the shooting started. Not from the reporters in the field. For the most part, I think, they did a wonderful job under the worst possible conditions. John Burns at the *Times* was especially excellent. It was the powers that be back home, the editors and the other "experts"—the pundits and commentators and at least one major network news anchor—who, once again, were giving ammunition to their critics.

The war had barely begun and the elites were going on and on about "quagmires," about whether the United States was getting itself into one by going to war in Iraq. But the real quagmire, the one we all should have been alerted to, didn't get even one second of airtime or a single drop of ink. That's because the quagmire that informed so much of the news coverage wasn't in the desert of Iraq but in the heads of the media elites. The real quagmire is one of liberal assumptions, which keep them mired in a certain narrow mindset that they can't seem to extricate themselves from.

It is a quagmire of biases, *and we see it in just about everything they cover.* If the subject is race, they tend to see the worst in the American people. If it's feminism, they see the worst in men. When they report on gay rights, they see opponents of even the most controversial issue as close-minded and bigoted.

In Iraq, the young reporters embedded with the troops didn't see quagmires. They saw movement and progress. But back home, the old guard was embedded in its own quicksand, showing no interest in escaping its gloomy preconceived notions. And whether the elites care or not, the American people noticed the endless tales of pessimism. As Dick Morris put it in his *New York Post* column on April 14, "In the Iraq War, the public may well have learned not to trust the broadcast networks or the establishment newspapers.

"Never before have Americans had the chance to watch the establishment media while also seeing the events unfold for themselves, live, on television. Our collective understanding of the dissonance between the two is breeding a distrust of the major news organs that will likely long outlast this war."

As much as I agree with that, let me be absolutely clear on one central point: I don't want journalists to be cheerleaders. Not for affirmative action or gay marriage or abortion—and not for the war in Iraq either. Personally, some of Fox News "fair and balanced" coverage, as our troops drove toward Baghdad, was a little too rah-rah, flag-waving for my journalistic taste. I didn't need to hear Shepard Smith refer to the Iraqi soldiers as "the bad guys." But the truth is, I can't get too worked up over it. Who would have been upset a generation ago if a reporter referred to the Nazis as "the bad guys"? And besides, Fox News anchor Neil Cavuto had a point when he told a professor who accused him of biased reporting: "Am I slanted and biased? You damn well bet I am, Professor. I'm more in favor of a system that lets me say what I'm saying here rather than one who would be killing me for doing the same thing over there."

So are we all. Still, I'm for fair and balanced reporting even when "we're" on one side and "the bad guys" are on the other. But I do understand what was motivating some of the more over-the-top, gung-ho journalists at Fox (and a few other places). Their "biases" are no mystery to me. "The puzzle is," as a *Wall Street Journal* editorial put it, "why some Americans, especially media and liberal elites, continue to wallow in pessimism about this [Iraqi] liberation." On the radio, Don Imus noticed the same gloominess. When the statue of Saddam came tumbling down, he said, it caused such sadness in some quarters at CNN that "a suicide watch has been put on Judy Woodruff."

Even before the war began, the pundits were busy doing what they do worst: making predictions. They may be wrong, these wise men and women, but they're never in doubt.

About one day into the war, National Public Radio correspondent Tom Gjelten went on *Washington Week in Review* on PBS and actually said this: "If the war is continuing a week from tonight, it's bad news."

A few days later, on ABC's *Nightline*, Ted Koppel in Iraq cautioned his audience to "Forget the easy victories of the last twenty years. This war is more like the ones we knew before."

The next morning, on *Good Morning America,* Diane Sawyer wanted to know if "this is going to be a long, protracted quagmire of a war?"

On March 30, 2003, *New York Times* analyst R. W. Apple, who, like so many journalists of a certain age, seems to have been trapped in his own quagmire since Vietnam, wrote that " 'Shock and awe' neither shocked nor awed."

It's not so much that the pessimists were pessimistic. It's that they were wrong! Remember, all this gloom and doom was being heaped upon us *during the early fighting stage of the war*—when everything was going remarkably well—not during the much more difficult *securing the peace stage,* which is a different story altogether. But still, the gloom-and-doom brigade kept chattering on.

Even the court jester was depressed . . . and depressing. On *60 Minutes* Andy Rooney looked more troubled than usual not long after the war began, telling his audience that "I've lived a long while now, and I don't remember any more unpleasant times than these." Let's see, Andy is in his eighties, which means he would have lived through the Great Depression, Hitler, Stalin, Punk Rock, and Jerry Springer. *But this Iraq thing was the worst of all?* "There aren't any good wars, but this one is especially bad. . . . The only real good news will be when this terrible time in American history is over."

When Baghdad fell, Andy changed his tune, telling Don Imus, "It appears as though [President Bush] did the right thing and I didn't think he was doing the right thing." Whatever you say, Andy.

And on Fox's *Hannity & Colmes,* former Secretary of State Lawrence Eagleburger dropped this bombshell: ". . . I was approached by the *New York Times* to write an op-ed piece. To make it very short, when I talked to them about it, I was told what we want is criticism of the administration."

At this point Sean Hannity jumped in to say, "They told you that?"

"Right out. Flat out," Eagleburger said. "He told me we want criticism of the administration. Needless to say, I did not write the op-ed piece."

When I told this story to a lapsed New York liberal pal of mine, he said something like "What's your point?" *What's my point?* This is a shocker, I told him. "Not for the *New York Times,*" he shot back.

And then there's Peter Jennings at ABC, who was by far the most relentlessly negative of all the anchors. Peter is a smart man who would say he wasn't being negative at all, just reporting the news wherever the facts led. But the day the statue came down in Baghdad, Peter felt the need to describe the celebrants as being part of a "*small* crowd." Couldn't Peter see how such a needlessly subjective word—*small*—would appear petty and slanted on such a day of celebration? And besides, in a country of 25 million people, the looters that Peter and everyone else kept showing on television also represented a "small crowd"—but I don't remember *them* being characterized that way.

And even in days of joy after Baghdad had fallen, in his "Photos of War" section at the end of *World News Tonight,* Peter ran a picture one night of a woman holding a sign that read, "KILL Bush, Blair, Rumsfeld and Powell NOT INNOCENT IRAQI CIVILIANS." Was it a real sign at a real antiwar demonstration? Yes. Was it news? Peter obviously thought so. But the woman holding up that sign was not in Iraq or Britain or the United States. She was in Nairobi, Kenya! Now compare that to how Peter Jennings handled another demonstration, just one day earlier—a demonstration *in support of American troops.* NBC and CBS News reported it on their evening newscasts; so did CNN, MSNBC, and Fox. But Jennings didn't mention the pro-America demonstration on his newscast. He didn't show even a single picture. Oh, and this one wasn't in Nairobi. It was a few miles south of Peter's studio, right there in New York City.

The "prophesies of doom and quagmire," as one conservative columnist put it, went on and on and on. "Two weeks ago these elites were predicting a long war with horrific casualties and global damage," the *Wall Street Journal* said in an April 16 editorial entitled

"Pessimistic Liberalism." "Then at the sight of Iraqis cheering U.S. troops in Baghdad, they quickly moved on to fret about 'looting' and 'anarchy.' Now that those are subsiding our pessimists have rushed to worry that Iraqi democracy and reconstruction will be all but impossible."

On that one, the jury is still out because the truth is that turning Iraq into a smooth-running free country clearly will be a difficult, long-term proposition. Just getting the basic necessities up and running—lights and clean water—was a major production. Add to that the perfectly legitimate question that wouldn't go away—the one about the weapons of mass destruction we were supposed to find—and the Bush administration was bound to take some serious heat from the media. Fair enough. But was it just me or did anyone else get the impression that none of those difficulties in Iraq have really displeased those on the Left, including more than a few journalists, who had been against the war from the outset?

Could it be that's why so many journalists have seemed so reluctant to report the good news out of Iraq in the months following Saddam's fall? For in the midst of all those heart-wrenching reports of American casualties—after the major fighting supposedly ended—an important fact regularly was overlooked: life in Iraq has indeed slowly been getting better. Granted, it may not always seem that way—especially when terrorists set off bombs that kill not only American soldiers but also Iraqi civilians—but the Iraqi people and world community really are better off now that Saddam Hussein is out of power. That this good news apparently hasn't been all that good to some Americans prompted the *Wall Street Journal*, in that editorial, to ask: "What is it that liberals find so dismaying about the prospect of American success?"

But before we get to that question, shouldn't we take into account, as the *WSJ* editorial did, the media's sorry track record when it comes to making predictions? Of course we should, if for no other reason than to have a few much-needed laughs. "Among the anticipated disasters that haven't come true: a 'nationalist' uprising against

U.S. troops á la Vietnam; the 'Arab street' enraged against us; tens of thousands of civilian casualties and a refugee and humanitarian crisis; bloody house-to-house urban combat; Iraq's oil fields aflame, rising oil prices and sending the economy into recession; North Korea ('the greater threat') using the war as an excuse to attack; the Turks intervening in northern Iraq and at war with the Kurds; and all of course leading to worldwide mayhem."

Can you imagine if they had had unrelentingly pessimistic anchors and pundits in air-conditioned Manhattan studios on D day, during the invasion of Normandy? If they had, we might have heard "expert analysis" like this:

"The weather is not good out there today. And the prospect of those troops proceeding onto the beach is just such a terrible military strategy. This is one bad war plan."

"Okay, the invasion went very well—I mean, we all knew it would—but what about now? There could be instability in the streets of Germany, the kind of thing we never saw when Hitler was in charge."

You know what? I *can't* imagine that kind of news coverage during World War II. Because back then, journalists *were* cheerleaders, if by that term we mean they were rooting for "the good guys" to win. Like the newsreel footage of the war, things were black-and-white back then. The Allies were right and the Nazis and the Japanese were wrong. By today's standards, that seems hopelessly simple and old-fashioned. Never mind that it was true. Vietnam, of course, changed everything. Just about everyone in charge was lying about something, and journalists, understandably, turned cynical. It was one of the casualties of that war that we don't hear all that much about.

So what about that question: "What is it that liberals find so dismaying about the prospect of American success?"

Brent Baker, the conservative vice president of the conservative media watchdog group the Media Research Center, has this theory: "I think the news media love to see failure."

This is a detestable observation. Too bad he's right.

"In the months leading up to the war," Baker says, "liberal opponents said it would be awful, and that the Iraqis wouldn't love us, and there would be blood in the streets. So when the actual war started, they actually believed their own fear-mongering. When anything went even a little bit wrong, they said, 'Aha. We were right.'"

Or as my friend Harry Stein, the author and journalist, put it in a very smart on-line piece: "The question, finally, must be asked: What is going on here? Do these people really despise America as much as they seem to?"

The answer, he says, is no and yes. "In fact, their professions of patriotism are earnest, for they can envisage an America to their liking, one that will, as the claim goes, live up to its creed—by which they mean stand as a model of their notions of 'freedom' and 'diversity' and 'economic justice.' They just despise America as it actually is."

This is not true of all liberals, of course, just too many liberals. The kind of liberals who, Stein says, "loathe George W. Bush with the same venomous passion they once brought to the hatred of . . . Richard Nixon. For them Bush is evil incarnate. And if he gets his way, only awful things will follow: not only in foreign affairs but (ultimately many of them care about this far more) on the domestic front."

But my guess is that even if the network news divisions are indeed slouching toward oblivion, they and the other elites will not let *any* of the criticism aimed in their direction or in the direction of their liberal friends puncture their bubble, where they remain insulated and content and convinced of their own virtue. Maybe that's a good thing. Because if they were shocked into silence at the mere sight of that United States marine throwing the American flag over Saddam's head, they would absolutely have choked on Dick Morris's closing thought in his *New York Post* column, appropriately called "Media Meltdown":

"This has been a rough war for tyrants and those who try to control the thoughts of their people. In Baghdad—but also in Manhattan, at the headquarters of the *Times,* NBC, CBS and ABC."

The Biggest Story the Media Won't Cover

S o, like the rest of the world, I tune in to watch Super Bowl XXXVIII, and before you can say "third quarter" we're watching Super Bowl 38-D.

Who knew?

Well, actually, we all should have known. Sex has been permeating our media culture for years, and sooner or later it was bound to show up in our living rooms on the most sacred day of all: Super Bowl Sunday. If you get in bed with MTV, as the NFL did, you had better expect to have sex. That's the business MTV is in.

Don't get me wrong. In the spirit of full disclosure, as we journalists like to say, and as a red-blooded American male, I'm all for seeing Janet Jackson's breast. Fact is, I'd like to see both breasts—and anything else she might want to show me.

Just not during the halftime of the Super Bowl, when all sorts of people are watching who may be offended—and not when tens of millions of American kids (a fifth of them children under the age of eleven, according to Nielsen) are watching, either.

And you know what? While we're at it, maybe we ought to get serious about a lot of other sleazy stuff that turns up on the tube when kids are sitting there, soaking it up. Maybe we ought to start making a serious fuss over all the soft-core porn and sexual innuendo that passes for harmless entertainment in our mainstream culture.

Turn on the CBS primetime program *Big Brother 4*, for instance, and you can watch as "houseguests hump beneath the covers," as *TV Guide* put it. You remember CBS? The Tiffany Network? The network that brings us the Victoria's Secret fashion show, also in primetime, each year, where beautiful women parade around in their underwear.

Or turn on NBC's *Will & Grace*, where it's one sexual joke after another, where Karen Walker, one of the show's main characters, tells this one about masturbation: "Since Stan and I split, I've done nothing but touch my muffin." Or how about her exchange with Jack, one of the gay guys on the show?

> JACK: Yeah. Oh, look! There he is. There's Bill. Isn't he dreamy?
> KAREN: Yeah, he's a slice of ice-cream cake. Now, when do I get to French kiss a girl? Come on, when" When?

Then again, it's almost pointless to single out particular shows in the barrage of cheesy double entendres and outright vulgarities that we find in primetime. And what's next? Probably real sex, that's what's next—and not "beneath the covers" and not on late-night cable TV, either.

But what gets lost in all this is that there's another story involving sex—a far more important story than Janet's dopey stunt. It is a story that impacts on countless American families, yet you probably don't know very much about it, because commercial television—still the main news source for most Americans—has given it so little serious attention.

It is the story of the sexualization of American children.

Cable reran the Justin/Janet "wardrobe malfunction" about a tril-
lion times. Thanks to television news, unless you were time traveling
through some other galaxy, you know about the Janet Jackson breast
episode. But here are a few things you probably don't know:

- Thirty-seven percent of ninth graders who attend suburban
  public schools in the United States say they have had sexual
  intercourse.
- When asked if they have ever touched another person's gen-
  itals—or been touched—in a sexual way, 59 percent of those
  ninth graders say yes.
- Six percent of suburban ninth graders say they have had anal
  intercourse.
- Seven percent of the suburban kids polled say they've been
  diagnosed with a venereal disease, like chlamydia, syphilis,
  gonorrhea, genital herpes, genital warts (or several others).
- Fourteen percent of suburban ninth graders say they've been
  pregnant.

I don't know about you, but I didn't know any of that—not until
I got a copy of a report called "Sex, Drugs and Delinquency in Urban
and Suburban Public Schools." It was put out in January 2004 by the
Manhattan Institute, a conservative think tank specializing in social
policy, which in its twenty-five-year history has helped shape American opinion on issues from welfare reform to tax policy. There's a lot
more in the report (which is based on data from the National Longi-
tudinal Study of Adolescent Health, one of the most comprehensive
studies regarding the behavior of high-school students in the United
States)—about underage drinking and illegal drug use—and none of
it is good news. This is how the report concludes:

> Parental concern about the rising influence of sex, drugs, and
> delinquency in urban schools has long been recognized as a
> significant fact in the last few decades' population flight from

the cities to the suburbs. Parents are fleeing urban schools not just because of low academic performance but also because they believe suburban schools are safer and more wholesome. But the results [of the study] suggest that fleeing from city to suburb doesn't produce much difference in the level of these problems one finds at the local school. The desks may be newer, the paint may be fresher, and the faces may be whiter, but the students are just as likely to have sex, use controlled substances, and break the law. The comforting outward signs of order and decency—shiny new schools armed with expensive textbooks and staffed by teachers who have mastered the latest educational fads—don't seem to be associated with substantial differences in student behavior.

In short, thanks to popular culture—not just TV and movies, but music and music videos and advertising—throughout America, what we used to think of as "childhood innocence" is gone. In fact, to hear experts on children's emotional and psychological health tell it, the change is deeply destructive. Given all the crap they squeeze into a half-hour network newscast, you'd think they might find a little time for this. You'd think this would be a great story for television, a medium that is otherwise obsessed with sex. As a friend of mine says, "Hell, I'm surprised we don't see specials all the time on how American kids are being sexualized, robbed of their childhood, things like that—just as an excuse to show *more* sex on the tube."

I'm not arguing that there's been a total news blackout on the subject. Sure, if you run a Nexis search of the networks over the last five years on all the variations you can think of on "kids and sex," you will come up with an occasional report that touches on the issue. During the Cinton sex scandal there were a spate of reports on how the president's behavior might influence children. And during 2003, both *48 Hours* and *Dateline* broadcast reports on teenage girls who sell nude shots of themselves on the Internet, and *20/20*'s John Stossel did a nice report about how preteenage girls were dressing up in "hooker wear," as some parents call it, desperately trying to look sexy beyond their years.

So yes, over the years, stories on the subject pop up every now and then. But what the mainstream media almost never do is cover the big picture—that is, *they almost never cover the story as the crisis it has become.* To those in the press, homelessness is a crisis, and AIDS, and American jobs going overseas. We know that because the Paul Reveres of the media defined them as crises. They pounded away at those stories constantly over weeks and months and even years, sounding the alarm, hoping to move society to meaningful action. But millions of ten-, eleven-, and twelve-year-olds acting in ways that would've been beyond unthinkable a couple of generations back? Apparently, that's no big deal. In fact, gay marriage—which directly affects a tiny percentage of Americans—gets far more play on television and page one in our newspapers.

Who does cover this vital story with energy and passion? You got it: mainly those far from the liberal camp. To his credit, Bill O'Reilly gets exercised about it all the time. So does Dr. Laura. But this is *not* only a conservative issue; it is one that affects liberals just as much. In fact, probably the best television report on the subject didn't come from the Right. It was on *Frontline,* on PBS, in October 1999. The program was called "The Lost Children of Rockdale County," a documentary that was shot in a prosperous suburb of Atlanta, Georgia. Think of it as one of those exceptions that prove the rule: For here, for once, television did not gloss over the crisis in our midst. Indeed, five years later, "The Lost Children of Rockdale County" remains one of the few serious, intelligent, and lengthy investigations on television involving children and sex.

After the program aired, a writer named Kay Hymowitz wrote a brilliant essay for the conservative magazine *City Journal,* titled "What's Wrong with the Kids?" What she wrote is worth quoting at length:

> The occasion for the show was an outbreak of syphilis that ultimately led health officials to treat 200 teenagers. What

was so remarkable was not that 200 teenagers in a large suburban area were having sex and had overlapping partners. It was the way they were having sex. This was teen sex as *Lord of the Flies* author William Golding might have imagined it, a heart-of-darkness tribal rite of such degradation that it makes a collegiate "hook up" look like splendor in the grass. Group sex was commonplace, as were 13-year-old participants. Kids would watch the Playboy cable TV channel and make a game of imitating everything they saw. They tried almost every permutation of sexual activity imaginable— vaginal, oral, anal, girl on girl, several boys with a single girl, or several girls with a boy. . . . During some drunken parties, one girl might be "passed around" in a game. A number of the kids had upward of 50 partners. Some kids engaged in what they called a "sandwich"—while a girl performs oral sex on one boy, she is penetrated vaginally by another boy and anally by yet another.

According to the producers, it was the profound loneliness of these children that led them to seek a "surrogate family" in the company of their peers. No one could dispute that these children are lonely. Some are the virtual orphans of broken and dysfunctional homes. Others were simply the children of part-time parents, who were out of the house working long hours to provide their children with lavish homes, cars, cell phones, and the latest teen fashions. Most of the sex parties took place after school between 3:00 P.M. and 7:00 P.M. in houses emptied of working adults. Other times kids slipped out of the house after midnight, without waking their exhausted parents.

But it gradually becomes clear that the absence in these kids' lives is not limited to office hours, and the loneliness they suffer goes beyond being left alone. Their parents, even when at home, seem disconnected. As the producers see it, one of the problems is that these families spend most of their time, including meals, in front of the television.

So, why have the mainstream media *not* taken the lead of the *Frontline* producers and Bill O'Reilly and Laura Schlessinger and Kay Hymowitz? Why, given the evidence of how important the story is, have the big mainstream media not given it "crisis" status?

That's a complicated question. Partly it's because, in general, reporters only recognize a crisis when the evidence is so obvious and so dramatic that it smacks them in the face. Even AIDS, the great medical crisis of recent decades, was only recognized as such once hundreds of people had died. Indeed, some reporters would surely say, with a straight face, that what happened in Rockdale Country was a story *only because of the syphilis outbreak.* Had it not been for that, it would have just been another American town where "boys will be boys and girls will be girls." Story? What story?

For, once again, we get back to the worldview of so many in the media. The truth is, a lot of liberal reporters are not really sure that kids having sex at an earlier age is all that bad. To the contrary, they're accustomed to thinking of those who regard it that way as prudes. After all, a lot of journalists came out of the sixties; and, like others of the Woodstock Generation, they're conditioned to think that violence equals bad and that sex equals good. Which is to say, they simply don't think about issues like this very deeply—or very well.

"So, you want to go back to Lucy and Ricky sleeping in separate beds?" is what I hear from liberal friends if I bring up the subject of all the degrading stuff on the tube. No, I say, but that doesn't mean I want to see people "humping beneath the covers" on mainstream TV during primetime, either.

"The prudes have always complained about whatever is new and edgy in the culture," my left-wing pals say. "They complained about Elvis, didn't they?" Yes, they did. But it's worth pointing out that there's a big difference between Elvis (who shook his hips) and Nelly (who grabbed his crotch) during the Super Bowl halftime show. Or Justin Timberlake—who, as part of the foreplay, gyrated his pelvis into Janet Jackson's ass while 140 million Americans, a lot of them kids, were watching.

In fact, many hip liberals will tell you, the outcry over the Super Bowl incident is just another example of the hypocrisy of Red State America. "What's the big deal over a little skin?" they ask. "Those right-wing boobs (excuse the expression) like to ogle naked women as much as anyone else."

The problem is that a lot of smart people, including a lot of otherwise intelligent journalists, just don't get it. Because they see the concerns of so many Americans—that their kids' innocence is being destroyed—as wildly exaggerated. Because, like so many other things, sex is one of those issues that the Left in general and the media elites in particular don't quite see the same way as a lot of other Americans do. Because, inside the elite liberal bubble, sex, drugs, and rock and roll are things to be celebrated, not fretted about. Because, to a lot of liberals in the media, the glass ceiling represents a national crisis—but twelve- and thirteen-year-old girls giving blowjobs in the boys' bathroom doesn't.

When I was at CBS News, I had a discussion with a liberal colleague, a producer based in New York, about sex and vulgarity in our mass media culture. "Doesn't all this crap on television bother you?" I asked him. "It's nothing more than a fart on the ocean," he replied. He wasn't endorsing vulgarity or gratuitous sex on TV. He just didn't think it had much effect in the real world. And in the world of big-time journalism, he isn't alone.

Nothing happens in a vacuum, of course. Everything in our culture is interconnected. No man is an island and all that. Casual talk about casual sex on television filters through the culture. What used to be risqué becomes mainstream. Calling somebody a "jerk-off" in primetime is no big deal. Talking about "getting laid" in a sitcom is no big deal. The real sex portrayed on reality shows is no big deal.

None of it is a big deal. Only the prudes and bluenoses think something is wrong with a media culture drenched in sex. Inside the bubble, everything is just fine.

Twelve Steps

'm an optimist. I believe people can change for the better. In fact, I'm so optimistic that I believe even the most arrogant, thin-skinned, and close-minded journalists can change for the better. Why not?

Unfortunately, there's an answer to that question.

Most journalists are extremely outer-directed. Introspection isn't their thing. And as every alcoholic knows, you can't get straight unless you look inward and honestly take stock of yourself first.

So, while I'm hopeful for their recovery, I'm not delusional.

Still, I do know that every journey begins with a single step—or in this case, twelve of them. And if a twelve-step program can help drunks . . . then why not journalists?

Step 1:
Face Up to
the Problem

I n difficult times, a philosopher once said, it is important to state the obvious. These are indeed difficult times for the media, so here goes: You cannot begin to solve a problem until you admit you have a problem.

Every recovering alcoholic who used to live in the dark world of denial understands this. So does anyone who used to be hooked on nicotine. You simply cannot smoke twenty packs a day and tell everyone you bump into that you can quit anytime you want, without coming off as pathetic.

This is what therapy is all about. You pay someone with a bunch of letters after his or her name a lot of money; you yak and yak for weeks and weeks about your miserable mother and how she loved your sister more than you; you run up a huge tab; then you finally see the light. Suddenly, it's as clear as can be, and for the first time, you acknowledge your problem—whatever it is—out loud.

Once you experience this life-changing breakthrough, you're on the road to recovery. Once you say that there really is something that needs to be fixed, you can finally go about fixing it. It's not easy, but a thousand-mile journey begins with that single step, right?

So the time has come for the media elites to begin their own long journey to recovery. It's time for them to say, "We humbly admit that we have a problem and we need help." For years the elites have lived in that dark world of denial. Someone says "bias," and instead of listening, they lash out. "Bias? What damn bias are you talking about, you right-wing bastard?"

I am convinced, for example, that some people on the Left *literally* get angrier with anyone who brings up liberal bias in the news than they get at Osama bin Laden for September 11. The intellectual Left always had excuses for Osama. How did *we* provoke *him*? they demanded to know. Wasn't American imperialism somehow at the root of worldwide terrorism? With so few haves on the planet and so many have-nots, what did we expect the terrorists to do, send us roses? But when the subject gets around to bias, there is no ambiguity, no such thing as two sides of the argument. The media elites—with the help of their enablers at all those Manhattan and Georgetown A-list dinner parties—close ranks; they close minds; they get angry and edgy, the way smokers do when the pilot comes on the PA system to say there are only ten more hours before we touch down in Tokyo where you can light up.

Anger for a journalist is not a good thing. It not only clouds one's ability to think clearly and to reason, but it also betrays the most sacred tenet of the profession—that journalists are supposed to be neutral observers *about everything*. Shouldn't the media remain calm, cool, collected, and professional even when the subject gets around to the one important American institution they rarely cover—themselves?

And so the media elites must be brave and take that first single step. They can thank me later.

Here's what I propose:

The evening stars must sit down with other media elites who are also addicted to bias and begin the arduous process of getting over it.

Picture it: The senior anchor of the group slowly rises from his chair. He solemnly looks around the room. Understandably, he is nervous and so remains quiet for a few seconds. All eyes are on the anchorman. Then, in that familiar voice we have come to know so well after so many years, he says the words that can change his life and, with a little help from a higher power, can change the lives of all the other elite journalists in the room.

"Hello," he finally says. "My name is Dan, and I'm a liberal."

Step 2:
Lose the Enablers

t's not just a cliché. Confession really is good for the soul. So now it's time to move on.

Literally!

Alcoholics need to smash the bottle. Druggies need to flush their stuff down the toilet. And the media elites need to leave New York City. Simple as that!

There is no way they can stay in New York and also expect to stay on the wagon. There are too many enablers in New York, too many liberals whom the media elites are shamelessly trying to please. As Don Imus has said over and over again: They're not doing the news for Middle America; they're doing it for their liberal pals who eat at Elaine's on the Upper East Side.

And what's worse is that these enablers keep telling their media friends that they don't have a bias problem, that they're doing just fine, that only those right-wing nuts think there's a liberal bias problem in the news. And after a while, even smart, decent guys like Rather, Brokaw, and Jennings start to believe it.

Journalists are supposed to be worldly people, and New York is just too provincial a place for them. In New York, journalists and their enablers can spend a typical day (week, month, year, life) and say, not unreasonably, that "I didn't run into anyone all day today who disagrees with me." So after a while, they think abortion on demand is not a liberal position at all, but merely a moderate, reasonable one. After all, "I didn't run into anyone all day today who disagrees with me." And then they think only homophobes are against gay marriage and adoption, because "I didn't run into anyone today who disagrees with me." After a while, they lose their sense of perspective. Everything to the right of center is conservative; everything to the left is middle-of-the-road. And all the while the enablers keep telling them, "You're fine; we're all fine; it's those losers in the Red States who have the problem."

I have met a lot of people in the past year or so who don't care all that much for Dan and Tom and Peter. But I say, have mercy! They mean well. They don't *intentionally* slant the news. They're just surrounded by so many like-minded people that they've lost their way.

So, my media friends, start spreading the news . . . you're leaving today.

And because I want to make this transition as easy as possible (in *Bias* I casually suggested they pick up and move to Omaha, but they thought I was kidding; I wasn't), I have come up with a list of *five* very nice places in this great country of ours, any one of which would be a good choice for ABC, NBC, and CBS to locate their new worldwide news division headquarters, far from the enablers in New York City.

Here's my list:
1. Tupelo, Mississippi
2. Mitchell, South Dakota
3. Oklahoma City, Oklahoma
4. Indianapolis, Indiana
5. Laughlin, Nevada

I fear that right about now there are many very important journalists in New York who have just thrown down this book and started shaking uncontrollably. I fear they are heading for the roof of their Park Avenue co-ops, so depressed that they would rather jump than leave their New York cocoon for any of those places. The anxiety is understandable; it's never easy saying good-bye to the enablers. But leaving New York is not the end of anything; it's the beginning—the beginning of a professional and maybe even a spiritual awakening.

To help smooth the way, I did some research. I found out all the good things about the places on my list. I hope it makes the move easier for my many friends in the media.

Tupelo, Mississippi

"There's little doubt that Tupelo is a city on the move." That's what the chamber of commerce says, so it must be true. "Vibrant growth, business diversification, and a solid quality of life have boosted the city's identity as an ideal place to live and work."

Want specifics? No problem.

Besides the Elvis Presley Birthplace and Museum and Elvis Presley Lake and Campground, there's the Tupelo Ballet *and* there is also the Tupelo Symphony. Admit it, you elitist snobs: In a million years you wouldn't have thought Tupelo boasted *either* a ballet company *or* a symphony.

What about food? you say. There's enough in Tupelo to make the elites forget Manhattan in a Mississippi minute. Some Tupelo hot spots are Bar-B-Que by Jim, Heavenly Ham, and Harvey's Sweet Pepper Deli. And did I mention that there are three—*three!*—Pizza Huts in Tupelo?

Theater? How about Tupelo's Pied Piper Playhouse?

Real estate is another plus. It's cheap compared to Manhattan and Westchester County. And there are only 34,211 people in Tupelo, which means no traffic jams (for your limo driver to worry about).

And finally, according to the chamber of commerce, "In recent years, Tupelo has received a growing amount of attention as one of America's best small cities, having twice been named an All-American City by the National Civic League."

But if the Deep South doesn't feel right, read on.

Mitchell, South Dakota

Mitchell is home of the "World's Only Corn Palace," as the Convention Visitors Bureau proudly proclaims. The Corn Palace is Mitchell's "multi-use center," the outside walls of which are covered with beautiful, colorful mosaics. And what, you ask, are these mosaics made of? Tiles? Don't be silly. They're made of corn, hence the name Corn Palace. They're also made of grain, grasses, wild oats, brome grass, blue grass, rye, straw, and wheat.

Take that, Guggenheim!

There are loads of restaurants in town, including three featuring South Dakota Mexican cuisine: El Garibaldi, Taco Bell, and Taco John's.

There's also the Middle Border Museum and Oscar Howe Art Center, which displays American Indian beadwork and porcupine quillwork.

Mitchell's motto is "Mitchell More than Ever!" I'm not sure what that means, but I could not agree more.

Oklahoma City, Oklahoma

Maybe the elites can argue that Mitchell is way too small for a big network news operation, but they can't say the same thing about Oklahoma City, which is just like New York City only different.

There's lots of culture in OK City, just like New York. They've got Ballet Oklahoma, the Canterbury Choral Society, and the Oklahoma

Opry, which is more than New York can say since, to my knowledge, there is no Manhattan Opry.

They've also got the National Cowboy and Western Heritage Museum, and Stockyards City, which is the largest stocker/feeder cattle market in the world!

Restaurants? There are too many to count, including the Bombay Club ("an intimate lounge with a relaxing atmosphere for quiet cocktails, with martinis, shrimp and crab claws on ice"), the Cattlemen's Steakhouse (established in 1910), and Earl's Rib Palace. (Earl says, "If you can find better BBQ, then eat it!")

Indianapolis, Indiana

Indianapolis is commonly known as the "Crossroads of America."

They say only Washington, D.C., has more memorials. They've also got the Indianapolis Art Center, the Indianapolis Museum of Art, the Indy 500, the Colts, and the Pacers.

Indianapolis is also known as the city of "endless possibilities."

And perhaps most important, courtside seats for the Indiana Pacers are a lot cheaper than courtside seats for the New York Knicks.

Laughlin, Nevada

"Near perfect year-round weather, an abundance of water recreation, exciting gaming and a variety of dining offered by eleven resorts and casinos makes Laughlin, Nevada, a complete adult destination," says the C of C.

No fewer than five couples each day get married in Laughlin. The chamber's Web site informs us that "Marriage ceremonies can be performed by the Laughlin justice of the peace. . . . Blood tests are not required and there is no waiting period. . . .

"A male and female person, at least 18 years of age, not nearer of kin than second cousins of half blood, may be issued a marriage license."

You can get good cake at Aunt Bea's Burnt Bun and good flowers at the Amor Wedding Chapel & Florist.

Laughlin has quite a rich history, too. It was named after its founder, and the owner of the Riverside Resort, Don Laughlin—way back in 1968.

This is surely a joke, the media elites will say, and not a very funny one at that. But why? These are all real places, where real people live with their real families. Granted, this is a part of America the media elites rarely see, except maybe when they're on the campaign trail, but there are lots of decent people in these towns and cities, and surely one of them would do just fine for a network's worldwide news headquarters.

And besides, wouldn't it be a good thing for the elites to live among people who have a different worldview than they do? Wouldn't it be helpful if the elites sent their children to *public* school with the children of people who work at the Corn Palace or at the Oklahoma Opry or at Don Laughlin's casino? What is so wrong with that? Are they afraid their kids will get cooties if they sit next to "regular" kids? And while we're on the subject, why would it be any worse than what we have now: elite parents sending their elite children to school with the elite children of other elite parents?

What kind of diversity is that?

By living in Mitchell or Oklahoma City or Tupelo the elites will get a whole new perspective on America, which will make them better journalists. Too many newsmen and newswomen don't know the kinds of people who live in places like that. Sadly, too many newspeople don't know very many people who aren't pretty much just like themselves. Living in Tupelo or Oklahoma City or Mitchell will make the elites a little less elite, which is a very good step toward recovery.

Yes, I know I said New York was too provincial a place for journalists, so what about the places on my list? Aren't they provincial, too? I guess they are. But an infusion of liberal New York media blood would be just the diversity everyone needs. You'd have the natives challenging (and moderating) the views of the newcomers, and vice versa. When one of the media people says he's for stricter gun controls, he'll get the other side from one of his gun-loving neighbors. When one of the elites finds himself in a chat at the church social and says he's for "a woman's right to choose," his neighbor might say, "Well, I'm pro-life; let's talk about it." When one of the journalists says she's for gay adoptions, her new neighbor will say, "I'm not so sure about that one; tell me why you're for it."

If this wonderful diversity of opinion existed in newsrooms in New York, as it should, there might not be any need for the elites to leave town. But it doesn't—not to any important degree anyway.

Granted, the elites won't be able to get the early edition (or possibly *any* edition) of the *New York Times* and the *Washington Post* in a lot of the places on my list. But this is a plus, not a minus. They will learn to think more for themselves instead of letting the *Times* and *Post* tell them what to think and how to think it.

And ten minutes after the elites hit town, they'll never again say, "I didn't run into anyone all day today who disagrees with me."

How can this be bad?

Step 3:
A Newsroom That
Thinks Like America

S ome of the steps proposed here will be very difficult for big-time journalists. Asking some of these people to look deep inside themselves and take inventory, to be honest about their own prejudices and biases, is something totally alien to their experience. In fact, they will find it disorienting. After all, it presumes they're not doing the very best, fairest possible job already when all their friends constantly assure them that they are.

But this step will probably be the most confusing of all. Because the one area in which they are *absolutely certain* that they've done the right thing is in making the newsroom more diverse. All you have to do is look around at the "glorious mosaic" that is the modern newsroom: women, people "of color," gays. Sure, there's still more to be done—Jesse Jackson and GLAAD, among others, will keep the heat on, and God bless them for it. But only a fool or a Neanderthal can fail to applaud the incredible progress that already has been made.

And I do. In many ways, today's newsroom is indeed a better place than it was a generation or two ago.

But millions of us are eager to see another kind of diversity, one that is also important and meaningful. It's past time that we moved from a newsroom that simply *looks* like America to one that *thinks* more like America—a newsroom that better reflects America in its highly varied beliefs and values and passions. Such a newsroom will welcome not only female reporters who proudly identify themselves as "feminists," but also those who have serious problems with feminist dogma. And such a newsroom will not only welcome black liberals but also seek out black conservatives.

And today's newsrooms also are in desperate need of some *class* diversity. News executives need to make a serious effort to go after the kinds of blue-collar kids that currently you almost never find in most American newsrooms. As Tim Russert says, news executives have to recruit kids not just from places like the Columbia School of Journalism but also from less tony and more conservative schools, like ones run by priests. They also need to find some kids who are smart and have a ton of enthusiasm but who didn't go to college at all. They need to find young men and women who served in the military. All of these kinds of people also have important perspectives to bring to the job.

Today, every single network news reporter you see on ABC, NBC, or CBS is making over a hundred thousand dollars a year. A lot of them are making *way over* a hundred thousand. Everyone on *60 Minutes* makes multimillions of dollars a year. The network anchors each make about ten million a year, give or take a couple of million.

I don't argue with any of that. I'm a capitalist. The problem is that the overwhelming majority of those reporters have *always* known privilege. I'm not saying they descend from the Rockefellers, just that many of them come from "comfortable" families and have degrees from prestigious colleges and probably haven't spent a lot of time with people outside their small, privileged realm. I worked with lots of people whose parents were doctors and lawyers and diplomats, but I can't remember any whose father was a plumber. Of course, Dan Rather and Tom Brokaw have spent time with regular folks. They come from working-class Middle American backgrounds. And I suspect Dan and Tom know better than most how right I am about this.

News Flash: The median income for all American workers over fifteen years old is $31,500. Lots of reporters have expense accounts larger than that.

The bottom line is that too many journalists have no real idea what life is like for tens of millions of people in America. To choose a small but telling example: Journalists at the networks and at major newspapers were at first bemused, then stunned, by the outpouring of emotion when Dale Earnhardt was killed in 2001. Many had only the vaguest idea who Earnhardt was. They certainly had no idea of what NASCAR means in parts of this country. And part of the problem is, there was no one in the newsroom to explain it to them.

But here's the point: If they don't even know this elemental fact about so many of their fellow citizens, how in the world are they possibly going to accurately and fairly cover their political views and social values?

The short answer is, it won't be easy. As Martin Baron, the editor of the *Boston Globe*, told David Shaw of the *Los Angeles Times*, "We live in other neighborhoods and we don't visit theirs. And I fear that there is a subtle disdain for their lives, their lifestyles, their material and spiritual aspirations."

One of the clearest examples of that disdain—not so subtle in this case—is when Evan Thomas of *Newsweek* went on a TV news talk show and dismissed Paula Jones as "some sleazy woman with big hair coming out of the trailer parks"—a nasty remark, which would never have been tolerated (by his bosses and other presumably civil people) if the prejudice were about race instead of class.

And there was the *Washington Post's* contemptuous dismissal (since apologized for) of Christian conservatives as "largely poor, uneducated, and easy to command."

So, while this quest for true diversity might seem pretty reasonable to most of us, those at the top echelons of the news business will find instituting real diversity in the newsroom the hardest step of all to take—because it involves a commitment to fundamental change in the newsroom culture, the very way journalists do business.

But that's also why it's so essential.

In January 2003, a woman named Sarah Pettit, the senior editor for the *Newsweek* Arts and Entertainment section, died of non-Hodgkin's lymphoma at the tragically young age of thirty- six. Having emerged from the gay press (she co-founded *Out* magazine), by all accounts she was a talented and passionate journalist. As *Newsweek* editor Mark Whitaker said, "She always had lots to say—often it was quite contrarian. It always forced us to sharpen our thinking about what we were doing."

He's right: Challenging unexamined assumptions is a good thing. Always. But, as a journalist friend of mine wrote me in an E-mail, "You know, I read this woman's obit and the admiring comments of her editor and my first thought was that this guy would *never* have such praise for a conservative who made a lot of noise in-house— even if he somehow got the job in the first place." It's only conjecture, of course, but for what it's worth, that was my thought, too. If a passionate conservative journalist who had lots to say had died, if his views were quite contrarian, if he made a lot of noise and at least tried to sharpen his colleagues' thinking about what they were doing, would his liberal media elite colleagues have honored his contributions in the same way? Who can say for sure? But I don't think so.

The fact is, I'm for challenging assumptions anytime we get the chance. Which is why I'm for the kind of diversity I've been writing about. I mean, can you imagine how robust the discussions around the newsroom water cooler would be when the subject got around to gay marriage or the death penalty or the aforementioned abortion and affirmative action if, in addition to welcoming gays and liberal blacks, the mainstream media sought out evangelical Christians and black conservatives? Think the news would look the same with that kind of diversity? Think it might be a lot more interesting? More authentic? *Better?*

Step 4:
No More Balkans

No more newsroom lobbies. No more caucuses organized by gender, race, and ethnicity. No more balkanization.

I'm not saying that journalists shouldn't have opinions or, as noted above, that they shouldn't argue their values in-house. But that's not the same as organizing into groups and pushing political agendas.

Sure, we know all the arguments: We're a professional association. We've been underrepresented in newsrooms. We just want to get more minorities like us into journalism for the sake of diversity.

Sorry, no sale. As we've seen, sooner or later—usually sooner—the professional organizations become wholly owned subsidiaries of liberal activist groups. Gay journalistic groups don't just make sure gay journalists are treated with respect like everybody else; they start pushing, however subtly, to get the kind of coverage of gay-related issues that gay civil rights group want. The black journalist groups are not just trying to get more blacks into the newsroom; they have de facto positions on a whole array of issues regarding race in America.

Yes, these professional organizations might work in theory. But in practice they're not good for journalism. As Michael Janeway, the former editor in chief of the *Boston Globe,* has written, it was after these race and gender and ethnic caucuses started popping up in newsrooms that "The politics of the street came into the newsroom. Suddenly, coverage of controversial stories had to be negotiated within the newsroom [with these caucuses] as well as outside [with more traditional civil rights groups]."

For all the noble intentions, this was inevitable given the way human beings and the organizations they form operate. And that's why there is only one solution: no more associations in the newsroom. No more associations of black journalists. No more organizations of women journalists. No more Hispanic or Asian or Native American caucuses. No more gay journalist groups. Just journalists, doing the most thorough and objective job they can.

Of course, saying it is the easy part.

Here's the tough part: The very same news executives who have long been too weak to tell the caucuses to back off when they go too far—afraid that they'll be called antiblack or antigay or anti-whatever—are the very same ones who must now find the backbone to say, "Journalists need to be independent. Period. End of story."

Step 5:
Teach the
Children Well

Since Columbia University Graduate School of Journalism, the Taj Mahal of journalism schools, has recently been "reevaluating its mission," the whole way journalism is taught in this country basically came under review.

This is a good thing—journalism education is way overdue for some serious rethinking. Unfortunately, more than a few of the all-star journalists and academics Columbia put together to come up with solutions are themselves part of the problem. Little wonder that instead of the no-holds-barred debate the subject requires, the discussion safely focused on ways to tinker with the curriculum, and things like whether teachers should be working journalists, how much to emphasize print versus broadcast journalism, and whether there should be room for courses on political theory and law.

It's time to get real. Those things may be worth talking about, but they don't begin to get to the heart of the problems with journalism education.

There are a number of matters that cry out for attention. For instance, in an increasingly technological world, journalism schools would do us all a favor by greatly beefing up their instruction in how to cover subjects about which too many journalists know almost nothing yet regularly shoot off their mouths anyway. For instance, who can doubt that students, many of whom are reflexively antibusiness, would benefit greatly by extended exposure to real-life businesspeople and their problems?

But the one thing that journalism schools *must* start instilling in their students is a genuine openness to diverse points of view. For too long, many of these supposed bastions of free thought have been exactly the opposite: purveyors of standard-issue PC where free and open discussion of controversial matters is squelched.

To be sure, most journalism schools, including Columbia, claim to stress ethics. As they should, they encourage discussion of objectionable press practices like sticking microphones in the face of some woman whose husband has just been killed in a plane crash. And they urge young journalists to pay attention to those (usually poor or minority) who traditionally have had little access to the media. They also celebrate those in the profession who've shown unusual perseverance or guts—people like Bob Woodward and Carl Bernstein, the *Washington Post* reporters who, at an age little older than that of today's students, did the breakthrough reporting on the Watergate scandal, which brought down the presidency of Richard Nixon.

But like the rest of the media elite, they conspicuously fail to address the one issue of journalistic ethics—bias—that millions of Americans care most deeply about.

I was not among those asked to join the committee evaluating the J-School, which is absolutely fine with me; I don't claim any special expertise on the subject. But I do have a modest suggestion that might help students (and more than a few professors) start to think harder about what real journalism is and what it should be.

Traditionally, the litany of questions a good reporter seeks to answer in covering a story is *who, what, why, where, when,* and *how.* Imagine if, applying that standard, would-be journalists were forced to compare and contrast the way the press covered two bombshell stories of the post-Watergate years.

First, the sensational revelation, just days before Clarence Thomas was to be confirmed to the Supreme Court in 1991, that a former employee named Anita Hill, who did not want to come forward publicly, had accused him of sexual harassment. That story was broken by Nina Totenberg of National Public Radio, who had been leaked the information by an aide to a liberal senator eager to undermine Thomas. When Totenberg's story hit the air, it provoked a maelstrom and led to Anita Hill's appearance at the Senate hearings on the nomination, and the memorable nationally televised melodrama that followed. Though in the end Thomas was confirmed, his reputation was permanently besmirched. For her part, Nina Totenberg became an instant superstar and received innumerable awards from journalistic organizations and women's groups.

The other story involves Juanita Broaddrick, an Arkansas businesswoman and former supporter of Bill Clinton, who at the height of the Clinton sex scandals gave an interview to NBC's Lisa Myers in which she charged that in 1978, when he was running for governor, then–Arkansas Attorney General Clinton raped her in a Little Rock hotel room. Broaddrick did not come forward with the allegation at the time, which is why there was no investigation by the local district attorney. And by the time she did tell her story to reporters, the statute of limitations had run out. In 1999, through his lawyer, President Clinton denied he had assaulted Broaddrick. But back in 1978, at the time of the alleged attack, she did talk to a number of friends about it and subsequently to a rape counselor who interviewed her. In addition to that, NBC's own investigation could unearth no discrepancies in her account. Nonetheless, the network held it—until the *Wall Street Journal* beat NBC on its own story. Dorothy Rabinowitz of the *Journal* interviewed Broaddrick, and only after the interview appeared in the paper did NBC News decide to run a truncated version of the story it once had exclusively. It got virtually no other mainstream coverage. Asked about the Broaddrick story in

2001 by Bill O'Reilly, Dan Rather said, "To be perfectly honest, I don't remember all the details of Juanita Broaddrick, but I will say that—and you can castigate me if you like—when the charge has something to do with somebody's private sex life, I would prefer not to run any of it."

Private sex life? That's an interesting way for anyone, let alone a journalist of Dan Rather's stature, to look at it. Juanita Broaddrick was not talking about a sexual frolic with her boyfriend. She was saying she was raped! And the alleged rapist was the attorney general of the state of Arkansas. By what twisted reasoning does that fall into the category of a woman's *"private sex life"*?

But Rather's strange take on the story aside, while the Juanita Broaddrick and Anita Hill episodes represented complicated cases, it would seem, at the very least, that a comparison between the two would lead to a lively, provocative dialogue and raise for students a number of vital and compelling questions:

WHO decides when a story is newsworthy and when it should be held?

WHAT are the factors that go into such a decision, and is partisanship ever one of them?

WHY is it reasonable to give major coverage of an unproven yet arguably credible allegation of dirty-joke-telling by a Supreme Court nominee yet bury an unproven yet arguably credible allegation of rape by a high-ranking state official who goes on to become president of the United States?

WHERE was the debate within the media itself about what many viewers and readers, rightly or wrongly, see as a double standard?

WHEN can we expect things to change?

HOW can we, as students about to enter the business, insure that things are fairer in the future?

Step 6:
Stop Following
the Leader

Remember, when we were kids, we played follow-the-leader? We were maybe five years old, and even then we probably thought it was a stupid game. So it's pretty sad that journalists all over the country are still playing it, traipsing around doing whatever the leader says. They need to stop.

As I've already discussed in some detail, it doesn't help that the leader they so slavishly follow is the *New York Times*. For journalists, the *Times* is not just a newspaper, it's a security blanket. It goes way beyond the fact that the *Times*, which hardly even tries anymore to disguise its agenda, is where journalists (especially in television) get so many of their story ideas. Maybe even worse, as anyone who has been on the inside knows, the *Times* tells journalists how to *think* about highly controversial issues like race or feminism, and this has a powerful effect on how they cover stories about, for instance, affirmative action or abortion.

It's fascinating, really, how narrow and provincial is the world that supposedly sophisticated journalists have chosen to live in, how little they expose themselves to thoughts and opinions that challenge their liberal assumptions.

Solutions? They're simple enough for any five-year-old to follow. First, journalists need to stop sucking their thumbs and drop their blankets. It's time for them to broaden their horizons and open themselves up to all sorts of fun, new ideas.

When liberals discuss one of their favorite subjects, diversity, they often talk about "fear of the other." This supposedly is a condition that afflicts only conservatives, who, I guess, are supposed to be afraid of anything different. The argument goes that we all have fears about the unknown, but once we're exposed to those fears, things start to improve—we see that "the other" isn't so bad after all and we become wiser, more compassionate, *better* people.

That makes sense to me. Which is exactly why journalists need to open themselves up to "other" ideas, ideas that for too long they simply dismissed as bizarre and scary.

Journalists, absolutely, should keep reading the *New York Times*, as well as the *Washington Post, TIME, Newsweek,* and whatever other mainstream publications offer them a familiar and comforting view of the world. I have no problem with that. But reporters and editors—especially if they're covering controversial social issues—should also regularly read the *Wall Street Journal* and subscribe to the *Weekly Standard.* And if they want even greater depth and analysis, they ought to read *Commentary* or *City Journal.* They should also check out Andrew Sullivan and Mickey Kaus on the Web, as well as columnists like John Leo, Charles Krauthammer, and Michelle Malkin.

And they shouldn't stop there. Journalists should read magazines from the hard Left, too, like *The Nation* and *Mother Jones.* There's tremendous diversity of opinion out there, and journalists need to take advantage of it and become familiar with it.

And while they're at it, it wouldn't hurt if every now and then they check out Rush Limbaugh. He's only the most popular commentator in America.

I can already hear some journalists griping that conservatives are no better than the kind of narrow liberals I'm describing, that conservatives aren't exactly open to alternative ideas, either. I agree! The difference, though, is that conservatives don't run the most prestigious newsrooms in America. Liberals do.

So I'll worry about conservative close-mindedness when they take over the newsroom—or when hell freezes over, whichever comes first.

Step 7:
Don't Stack the Deck

Too many journalists come to the table not only with too many assumptions but also with too many tricks. They're like a bunch of Houdinis trying to sneak one by the unsuspecting audience. It's so unconscious, they do it pretty much as a matter of habit. They already have determined, reflexively, who will wear the white hats and who will wear the black hats before they even begin reporting a story; but they obviously can't admit that, so they need to find a way to flimflam the audience. How do they do it? They dig way down into their bag of tricks and come up with the old "warning label" illusion. Then they casually stick it on the bad guy in the story and hope nobody notices what they did or how they did it.

I have written about this particular little trick before, one that is a glaring example of bias in the news. But to understand its importance, first you must understand the sleight of hand involved.

Reporters, you see, label conservatives in their stories far more often than they label liberals, and nowhere is this more obvious than on television. Consider this: Of all the "conservative" or "liberal" ideological labels used on all the network evening newscasts for the five years between 1997 and 2001, according to the Media Research Center, conservatives got 79 percent of the labels on ABC, 80 percent on NBC, and 82 percent on the *CBS Evening News* with Dan Rather.

Why is that? Why should we care? And what, exactly, do labels have to do with bias, especially if they're accurate?

The simple fact is, labels are not neutral. They mark an individual as a true believer pushing an agenda rather than as fair-minded and neutral, and because of that they impact tremendously on the key issue of credibility. For example, if a journalist goes on the air and says, "Joe Jones, a conservative professor at Johnson University . . . ," your antennae go up; the word "conservative" sends off signals. *Listen carefully,* you've just been told whether you realize it or not, *Professor Jones is not neutral; he has an ax to grind, and his views most definitely are not middle-of-the-road.* So far so good, especially since, in this little example, it's true. The same story about the same professor, *without* the conservative label, gets you listening in an entirely different way. No antennae go up. You assume you're about to hear from a nonpartisan expert with no agenda. So when labels are used, and how often they're used, and in what context they're used, matters a lot—even (make that especially) when the people in the audience don't quite know how they've just been manipulated.

And the way labels are used by mainstream journalists, the term "conservative" is a lot like a warning label on a pack of cigarettes—not so coincidentally because that's what many journalists actually believe, that conservative views may be hazardous to your health.

So when a reporter interviews someone whose conservative opinions the reporter finds alien and backward—the black hat of the piece—he will routinely be identified as a "conservative."

Of course, the case can be made that there's nothing wrong with labeling. In fact, I would have no trouble making that case myself. Labeling, after all, is a good shorthand way to tell the audience where someone fits in, ideologically, in the big scheme of things. I could—and would gladly—make that case . . . *if only reporters were consis-*

tent. After all, the term "liberal" also carries its fair share of baggage. But remember, when reporters use an ideological label, about eight out of ten times they're using it to identify conservatives, not liberals. So, guess how many network journalists labeled Al Gore as a liberal during the *entire* 2000 campaign. Try *none!* In fact, during the entire presidential race, only one network reporter, NBC's Lisa Myers, ever used the word "liberal" to identify liberal Democratic candidate Bill Bradley.

You see, conservatives need to be labeled so you know they're not neutral. Liberals need no labels because—at least according to a lot of journalists—they *are* neutral. I know it sounds silly, but this is how they think.

But then, conservatives are *lucky* if they get off just with the "conservative" label. When Phil Jones, once of CBS News, covered Senator Jesse Helms, Helms got the "ultraconservative" label. (Not that Jones was alone: According to Nexis, "ultraconservative" was attached to Helms's name in 506 stories!) When Eric Engberg, also formerly of CBS News, reported on House Republican Tom DeLay, he identified DeLay as a "conservative hard-baller." Dan Rather referred to Dick Cheney's "hard-line conservative congressional voting record."

I wouldn't be bothered by any of that—*not in the least.* All I ask is that reporters be fair. So I ask: When was the last time you heard a network television reporter identify Ted Kennedy or Jesse Jackson as a "liberal hard-baller"? When have they ever called Nancy Pelosi "a hard-line liberal"? When was the head of NOW ever described as an "ultraliberal"?

You see how the sleight of hand works? You see how they say conservatives are the bad guys without ever quite using those words?

And this business of selective labeling doesn't apply just to individuals. The Concerned Women for America was called "conservative" in 41 percent of the stories broadcast about that group. The National Organization for Women got the liberal label just 2 percent of the time. Translation: Conservative women need to be identified because they are, well, conservative, and therefore (according to the mainstream media) out of the mainstream. But liberal women are *presumed* to be middle-of-the-road; after all, they are, in many ways, just like the women in the newsroom who are reporting about them, and therefore they are the very essence of mainstream and, therefore, need no warning labels.

This obsession with identifying conservatives reminds me of the bad old days when journalists identified a criminal by race only if he was black. Even though not all reporters and editors were bigots, at some level they saw blacks as different, as alien, as more dangerous, as out of the mainstream and, of course, as inferior. I think that's why journalists identify conservatives so often today: because they see them as different, as alien, as out of the mainstream, maybe even as dangerous and inferior.

So here's a helpful, easy-to-follow hint that will help journalists be evenhanded: *Always* identify the following groups and individuals as "liberal": NOW, the NAACP, People for the American Way, the ACLU, Ted Kennedy, Jesse Jackson, Hillary Clinton, Tom Daschle, and Nancy Pelosi.

I would offer up a similar list for conservative individuals and groups but the media have never had a problem identifying them.

Perhaps the best example of how reporters play tricks with labels is the case of one Larry Klayman, the head of a conservative group called Judicial Watch. During the Clinton years, Klayman made a name for himself—and incurred the wrath of liberals everywhere— by filing innumerable lawsuits aimed at forcing Clinton administration officials to release documents linked to possible illegality. In news reports, he was always identified as conservative, which, as I say, is accurate enough. But the not-so-subtle point was to dismiss Klayman as just another right-wing Clinton-hater. As a story in *TIME* magazine began, "Even in the fang-baring world of Bill Clinton's most dedicated pursuers, Larry Klayman is in a class by himself."

But then—surprise—in the summer of 2002, Judicial Watch filed still another lawsuit. But this time it wasn't against Bill Clinton or any other Democrat. This time it was against the Halliburton Energy

Corporation and its former CEO, a fellow by the name of Dick Cheney. The charge: allegedly cheating investors by overstating the company's income. Suddenly, magically, Klayman's black hat disappeared. Now that the elites approved of what he had done, Judicial Watch was "a public interest group" or a "legal advocacy group" or a "watchdog group." Suddenly, the characterization of Judicial Watch and Larry Klayman as "conservative" also disappeared—presumably not to be resurrected until the next time Judicial Watch went after a prominent Democrat.

Houdini would be proud.

This lopsided labeling should embarrass journalists. And of all the bias-related problems, this one should be by far the easiest to fix. All it takes is a little fairness: If reporters are going to label conservatives (Fine!), then also label liberals. What could be easier? So why hasn't it been done? The answer to that, I'm afraid, is not an easy one for all those journalists who routinely claim that they have no biases and that they really do care about fairness.

Step 8:
Tell the *Whole* Story

I t's not just what reporters put into their stories that matters. It's also what they leave out—or *choose* not to include.

I don't use that word *choose* by accident. Every news story involves a series of choices: whom to interview; what interviews to use; which ones to discard; where to put the quotes in the story, near the top or the bottom. All of this goes to the impression the story leaves—*and is intended to leave*—on the reader or viewer.

Quite simply, reporters do not come to stories that involve the big issues of the day as blank slates. They have opinions on everything. They more or less know how they feel about every controversial story before they even start.

That's why good reporters make a point of monitoring themselves closely. "Every time you do a story," Tim Russert advises, "take out a piece of paper and draw a line down the middle and put on each side the best arguments for or against that particular issue. Then make sure you describe and define those issues, those arguments, in a fair and objective way. You'll be amazed by how much it forces you to check the instinct to drift into potential bias."

Even then bias can be easy to drift into, because, by its very nature, it is ingrained and hard to see.

And in no way is it more insidious than in influencing what reporters *fail* to include in their stories. When it comes to the big, important, culturally divisive subjects of gender, sexuality, and race, the mainstream media have a long record of ignoring (or at least underplaying) information that is troublesome to the larger liberal agenda. How else to explain the insistence on covering AIDS, in the face of so much evidence to the contrary, as a disease on the verge of ravaging Main Street heterosexual America? How else to explain the media's longtime failure to challenge the feminist claim that late-term (or partial-birth) abortion was rare and almost always performed to save the life of the mother? How do we explain the media's reluctance, even now, to examine such issues as teenage pregnancy and fatherlessness as major reasons for black inner-city poverty?

Then, too, there are times when telling the whole truth makes it harder to paint certain individuals as good guys or bad guys. Take the coverage of the most damning charge leveled by liberal opponents against Judge Charles Pickering, the white conservative Mississippian nominated by George Bush to the United States Court of Appeals in 2002: that he was soft on racial bigots.

As CNN'S Jonathan Karl reported, in a 1994 case "Judge Pickering was seen as trying to fight for a more lenient sentence for the person who was convicted of a cross-burning . . ."

That was it—no details, no further elaboration, just that Judge Pickering "was seen" as fighting on behalf of a convicted cross-burner. I was following the story—the case involved a cross-burning in the front yard of a mixed-race couple—and like most Americans hearing such reports, I was pretty taken aback. What business did someone who sympathized with a cross-burning bigot have sitting on the second highest court in the land? And—the unspoken question—what kind of president would even consider making such a nomination?

Millions of other viewers undoubtedly had the same reaction.

After all, every element—Mississippi, a cross-burning, a white judge going easy on a racist defendant—played into all the preconceived notions. On the face of it, this was something out of the nation's darkest past.

Democrats out to quash the nomination and damage President Bush couldn't have come up with more potent ammunition. As Illinois Democratic Senator Richard Durbin put it, Pickering's decisions on the bench "have raised some serious questions. One in particular involved the cross-burning case . . . which frankly raises many ethical questions."

And the mainstream press, parroting Democratic talking points, duly raised those questions again and again. Typical of the coverage was Carole Simpson's report on ABC that "his critics say as recently as 1994, Judge Pickering engaged in extraordinary lobbying to try to get a reduced sentence for a young man who participated in a cross-burning. The White House says the judge is being unfairly maligned."

According to the rules of network news coverage, that last sentence represents the obligatory nod to "balance" and, theoretically at least, gets the journalist off the hook.

But of course, it provides no explanation at all for Pickering's action. In fact, the White House itself might well be seen as insensitive (if not racist) for continuing to defend such a person!

I personally have no brief on the merits of the Pickering nomination. But I do have one for fair and honest reporting. Context matters. It matters a lot. And I don't know about you, but I didn't catch very much context on the evening newscasts on Pickering and the cross-burning story. What I did catch were all the familiar assumptions about race and about bigoted white men in the South, and a story that meshed with the liberal newsroom template on such matters.

But it turns out that there is a context, a very important one—one I didn't hear until President Bush renominated Pickering in 2003 (the first nomination was killed by the then Democratic-controlled Senate Judiciary Committee). One night I turned on *Special Report* with Brit Hume, on Fox, and there was Byron York, the White House correspondent for the conservative *National Review,* providing the details of the case the mainstream press had systematically ignored.

Three men burned the cross on the couple's lawn in January 1994. One of the three was a young man with an abnormally low IQ; prosecutors reduced the charges against him, and he got no jail time. The second was a seventeen-year-old who was the ringleader of the gang, a vile bigot who earlier had fired a shot into the home of the couple. The last was twenty-year-old Daniel Swan, who had no prior criminal record.

The seventeen-year-old, York was saying, made a deal with the Clinton Justice Department (cross-burning falls under the federal hate crime laws) and got no jail time, despite the fact that he clearly was motivated by racial hatred, had tried to shoot the couple in their own home, and was in charge that night. What troubled Judge Pickering is that the same Clinton Justice Department was demanding that Swan, the twenty-year-old, get a mandatory sentence of seven and a half years, despite the fact that he was not the ringleader and had nowhere near the racial animus of the seventeen-year-old and had never shot at anyone inside the house.

There was no question that Swan would go to prison. Pickering wasn't against that. Quite the contrary; he felt strongly that Swan should be locked up. But was seven and a half years fair, given that the ringleader got no prison time at all?

At one point Judge Pickering explained his thinking in a letter to Senator Orrin Hatch, the ranking Republican on the Judiciary Committee. "I have consistently sought to keep from imposing unduly harsh penalties on young people whom I did not feel were hardened criminals." Swan, remember, was a first-time offender. Pickering went on to explain that while on the bench he had reduced the sentences of other first-time offenders from the mandatory minimums required by law for black defendants, too.

Judge Pickering let his concerns be known to the Justice Department in Washington, and just before final sentencing, officials there backed off on their recommendation that Swan be sent away for

seven and a half years. Pickering then sentenced Swan to twenty-
seven months in prison and at the sentencing hearing delivered a
stern lecture. "You're going to the penitentiary because of what you
did," he told Swan. "We've got to learn to live, races among each
other. And the type of conduct that you exhibited cannot and will not
be tolerated. . . . You did that which does hinder good race relations
and was a despicable act. . . . I would suggest you do some reading on
race relations and maintaining good race relations and how that can
be done."

I don't like it, but I understand the hardball actions of President
Bush's Democratic opponents and those in the civil rights community
who oppose Pickering's conservative views. That, unfortunately, is the
nature of rough-and-tumble politics. But I do fault the press, big-
time, for simply echoing the liberal view and presenting it as objective news.

I should note that there were exceptions to the sorry rule. When
George Stephanopoulos, like Russert a former Democratic operative,
questioned Tom Daschle in January 2003 on ABC's *This Week* about
the charge that Pickering has been insensitive on civil rights, he noted
that "defenders of Judge Pickering say that the Democrats are just
race-baiting. They point out, for example, the Democrats have made
a big deal about the fact that Judge Pickering reduced the sentence
of someone convicted of cross-burning, but he also reduced sentences in cases for African-Americans, so it has nothing to do with
race."

But far more typically, there was Democratic Senator Joseph
Biden's appearance on the CBS News program *Face the Nation,*
wherein Biden used the links between Pickering and fellow Missis-
sipian Trent Lott to hammer the Republicans on civil rights in general. "The whole context of how the president responds, not only to
Lott but to who he sends up to us—I mean, you know, Pickering was
mildly insensitive on cross-burning when people put a cross in some
black family's lawn. You know, you can't hold Lott accountable for this

insensitivity and not the policies as well. But—but that's a Republican deal here . . ."

While Biden went on, sitting there listening to it, surely by then well aware of the facts of the case, were Bob Schieffer and his CBS colleague Gloria Borger, neither of whom challenged a word of it—this from journalists who pride themselves on their sense of fair play as well as their skepticism and toughness.

Then on January 18, 2003, long after he, also, certainly knew the facts, Frank Rich, the *New York Times* columnist, wrote about "Charles Pickering's strenuous effort to reduce the sentence of a convicted cross-burning hoodlum." Four days later, Maureen Dowd, in her *New York Times* column, joined the party, referring to Pickering as "a federal judge with a soft spot for cross-burners."

Ms. Dowd, who has a soft spot for cheap shots, could not have written anything that vicious and that dumb by accident. Like Rich, she was simply being mean-spirited, because columnists can write just about anything and get away with it, especially at the ideologically driven *New York Times.* Frank Rich and Maureen Dowd misled their readers, and they did it only because it fit their biases to do it. Commentators or not, there's a name for that: bad journalism.

The bottom line is that it is the obligation of any journalist worthy of the name to play fair—to report and, in the case of columnists, to comment, on every story as honestly as possible. Liberals rightly condemn Joseph McCarthy and the politics of half-truth and innuendo. It's time for them to learn that the ethical rules apply to them, also.

Step 9:
Don't Confuse *Journalist* with *Activist*

Years ago, when Abe Rosenthal was ringmaster at the *New York Times*—his official title was executive editor—legend has it that he summed up one of journalism's golden rules with characteristic brevity and style. "I don't care if my reporters fuck the elephants," Abe reportedly said, "but if they do, they're not covering the circus."

In other words—in case we actually need *other* words—if a reporter takes sides in a controversial issue, the reporter cannot be allowed to cover news regarding that issue.

Who could argue with that, right? It's so obvious I hesitate even to bring it up. Except for the fact that some very important people in the world of big-time journalism seem not to get it.

Case in point: On December 8, 2002, Bob Simon, the CBS News correspondent, reported a story on *60 Minutes* about how the Bush administration is using an arsenal of advertising techniques to sell Americans on war with Iraq. "Simon reminds viewers," the CBS News Web site tells us, "that a horrible story spread widely by the first Bush administration prior to the Gulf War about Kuwaiti babies pulled from incubators by invading Iraqis turned out not to be true. The current Bush administration may be also misinforming the public in its efforts to justify a possible second war with Saddam Hussein."

Anytime a reporter suggests that the president of the United States may be "misinforming" the American people on the question of going to war, it's important news. And in this case, the overall tone of the story was that President Bush wants to go to war with Iraq so badly that he and his people will tell all kinds of stories just to get the American people to support the war effort.

I have no problem whatsoever with a tough report like that, assuming it's well sourced. And given how many questions have been raised about President Bush's motives for taking America to war in Iraq, I'm glad Bob Simon did the story. But I do have a problem with Bob, who I know is an intelligent and courageous reporter, covering the circus after getting intimate with the elephants.

You see, Bob Simon left one not-so-little detail out of his story. Bob failed to mention that he had already taken a very *public* position on whether America should go to war with Iraq. Two months before his *60 Minutes* piece aired, on October 3, 2002, right smack in the middle of a national debate on the wisdom of attacking Iraq, Bob Simon told *USA Today* that "I don't think that going to war with him [Saddam Hussein] is the right thing to do right now."

And Bob added that "Saudi Arabia should be at the top of the list, not Iraq."

For what it's worth, I think Bob Simon made some very good points. Still, going public the way he did is very unusual. Reporters have no business giving public opinions about whether going to war "is the right thing to do"—and they sure as hell have no business giving their opinions *just eight days before the United States House of Representatives and the Senate are going to vote on that very question.* But if, for whatever lapse of judgment, they do, they certainly have no business then doing stories about how the Bush Administration "may be . . . misinforming the public in its efforts to justify . . . war with Saddam Hussein."

And it's not just because *I* say so. CBS News says so! Its own book on standards says the following:

> A CBS News employee who takes a public position on a controversial issue outside of work runs the risk of compromising his or her reputation for impartiality and fairness, and, in so doing, may damage the overall credibility of CBS News.
>
> Accordingly, employees should generally:
>
> • Avoid identifying themselves with any side of a controversial issue.

It's good to have standards, but it's even better to take them seriously, especially when the issue involves war and peace.

By the way, almost everyone in both Houses of Congress who voted against the War Resolution—who, like my former colleague Bob Simon, thought going to war was not the right thing to do—were Democrats, many of them liberal Democrats. Is that what Bob Simon is, too? I don't know and I don't care, though I'll bet a lot of Americans who read what Bob said have their suspicions. And now do you see why it's so important to stay away from the circus if you have a relationship with the elephants?

And then there was the time that Katie Couric ran off and joined the circus.

If there's a more controversial subject on the American agenda than abortion, I don't know what it is. So, should supposedly objective reporters be allowed to march in pro-choice or, for that matter, pro-life rallies?

Of course not!

And if they violate their own news organizations' standards and demonstrate anyway, should they then be allowed to do interviews on the subject?

Another dumb question, right?

Then how do we account for this exchange (taken down verbatim by those right-wingers at the Media Research Center) between Katie Couric and Whoopi Goldberg, who had just written a book, on the *Today* show a few years back?

KATIE COURIC: Let's talk about the chapter you write called "Choice"—it's a very, very personal chapter about getting a call from your fourteen-year-old daughter telling you, "Hey, Mom, guess what?"

WHOOPI GOLDBERG: "I'm pregnant." Yes, shock, but relief that she told me.

COURIC: Then she gave you a double whammy and said, "Mom . . ."

GOLDBERG: ". . . I'm gonna keep this baby."

COURIC: So you write about choice meaning what?

GOLDBERG: Well, because, you know, when you get out there and you march, because we've marched together . . .

COURIC: [*feigning ignorance*] No-o-o. I'm not allowed to do that. [*She giggles.*]

GOLDBERG: [*playing along, staring upward*] Oh, no, that's right. We have not marched together. It was somebody that looked like you.

"At this point," the Media Research Center reports, "Couric is staring at Goldberg, who is laughing as are others off-camera as Goldberg acknowledges her error in making a public mention."

GOLDBERG: Uh, I forgot where I am sometimes.

There was no uproar over this. But suppose some journalist marched in a pro-life parade and then had the gall to do interviews on the subject. Think everyone would be so nonchalant then? Think NBC News would be silent on the subject?

For that matter, think Katie Couric herself would be?

Step 10:
Make Bias a
Punishable Offense

There need to be sanctions. There needs to be some way to impose what the Jamaicans charmingly call "heavy manners" on those journalists who blatantly abuse their power.

After all, punishments are meted out to journalists all the time, for all kinds of transgressions.

There was punishment for Bob Greene, the *Chicago Tribune* columnist, after it came to light he had once interviewed a seventeen-year-old Catholic high school girl and soon thereafter was in a hotel room with her having sex. Never mind that the girl was "of age." Never mind that the liaison happened fourteen years earlier and that she complained about it only when she was about thirty; never mind that Bob had been at the paper for twenty-five years. The *Tribune* forced him out. Since the girl wasn't an intern, Bob couldn't even use the "It was a private matter" defense.

There was punishment, too, for Janet Cooke of the *Washington Post,* who won a Pulitzer for a story entitled "Jimmy's World" about an eight-year-old heroin addict. When it came out that there was no Jimmy, she was gone from the *Post.*

And then there was the case of Stephen Glass of the *New Republic* magazine, a reporter who made Janet Cooke look like Walter Cronkite. The *New Republic* gave Glass his walking papers after determining that he had fabricated six articles in their entirety . . . and parts of twenty-one more.

And, of course, there's Jayson Blair, formerly of the *New York Times*.

Why, then, is there no punishment for the most serious offense of all: abusing your power as a journalist to go after an ideological foe or to further a social agenda? Shouldn't *something* be done to journalists who, for whatever reason, don't play fair when the subject is one they care deeply about?

Ideally, such punishment should be imposed in-house. Some newspapers already have ombudsmen, journalists who supposedly, without fear of repercussions, write about their own papers' coverage of certain controversial stories. This is a great idea. The only problem is that a lot of ombudsmen are even further to the left than the people they're supposed to be keeping an eye on. They're the sort of people more likely to get upset when someone says "ombudsman" instead of "ombudsperson" than when liberal bias smacks them in the face.

So, I say it's time to go way beyond the concept of ombudsmen and ombudswomen. It's time to impose heavy manners on the most brazen of the journalistic transgressors. I say some of these people have felt invincible and untouchable for too long.

John McWhorter, the scholar and author, came up with an actual humiliation plan in an op-ed he wrote for the *Wall Street Journal*. McWhorter was upset by the way the *Washington Post* handled two profiles of leading black Americans that had appeared in the paper only days apart—one about Clarence Thomas, the black conservative justice of the Supreme Court, and the other about Cornel West, the liberal black scholar and social activist.

Guess which was a valentine and which he saw as a journalistic hit job.

The piece about Justice Thomas quoted just about everyone in North America who had something bad to say about him, naturally including many who consider him a sellout and an Uncle Tom. The piece about the liberal Cornel West, on the other hand, was a kiss on the cheek, lauding him as a strong and independent black man who doesn't take crap from anyone.

"A fourth-grader could see this is not balanced coverage," McWhorter wrote. "It is an alternation between character assassination (of Thomas) and puff-piece drivel (about West)."

So McWhorter came up with a really good idea. "I wish a foundation would dedicate a grant to writing profiles of profile writers themselves," he said in his op-ed, "especially of anyone who has written about race. For some . . . it would be a hit job, reveling in minor inconsistencies in their writing and low moments in their lives, mentioning a few strengths for 'balance' but matching each with an acrid quote from an ex-lover or childhood friend. Maybe, just maybe, such writers would then understand the difference between 'balance' and fun-house-mirror distortion—and think twice before contributing to the swill that passes for coverage of some of our most important black thinkers today."

It's a lovely thought, isn't it, letting these people occasionally know exactly how it feels to be savaged in print? If all journalists actually faced a realistic prospect of being exposed *themselves*—of seeing their biases and petty natures revealed before the world, of knowing beforehand there are those out there ready to call them to account—I'm betting most would actually be more careful before taking irresponsible potshots at someone the next time.

This doesn't mean that journalists should go soft, should stop asking tough questions, or should stop being skeptical. This is about reporters who cross the line. It's about using the incredible power journalists have to consciously or subconsciously pursue an agenda, to go easy on people and causes they like and hard on people and causes they don't like.

I like the McWhorter idea a lot. It just needs a little tinkering.

Rather than get a foundation to offer grants, how about a simple Web site dedicated to peace, justice, the American way—and fair journalism? Let's call it www.newsjerks.com.

Newsjerks would not engage in partisan hit jobs—that would defeat the whole purpose—but it sure as hell would expose anyone who did. In fact, it would expose just about anything juicy, big or small, about any important journalist who abuses power, just as long as the information is accurate. Let's not think of this as revenge but as therapy. As T. S. Eliot once said, "You will find that you survive humiliation, and that [it's] an experience of incalculable value."

So, where to begin?

Do you think that any reporter who has gone after some politician for alleged corruption ever cheated on his own expense report?

Do you suppose there might be a couple of journalists out there guilty of the sort of hypocrisy they find so shameful in others—say, editorializing against vouchers for poor kids while sending their own children to pricey private schools?

For that matter, is it possible that Bob Greene isn't the only journalist to have sex with someone he's written about?

See how it works? Read all about it at newsjerks.com.

Pretty tough stuff, you say. And your point would be . . . ?

Step 11:
Expand Your Rolodex

I t is not necessarily bias that makes so many reporters tilt stories in a liberal direction. For some it's just force of habit. When there's a story related to a "women's" issue, they think NOW; for one involving race, it's the NAACP.

Either way, denying conservatives full and fair coverage is bad journalism. It is also suicidal. It alienates readers and viewers in droves and exacts a cost in credibility that can never be measured.

And at this point there is absolutely no excuse for it. There are conservative groups out there working on a broad range of issues eager to contribute to the national debate. Just to make it easy on reporters, I offer the following starter list, broken down into broad categories. While I personally do not agree philosophically with the agenda of every group on the list, each represents the views of a great many Americans and deserves to be heard by a broad audience.

General Interest Conservative Organizations, Think Tanks

Acton Institute for the Study of Religion & Liberty
161 Ottawa NW Ste 301
Grand Rapids MI 49503
616-454-3080
fax: 616-454-9454
E-mail: info@acton.org
Focus: Promoting a "free and virtuous society characterized by individual liberty and sustained by religious principles."

American Enterprise Institute for Public Policy Research
1150 17th St NW
Washington DC 20036
202-862-5800
fax: 202-862-7177
Focus: Limited government, private enterprise, and a strong foreign policy and national defense.

Americans for Tax Reform
1920 L St NW Ste 200
Washington DC 20036
202-785-0266
www.atr.org
Focus: Lower and fairer taxes; simplification of the tax code.

Cato Institute
1000 Massachusetts Ave NW
Washington DC 20001-5403
202-842-0200
fax: 202-842-3490
Focus: Libertarian think tank; individual liberty and limited government.

Center for the Study of Popular Culture
4401 Wilshire Blvd
Los Angeles CA 90010
800-752-6562
Focus: Leftist influence in American culture; biases at colleges and universities; immigration. Founded and headed by ex-leftist radical David Horowitz.

Claremont Institute
250 W 1st St Ste 330
Claremont CA 91711
909-621-6825
fax: 909-626-8724
E-mail: info@claremont.org
Focus: Limited and accountable government that respects private property, promotes stable family life, and maintains a strong defense.

Competitive Enterprise Institute
1001 Connecticut Ave NW Ste 1250
Washington DC 20036
202-331-1010
fax: 202-331-0640
E-mail: info@cei.org
Focus: Free enterprise and limited government; regulatory and environmental issues.

Discovery Institute
1511 Third Ave Ste 808
Seattle WA 98101
206-292-0401
fax: 206-682-5320
Focus: Promoting the free market and individual liberty; the environment and the economy.

Empower America
1701 Pennsylvania Ave Ste 900
Washington DC 20006
202-452-8200
Focus: Individual responsibility, economic freedom, and education.
Cofounded by Bill Bennett.

Ethics and Public Policy Center
1915 15th St NW Ste 900
Washington DC 20005
202-682-1200
fax: 202-408-0632
E-mail: ethics@eppc.org
Focus: To "clarify and reinforce the bond between the Judeo-Christian moral tradition and the public debate over domestic and foreign issues."

Federalist Society
1015 18th St NW Ste 425
Washington DC 20036
202-822-8138
E-mail: fedsoc@radix.net
Focus: Strict interpretation of Constitution; ground zero for judiciary battles.

Heritage Foundation
214 Massachusetts Ave NW
Washington DC 20002
202-546-4400
www.heritage.org
Focus: Conservative social values. Offers media hotline (202-675-1761), which is available 365 days a year.

Hoover Institution
Stanford University
Stanford CA 94305
650-723-1754
fax: 650-723-1687
E-mail: horaney@hoover.stanford.edu
Focus: Ideas defining a free and peaceful society.

Institute for Foreign Policy Analysis, Inc.
Central Plaza Bldg 10th flr
675 Massachusetts Ave
Cambridge MA 02139
617-492-2116
fax: 617-492-8242
E-mail: mail@ifpa.org
or
1725 DeSales St NW Ste 402
Washington DC 20036
202-463-7942
fax: 202-785-2785
E-mail: dcmail@ifpa.org
Focus: National security, foreign policy, political economics, and government-industrial relations.

Institute for Justice
1717 Pennsylvania Ave NW Ste 200
Washington DC 20005
202-955-1300
fax: 202-955-1329
Focus: A conservative ACLU, dedicated to protecting individual rights rather than expanding government.

Intercollegiate Studies Institute
3901 Centerville Rd
PO Box 4431
Wilmington DE 19807
302-652-4600
Focus: Encouraging conservative voices on the nation's campuses; generating "understanding of the values and institutions that sustain a free society."

John M. Ashbrook Center for Public Affairs
Ashland University
401 College Ave
Ashland OH 44805
419-289-5411
877-289-5411 (toll free)
E-mail: info@ashbrook.org
Focus: Defense of individual liberty, limited constitutional government, and civic morality.

Justice For All
713-935-9300
E-mail: info@jfa.net
Focus: Victims' rights and criminal justice reform.

Landmark Legal Foundation
445-B Carlisle Dr
Herndon VA 20170
703-689-2370
fax: 703-689-2373
E-mail: info@landmarklegal.org
Focus: Conservative public interest law center. Founded by Mark Levin.

Manhattan Institute
52 Vanderbilt Ave
New York NY 10017
212-599-7000
fax: 212-599-3494
E-mail: mb@manhattan-institute.org
Focus: Urban social policy. Affiliated with experts in a variety of areas, including Kay Hymowitz (children and family), Heather Mac Donald (police; racial profiling), and John McWhorter (race and ethnicity).

National Association of Scholars
221 Witherspoon St 2nd flr
Princeton NJ 08542-3215
609-683-7878
fax: 609-683-0316
E-mail: join@nas.org
Focus: Higher education. The NAS is "deeply concerned about perspectives within the academy that reflexively denigrate the values and institutions of our society."

Pro-Life/Antiabortion

National Right to Life Committee
419 7th St NW Ste 500
Washington DC 20004
202-626-8800
www.nrlc.org
Focus: Leading pro-life with branches nationally.

Concerned Women for America
1015 15th St NW
Washington DC 20005
202-488-7000
www.cwfa.org
Focus: Christian-based, pro-life, working to "restore families to their traditional purpose."

The Nurturing Network
627 Innsbruck Ave
Great Falls VA 22066
703-759-7090
www.nurturingnetwork.org
Focus: International charitable organization that sets "politics and rhetoric aside" and provides "practical, life-saving services to women facing the crisis of an unwanted pregnancy."

Catholic Information Center
1501 K St NW Ste 175
Washington DC 20005-1401
202-783-2062
Focus: The CIC is an agency of the Archdiocese of Washington, D.C. Its director, Father John C. McCloskey, is an excellent source for traditional Catholic perspective.

National Organization of Episcopalians for Life (NOEL)
405 Frederick Ave
Sewickley PA 15143
412-749-0455
E-mail: NOELInfo@NOELforLife.org
Focus: A para-church organization within the Episcopal/Anglican tradition seeking to develop and strengthen pro-life and pro-family ministries in the Episcopal Church and the culture at large.

Individual Sources on Abortion-Related Issues

Professor Jean Bethke Elshtain
Laura Spelman Rockefeller Professor of Social and Political Ethics
University of Chicago
Swift Hall Rm 202
1025 E 58th St
Chicago IL 60637
773-702-7252
A noted political philosopher, Professor Elshtain has written widely on the links between religion and public policy.

Professor Elizabeth Fox-Genovese
Eleonore Raoul Professor of the Humanities
Emory University
History Dept
205 Bowden Hall
Atlanta GA 30322
404-727-4063
Founder of Emory's Institute for Women's Studies and noted scholar of women's history. Believes "abortion has failed women."

Professor Robert P. George
McCormick Professor of Jurisprudence
Princeton University
371 Prospect Ave
Princeton NJ 8540
609-683-1304
Member of the President's Council on Bioethics. Professor George is the author of *Making Men Moral: Civil Liberties and Public Morality.*

Dr. Bernard N. Nathanson
133 E 73rd St
New York NY 10021
212-861-1417
Cofounder of pro-choice National Abortion Rights Action League
(NARAL) and former abortion provider (having performed the procedure over five thousand times); he now rejects abortion.

Other Women's Issues

Independent Women's Forum
PO Box 3058
Arlington VA 22203-0058
703-558-4991
www.iwf.org
Focus: Broad range of equity-related issues. National Advisory Board
chairman is renowned "equity feminist" Christina Hoff Sommers.

Eagle Forum
316 Pennsylvania Ave Ste 203
Washington DC 20003
202-544-0353
fax: 202-547-6996
E-mail: eagle@eagleforum.org
Focus: American sovereignty, traditional values, education, combat-
ing radical feminists. Headed by Phyllis Schlafly.

The College Sports Council
Eric Pearson 202-429-2097
Jim McCarthy 202-333-8810
www.savingsports.org
Focus: Damaging effects of Title IX.

Center for Military Readiness
PO Box 51600
Livonia MI 48151
202-347-5333
E-mail: info@cmrlink.org
Focus: Women in the military.

Clare Booth Luce Policy Institute
112 Elden St Ste P
Herndon VA 20170
703-318-8867
www.cblpolicyinstitute.org
Focus: Preparing young women for conservative leadership.

Employment Policy Foundation
1015 15th St NW
Washington DC 20005
202-789-8685
www.epf.org
Focus: Gender-related employment issues.

Employment Policy Institute
1775 Pennsylvania Ave NW
Washington DC 20006
202-463-7650
www.epinet.org
Focus: The purported wage gap between men and women; other employment-related issues.

Women in the Economy
12655 N Central Expy Ste 720
Dallas TX 75243-1739
972-386-6272
fax: 972-386-0924
www.womenintheeconomy.org
Focus: Women in American economic life.

Marriage, Family, and Children; Gay Rights

Family Research Council
801 G St NW
Washington DC 20001
202-393-2100
www.frc.org
Focus: Traditional family; marriage.

Focus on the Family
8605 Explorer Dr
Colorado Springs CO 80995
800-232-6499
fax: 719-531-3424
Focus: Traditional family, homosexuality, pro-life. Christian-oriented, headed by Dr. James Dobsen.

American Family Association
PO Box 2440
Tupelo MS 38803
662-844-5036
Focus: Pro-life, traditional family values. Fundamentalist Christian organization headed by the Rev. Don Wildmon.

Toward Tradition
PO Box 58
Mercer Island WA 98040
206-236-3046
fax: 206-236-3288
Focus: Jewish-Christian coalition concerned with traditional American values observed through prism of faith. Michael Medved is affiliated.

Agudath Israel of America
Rabbi Avi Shafron
Director of Public Affairs
212-797-9000
Focus: Traditional Orthodox Jewish perspective. Rabbi Shafron is a frequent contributor to *Jewish World Review* (jewishworldreview. com), another excellent source for conservative commentators on the issues of the day.

Race

American Civil Rights Institute
PO Box 188350
Sacramento CA 95818
916-444-2278
fax: 916-444-2270
www.acri.org
Focus: Educating public about racial and gender preferences; fostering race-blind public policy; monitoring implementation and legal action on California's Proposition 209. Founded by Ward Connerly.

African-American Republican Leadership Council
The Ronald Reagan Bldg
1300 Pennsylvania Ave NW Ste 700
Washington DC 20004
212-675-8338
Focus: Finding common ground between conservatives and the African-American community.

Brotherhood Organization of a New Destiny (BOND)
Media inquiries: 323-782-1980
Focus: Headed by the Rev. Jesse Peterson. A nonprofit religious organization dedicated to "Rebuilding the family by rebuilding the man."

Center for Equal Opportunity
14 Pidgeon Hill Dr Ste 500
Sterling VA 20165
703-421-5443
fax: 703-421-6401
www.ceousa.org
Focus: Promoting color-blind equal opportunity. Headed by Linda Chavez.

Centre for New Black Leadership
202 G St NE
Washington DC 20002
202-546-9505
www.cnbl.org
Focus: Public policy and economics.

Congress of Racial Equality
317 Broadway
New York NY 10003
212-598-4000
fax: 212-598-4141
E-mail: core@core-online.org
Focus: Formerly mainstream civil rights organization, now considered conservative. Urges color-blind society. Headed by Roy and Niger Innis.

National Center for Neighborhood Enterprise
1424 16th St NW
Washington DC 20036
202-518-6500
fax: 202-588-0314
E-mail: Info@ncne.com
Focus: Empowering "neighborhood leaders to promote solutions that reduce crime and violence, restore families, revitalize low-income communities and create economic progress. . . . Societal problems addressed by NCNE's grassroots network include youth violence, substance abuse, teen pregnancy, homelessness, joblessness, poor education and deteriorating neighborhoods." Founded by Robert Woodson.

Step 12:
Stop Taking
It Personally

Benjamin Franklin said it more than two hundred years ago, and his fellow journalists today need to take his words to heart: "Our critics are our friends, they show us our faults."

A Final Word

emember the movie *High Noon*? The bad guys were coming to town, and no one but Gary Cooper, playing the sheriff, would stand up to them. No matter how hard he tried, he couldn't get the good people of the town to do the right thing. They had too much to lose, they figured.

That'll give you an idea of how it is in too many newsrooms.

George Orwell, the British essayist and author of *Animal Farm* and *1984,* once wrote about how societies censor themselves. "At any given moment there is a sort of all-pervading orthodoxy, a general tacit agreement not to discuss large and uncomfortable facts." He might just as well have been talking about the orthodoxies and the agreements that pervade America's most elite newsrooms.

Fair-minded reporters see and hear things all the time that they know just aren't right, large and uncomfortable facts they tacitly agree not to discuss. It doesn't take a genius to understand that certain issues aren't covered with equal respect for all points of view. The American people know that powerful assumptions about right and wrong, good guys and bad guys, influence and often distort the way certain stories are handled.

One of the most telling examples is how the media cover the abortion story. Every poll shows that Americans are sharply divided on the issue, regarding it as deeply troubling ethically and morally, and that while a majority support the right to legal abortion in the first trimester, large segments of the population favor important restrictions on the procedure.

But in many newsrooms—including the most powerful news organizations—such doubts are almost never heard. Those on the pro-life side are assumed to be fanatics, religious and otherwise. They are anti-women. They are the enemy.

And while it is almost never expressed explicitly, a rare revealing slip was Dan Rather's question to a U.S. senator, wondering if he thought Supreme Court Justice David Souter's views were "antiabortion or anti–women's rights, whichever way you want to put it," as if the two were one and the same. But even when it's not so blatant, those on the other side can read between the lines, and they are justly offended. As *New York Times* science writer Gina Kolata told an interviewer, "Anybody who reads the *New York Times* who doesn't think the *New York Times* is pro-choice, they are out of their minds. . . . We send messages all the time about what we think."

But the fact is, there are many, many journalists more troubled by the prevailing atmosphere than they let on. Some actually differ with newsroom sentiment on the most controversial issues of the day; others just recognize the crucial importance of a lively ongoing debate. But either way, they are more silent about their feelings than they should be.

That is the nature of peer pressure. Everyone understands that it's good for your career if you're a team player. No one wants to be seen as a troublemaker—or worse, as a right-wing crazy.

That has to change. Reporters need to start standing up to newsroom orthodoxies, not merely because it's right, but also because it's good policy. An ongoing civil conversation in the newsroom about contentious issues, challenging pat assumptions and unexamined beliefs, by its very nature will start to open minds. Inevitably it will make for fuller, fairer coverage of the news.

The next time a *Washington Post* reporter writes that the pope at times "speaks with the voice of a conservative crank" because he won't budge on issues like abortion and birth control, someone in the newsroom needs to say that using language like that is not just wrong—it's also deeply offensive.

When an ABC News reporter offers the view that while, since September 11, *terrorist* has come to mean *Islamic and foreign,* "many believe we have as much to fear from a homegrown group of anti-abortion crusaders," someone in the newsroom needs to stand up and say, "Really? You *really* believe many Americans think antiabortion crusaders pose as big a threat to Americans as Osama bin Laden?"

And if Dan Rather repeats that the Republican Congressional agenda will "demolish or damage government programs, many of them designed to help children and the poor," someone needs to stand up and say, "You know, Dan, that kind of language is way over the top and offends a lot of people who aren't even Republicans."

I'm not saying there will never be consequences. Some of the biggest names in journalism are also some of the biggest bullies. They confuse even mild dissent with disloyalty. But reporters like to pride themselves on their guts. Ask a reporter to name his or her favorite movie, and the chances are good you'll hear *High Noon* or *To Kill a Mockingbird*—movies built around brave figures risking everything on principle. That's why they're so quick to condemn cops who won't speak up against other cops who step out of line, and doctors who won't speak out against other doctors; and priests who overlook wrongdoing in their ranks.

They're right—principle matters. Fairness matters. Standing up for those things is how character is defined.

Many journalists, of course, have shown remarkable courage covering wars and insurrections. It's now time for many more to be brave enough to stand up in their own newsrooms and say, "I think this is wrong. Let's talk about it."

Will they? I'm with Yogi Berra. It's tough to make predictions, especially about the future. All I know is that if history is any guide, it's going to be a tough road. Arrogance, after all, is a powerful and destructive force. But choosing to remain the elite armies of condescension, marching down the street with their privates swinging in the breeze, is a losing strategy, no way to win back the respect and trust of the American people.

That's why the media elites should use no one less than Edward R. Murrow, the legendary CBS News correspondent, as their guide. Back in the 1950s, when Senator Joe McCarthy was running rampant and threatening opponents with destruction—including Ed Murrow himself—he did a memorable broadcast on the senator and his methods. "We are not descended from fearful men," Murrow said in his commentary at the end of the program, "not men who feared to write, to speak, to associate and to defend causes which were for the moment unpopular. This is no time for men who oppose Senator McCarthy's methods to keep silent. We can deny our heritage and our history, but we cannot escape responsibility for the result."

Index